“Terribly at the Mercy of His Mind”

Henry James in the 1890s

“Terribly at the Mercy of His Mind” Henry James in the 1890s

Printed in Seoul, Republic of Korea

Marcus Klein
12896 Rock Ridge Lane Valley Center, CA 92082 (760) 751-3094
Mnklein@aol.com

Seoul National University Press
599 Gwanak-ro, Gwanak-gu, Seoul 151-742, Republic of Korea

E-mail: snubook@snu.ac.kr
Home-page: http://www.snupress.com

First Printing: Mar. 15, 2010
ISBN 978-89-521-1081-7 93840

"Terribly at the Mercy of His Mind"
Henry James in the 1890s

MARCUS KLEIN

Seoul National University Press

ONCE AGAIN, FOR MARIAN, JENNY, AND ERIC

Acknowledgments

Sections of this book have appeared previously in *Arizona Quarterly* and *New England Review*. In slightly different version the remarks on 'The Turn of the Screw' appeared in *The Hudson Review* under the title 'Conventions and Chaos in The Turn of the Screw'. The author wishes to thank these journals for permission to reprint.

CONTENTS

Preface

For his principal biographer, Leon Edel, the latter half of the nineties had been the time of "The Treacherous Years". James, said Edel, "may be said in these years to have suffered a kind of 'nervous breakdown'". Haunted by private demons, he wrote stories and novels which are to be read as acts of exorcism. This, the later nineties, was a time, said Edel, which, moreover, had followed upon a previous five years, the theater years, 1890 to 1895, when James had suffered "a state of malaise and often of acute anxiety". In a slightly different way of looking, for James' biographer Fred Kaplan the years 1888 to 1895 were those of "The Dark Abyss," marked by deaths: James' sister Alice, who succumbed to cancer in 1892, and his friend Constance Fenimore Woolson, who committed suicide in 1894. Again, for Oscar Cargill the years 1896 to 1901 were those of "The Augean Stable," when—as had earlier been pointed out by Edmund Wilson—sex began to appear in James' works "in," as Wilson had said, "a queer and left-handed way". For F.W. Dupee the nineties was "The Awkward Period". And as for technical matter, of style and point of view, for the critic Walter Isle the tales and novels James published in the years 1896 to 1901 are to be regarded as "experiments in form" looking forward to "the final achievement of 'the major phase' after 1900". For Edward Wagenknecht, among the relatively few who have given concentrated attention to the period as such, the novels of the nineties constituted "Transition," looking forward to "The Masterpieces" to come after the turn of the century.

Which is to say that in one way and another consensus has

occurred, that the 1890s, that peculiarly (and decimally) bracketed moment consisting of five years of playwriting followed by five years of experimental or transitional fictions, was a signal moment of the Master's faltering, nerve-wracked and burdened by grief, from which time he recovered and after which he fulfilled himself.

This is a book about James' writings in the nineties, both plays and fiction, regarded—following James' own estimation—as being distinct from past work, but read here as neither symptom of "cerebral lesion" (in the words of the narrator of *The Sacred Fount*) nor as transition to "The Masterpieces". To the contrary, this production (but finally everyone does agree to this) gives us James at his most challenging. Here is James, by way indeed of considerable break from his past, at the work of a tricky and most unsettling business involving basic questioning of literary and moral conventions, involving especially in the longer fictions ever more probing investigation of the depths and perversities of personality. The work is intense, and is unyielding, and is knotty, and, as well, at the same time is peculiarly bold and joking, and not infrequently is raw in a way not often thought to be "Jamesian". Close attention is demanded, especially to the way the novels of the period unfold, but here is Henry James, taking the writings of the period as a whole, who is something other than and more exciting than masterful. Rather, he is relentless, and, as he himself would indicate, is at the service of his intelligence. And no doubt it needs to be said that he is intelligent beyond *Tendenz* of any tendency, that—at least in these late works—he is beyond capture by any party whatsoever, nor by any single idea. James' novel *The Sacred Fount*, coming at the end of the decade, is, relevantly, to be seen to deal specifically with the comedy and, to put the matter as bluntly as does the novel, the insanity of thinking-by-theory.

Life did bear down upon James in the nineties. There were the deaths. He had been at Alice's bedside when she died. About Fenimore's suicide he may have felt guilty for having raised expectations and perhaps therefore for having been a cause of her suicide—the matter is debated—but, guilty or not, for a certainty he was affected.[i] He found himself put to the task of clearing out her apartment in Venice. In a grotesque incident, with the help of a gondolier he threw her clothing into the canal only to have the garments repeatedly billow up until finally they sank.[ii] And there were other deaths: James' old family friend James Russell Lowell, in 1891; a young friend and sometimes literary agent, Wolcott Balestier, whose funeral he attended, traveling to Dresden; Robert Louis Stevenson in 1894; Fanny Kemble in 1893; George DuMaurier in 1896.

And these were the years, of his maturity, when James seems to have become aware of his being attracted to certain young men, while the more certainly these were years of his realization of his loneliness. One of the young men was Morton Fullerton, to whom, in October of 1900, James addressed one of the most painful letters in all of his printed correspondence. "I wish I could help you," he wrote, apparently in response to a request made by Fullerton, "by satisfying your desire to know from 'what port,' as you say, I set out."

> And yet, though the enquiry is, somehow, of so large a synthesis, I think I *can* in a manner answer. The port from which I set out was, I think, that of the *essential loneliness of my life*—and it seems to be the port also, in sooth to which my course again finally directs itself! This loneliness, (since I mention it!)—what is it still but the deepest thing about one? Deeper about *me*, at any rate, than anything else; deeper than my "genius," deeper than my "discipline," deeper than my pride, deeper, above all, than the deep countermining of art.

And, "May that amount of information about it give you a lift!" he added, with nice irony. Money, moreover, was a constant concern, as is indicated by the letters. Certainly he was not poor. Alice's death had in fact freed some American income for him. But he was very much a freelance, writing for a living, and for all of the esteem in which he might have been held, he did not have anywhere near the financial success of other writers, whom he knew and did not necessarily himself esteem. Relative to those of others—his friend Francis Hodgson ("Fluffy") Burnett, for one particular instance—his novels and story collections did not do well. In January of 1888, reflecting on the commercial failures of *The Bostonians* and *The Princess Cassimassima,* he was writing to William Dean Howells, "I have entered upon evil days." The desire and demand for his productions, he said, had been reduced to zero. Editors had been keeping back his materials for months and years "as if," he said, "they were ashamed of them, and I am condemned apparently to eternal silence." Then again, seven years later, in 1895, he was saying to Howells that "periodical publication is practically closed to me—I'm the last hand that the magazines, in this country or in the US., seem to want.... I'm utterly out of it *here*—and *Scribner,* the *Century,* the *Cosmopolitan,* will have nothing to say to me—above all for fiction. The *Atlantic,* and Houghton and Mifflin, treat me like the dust beneath their feet." His bitterness, and jealousy, became anguish when, in 1899, Lamb House came up for sale. He had been leasing the country home in Rye—"a haven of rest," he wrote to his brother William, "out of which I pray heaven I may never shift for all the rest of my days." Now he could have it outright, but, at least for the moment, he didn't have the money, and William had advised against the purchase. "My whole being cries out aloud for something that I can call my own," he wrote, "and when I look round me at the splendour of so many of the 'literary' fry my confrères (M. Crawfords, P. Bourgets, Humphry Wards, Hodgson Burnetts, W.D. Howellses etc.) and I feel that I may strike the world as still, at fifty-six, with my long labour and my genius, reckless, presumptuous and unwarranted in curling up (for more assured peaceful production), in a poor little $10,000 shelter—once for all and for all time—*then* I do feel the bitterness of humiliation, the iron enters into my soul, and (I blush to confess it), I *weep!*"

Certainly money had much to do with his decision to try the theater. That's where the money was. Other fiction writers—Fluffy Burnett, for one—had fared well financially. At the end of 1888 he had been approached for a dramatic version of The American, which he wrote the next year, giving it a happy ending at the demand of the theater manager. It was produced in 1891, first in the provinces and then in London. It was not a financial success but it had had what James would characterize as an honorable run, and for the next four years, then, he worked at being a playwright. He wrote plays and he closely associated himself with the London theater and with theater people. By how much indeed this latter is suggested, to cite one evidence, in the record published later by the actress Elizabeth Robins, consisting of some one hundred fifty letters and notes written to her by James, with an additional many addressed to Florence Bell, a friend and playwright. Robins was an American who had established herself in England. She had been instrumental in introducing Ibsen to London audiences and for most of her life was engaged in establishing theatrical companies and bringing new plays and playwrights to the English stage. James' letters to her and to Bell are not in fact, any of them individually, especially informative, or even substantial, but just so they are the more illuminating as they provide evidence of the kind of James' continuous involvement in the ordinaries of the professional theater. Just as Robins herself would say in her introduction, they provide "a record of Mr. James' preoccupation with the theatre—apart from his personal adventure as a playwright.... There is evidence of his knowledge of plays, playwrights and acting, not only English. ..." For one instance, a lengthy exchange deals with James' doing apparently extensive editing and rewriting of a play, Mariana, by a Spanish playwright, José Echegaray, in order to make the translation adaptable to the English stage.[iii]

James would write his other plays and would have other dealings with the theater, but his intention to be primarily a playwright ended (famously, notoriously) the night of January 5th, 1895, with the opening, in London, of his play *Guy Domville.*

Guy Domville was only the second of his plays to be produced and was his one serious play, in the usual sense of "serious"—the others, his "theatricals," as he called them, had all been comedies. Following the many frustrations connected with the theater, and the griefs which otherwise had come upon him, he had had great hopes for this play, which then were all but obliterated by the first-night audience, at least by the larger part of it. He had come to the theater only as the play was ending and did not know that it had earlier been interrupted by the jeers of a rowdy audience. He did have friends in attendance, who at the final curtain called for "Author, author," in all good will, but catastrophically. The theater manager and leading man, George Alexander, had led James to the footlights, where he had been greeted, in the words of James' friend Edmund Gosse, by "a storm of hoots and... catcalls from the gallery, answered by loud and sustained applause from the stalls, the whole producing an effect of hell broke loose, in the midst of which the author, as white as chalk, bowed and spread forth deprecating hands."[iv] That January evening, James would say, had made for "the most horrible hours of my life."[v]

For F.O. Matthiessen, who in 1944 had sole possession of the as-yet-unpublished Notebooks, "Eighteen Ninety Five was the great turning point in James' career".[vi] In 2004, oddly and coincidentally, two notable novels about James in the 1890s appeared, almost simultaneously: *The Master* by Colm Tóibín and *Author, Author* by David Lodge. For both writers the nineties was a time of despair for James with, for both, the crucial moment being the *Guy Domville* episode. And for both writers, as for F.O. Matthiessen sixty years earlier, and as indeed for almost all of James' biographers, the episode was taken, in effect, to confirm a paradigm, implied but nonetheless compelling, of sickness, climax, and gradual recovery, into a kind of bronze distinction. For Colm Tóibín, James in the nineties was greatly ruminative about past errors, and was lonely, yearning for young men, and feeling guilty, mostly about Fenimore Woolson. For David Lodge, a principal subterranean motive of the nineties was jealousy of the popular and commercial success of others, particularly of Woolson and of James' young friend George Du Maurier.

So it seems to be necessary to recall that James was a writer first of all. No doubt that the *Guy Domville* incident marked a crisis in his life, but the crisis, as such, did seem to pass, or at least he was not paralyzed by it.[vii] Not at all long after the January 5th incident, on January 23rd of 1895, James was writing in his Notebook:

> I take up my own old pen again—the pen of all my old unforgettable efforts and sacred struggles. To myself—today—I need say no more. Large and full and high the future still opens. It is now indeed that I may do the work of my life. And I will. x x x x I have only to *face* my problems. x x x x But all that is of the ineffable—too deep and pure for any utterance. Shrouded in sacred silence, let it rest. x x x x

The idea, furthermore, of an endlessly ruminative, self-absorbed, guilty, frustrated James, in the time of the nineties, is at least challenged by the fact that during the decade, in addition to six full-length plays (all but one of them comedies, it is to be noted), he wrote and published thirty-odd stories, some forty essays of varying length, and five novels, or seven depending on how one counts the long fictions *In the Cage* and *The Turn of the Screw*, or eight if one counts *The Sense of the Past*, much of which was composed in 1900. If nothing else, the amount of the activity will testify to the sheer vitality and strength of the man. (Despite his gout and his dental troubles and his deteriorating arthritic hand and his constipation and his tendency to weight, he had athletic inclinations. In 1888 he had been taking fencing lessons twice a week and lifting weights. In 1895 he bought a bicycle. And there is other kind of evidence of the immense energy and stamina of the man in the sheer amount, density, extensiveness, and intricacy of his social life, as may be seen by glancing, merely, at his letters of the period, as so far published.)

Nor except in a handful of instances—the stories about writers, primarily—is it possible to make simple and direct connections between the fiction and the life. James wrote out of himself, perforce, but he was not a confessional writer, time of troubles or not. The primary lesson to be taken from the Notebooks, which begin in 1878, is that he was a writer constantly on the lookout, *elsewhere*, for materials for fiction. That, mostly, is what the Notebooks are about.

Nonetheless, the writing in the nineties is distinctly different—tonally, thematically, technically, and in terms of moral judgment and perspective, which is to say in evidence of basic beliefs or, more particularly, basic dubieties. The prose is provocative, treacherous. The themes, in no particular order, are: lunacy, incest, pedophilia, infanticide, sadism and sexual perversity, infant eroticism, adultery, bastardy, blackmail, and others similar. (The one exception of any significance is *Guy Domville,* and any fair reading of that play will suggest that the vulgarians among the first-night audience were not more than overly expressive.) When in 1898 his young friend Arthur Christopher Benson asked James about the possibility of his writing a sequel to *The Portrait of a Lady,* James said no, "It's all too faint & far away—too ghostly & ghastly," and added, "I have bloodier things *en tête*. I can do better than that!"[viii] The irony now is more constant than heretofore, and much more chill. The techniques are more intricate (in the "theatricals" as well as in the fictions) and, in the fictions, more devious. Characters are now primarily objects of interest rather than of sympathy, and their interest is in the way they gradually unfold, both for the reader and for themselves. The great trick of *What Maisie Knew,* for instance, is just that, darling of a little girl that she is, and bedeviled as she is, James most of all is *interested* in her, not in love with her, and we watch as gradually Maisie achieves an expression of the sexual knowledge which she has possessed since earliest childhood. Possessed and finally expressive of her own perversities, she is not Pansy Osmond.

The language of the fiction is distinctly different, especially in the novels. Certainly it has become more difficult for the reader, but manifestly for the reason that the language is under greater pressure. Very subtle readers profess to discover the exact moment, in 1897, during the composition of *Maisie,* when James turned to dictation from writing by hand, with the result, it is said, of a general loosening of the prose. But evidence for that is less than persuasive, and is also easily contradicted. It is the case, rather, that despite the occasional elaboration of sentences, the usual direction is towards concision and compaction, with a playfulness within.

The practice is not new, but, for instance, now especially James will like to bear down on clichés, to reveal the surprises in their literalness. Something of his intention may be inferred from a remark about Flaubert in an essay of 1893, meant as ridicule: "The horror, in particular, that haunted all [Flaubert's] years was the horror of the *cliché*."[ix] For James the cliché is an opportunity for doubling. "Increasingly," as F.W. Dupee pointed out, "the language rejoices in sudden colloquialism, raffish jargon, and a habit of turning abruptly and alarmingly concrete." The metaphors tend, moreover, to be startling in their concreteness. To cite one of Dupee's examples: "Mrs. Wix gave the jerk of a sleeper awakened or the start even of one who hears a bullet whiz at the flag of truce." As Dupee also said, they "connect James' refined-appearing world with the realm of the physical and the elemental, of latent horror, of what he described as 'the thing hideously *behind*.'"[x]

The change (in mood, in perspective, in concerns, in technique), which is certain, doubtless had many promptings, James' many griefs during the nineties perhaps among them. But there were others.

There was the theater experience in itself. As James himself would several times say, the theater taught him "the divine principle of the Scenario," which would have an effect beyond simply plotting entrances and exits or restricting actions to a single scene, as in a play. More significantly for the fiction, as in a play according to the principle of the Scenario, the author would be absent. There would be no outside commentary nor on the other hand, as James put it, would there be any "going behind". And that would mean that characters would be on their own and engaged necessarily in self-revelation—meaning that a character's performance was a continuing act of irony, to be regarded distantly and objectively, not even critically, except as steady and cool objectivity was in itself critical. And if what characters revealed, as they talked, was more often than not a suppressed or frustrated or illicit sexuality, that was an ore which James' contemporary Freud was assaying at exactly the same time, but for James, in the theater, it was a basic material of comedy. That—frustrated or illicit sex—was what the comedies were largely about, those that he was seeing and those that then he wrote. And the very environment of the theater encouraged, furthermore, a license of expression, now that he was in it. Already in *The Tragic Muse* he had taken the theater to be a site of easy impropriety. Biddy Dormer, for instance, reflecting on Peter Sherringham's passion for the actress Miriam Rooth, is caught in being about to say that for actresses, marriage is no impediment. Altogether in the theater half of that novel, morals are loose and the milieu is tawdry.

And there was the matter, simply but not so simply, of the length of the compositions of the nineties. *The Tragic Muse*, a "massive" and an "interminable" novel, as James described it, had been serialized 1889–1890. In the middle of writing it, in 1888, James had sent a letter to Robert Louis Stevenson saying that after he had done with this novel he proposed to do nothing but short lengths. In January of 1895, following the *Guy Domville* disaster, he was writing to William Dean Howells: "I shall never again write a *long* novel; but I hope to write six immortal short ones."[xi] James' motives were different early and late. The letter to Howells was propelled by bitterness and wounded pride while the earlier one was perhaps expression of sheer weariness—as usual, a novel had been getting away from him just when, at the same time, he had contracted for several essays. After the turn of the century, by way of his "major phase," James would of course change his mind and complete three very long novels. But meanwhile the matter of the length first of the plays and then of the novels of the nineties, itself compelled a shift of perspective. In his letters James complained mightily and continually about the restrictions put upon him both by theater managers and by the editors who were serializing his fictions. Each of the short novels he published between 1895 and 1901 got away from him. The letters and the Notebooks so indicate. He had carefully prepared his scenarios, sometimes at great length and in great detail, and as the stories and characters exfoliated, he had forced himself to compress, thereby reinforcing the withholding of explanations and backgrounds, even as his characters were themselves the more forced to divulge. And if dialogue or other expression was often truncated or otherwise ended in ambiguity, so that the divulging often seemed to end in a confession of unutterability, that too was one likely effect of compression. So Cynthia Ozick is led to observe that "the pivotal truth about the later Henry James is not that he chooses to tell too little—that now and then he deliberately fires blanks—but that he knows too much, and much more than we, or he, can possibly take in." James' own remarks about Turgenev in an instance, in 1896, are to the point here. He praised Turgenev for his "concision," and added: "He understands so much that we almost wonder he can express anything."[xii]

And then there was the matter of his intended audience. Following the *Guy Domville* disaster he would several times complain, in letters and in fiction, and in the same words, that "You can't make a sow's ear out of a silk purse". Try as he might, he would not be able to please the masses. And it was true that mostly he didn't, but not for lack of trying. Complain as he would, that the established magazines like *Century, Scribner,* and *Atlantic* had turned their backs on him—which was not altogether true—it made a difference in the nineties that he pursued and was published in journals which entirely were in the business of pleasing the masses: *Illustrated London News,* for one, which serialized *The Other House,* and *Harper's Weekly,* for another, which serialized *The Awkward Age. Harper's* had previously taken the essays which, with some others, were to be collected as *Notes on Novelists.* Those publications no doubt wanted James' prestige, while he wanted the money. *Harper's Weekly* paid him especially well. But in any event, James did endeavor to provide what they wanted. In February of 1896, seeking to make arrangements for the serial publication of *The Other House,* he was writing to the editor of *Illustrated London News,* "I should be very glad to write you a story energetically designed to meet your requirements of a 'love-story,'" and immediately subsequently, "I shall endeavour to be thrilling." And while "the ghostly and the ghastly" did not really constitute a new reservoir of imagination for him, the popular market as he came to know it in the nineties would have encouraged the darker excitements, would have licensed the lurid.[xiii]

He also published stories in—and for—*The Yellow Book,* that principal site of self-defined decadence, founded and presided over by Henry Harland and Aubrey Beardsley. In a letter to his brother William he professed to hate "the horrid aspect and company of the whole publication," but in fact he was on friendly terms with Harland, and knew Beardsley. His tale "The Death of the Lion" had appeared in the first issue of the quarterly and, as he also said to William, it had had "for a thing of mine, an unusual success." Moreover, hate the aspect and company as he might, he continued his association. "The Coxon Fund" was in the second issue. "The Next Time" was in the sixth.[xiv] There was also to be an essay on George Sand, in 1897. None of this inscribed him in the decadent movement as such, with its sexy assault on propriety, but at the least he did not separate himself from it, either, except in private communication with his brother. James moved in numerous circles, this one among them.

The themes, once again, were dark: lunacy, pedophilia, prepubescent sexuality, sadism, infanticide, among them. And once more again, James' way with characters generally was to allow them to erupt. To Arthur Benson he was writing in 1896 that he saw "life indeed as ferocious and sinister."[xv] But for all of that, and by way of greater complication, the writing was not even solemn. The trouble with Flaubert, so James would observe, "beating about the bush to deal death to the abominable assonance," was that he was never funny. In a lengthy essay, in 1893, he would say that "in [Flaubert's] deepening vision of the imbecility of the world any remedy would have deprived him of his prime, or rather, of his sole amusement. The *bêtise* of mankind was a colossal comedy, calling aloud to heaven for an Aristophanes to match, and Flaubert's nearest approach to joy was in noting the opportunities of such an observer and feeling within himself the stirrings of genius." Similarly, in an essay about George Sand (about whom he wrote more than about any other novelist), he would say that when she failed it was "by excess of indulgence and by absence of the humorous vision, a nose for the ridiculous—the fatal want, this last almost always, we are reminded, the heel of Achilles, in the sentimental, the romantic estimate."[xvi] In his own writing he could dare to be crude—there are the many "fanny" jokes, for obvious instance, discussed below. He invented ridiculous characters, and made fun of them. (See, for instance, the story "Glasses," discussed in the following pages, along with repeated instances in the plays.) The scenic techniques which disallowed straightforward exposition also required constant indirections and insinuations, making for a game between author and reader, a fact which James very well knew and exploited. The very act of communication between author and reader, that is to say, involved a kind of game. That was why, for instance, for him *The Turn of the Screw* was an *amusette*, as he said in his Preface to the tale. The infinitely teasing novel *The Sacred Fount* was, he insisted, a joke. But the comedy was even the more persistently inherent in the pressured language of the late style. He played with diction—thus the formalities of the language dropping into abrupt colloquialisms, and thus to the same effect the formal pressure put upon colloquial clichés. James' language had always tended to, at least, archness. Linguistic irony was his note—in contemplation of Niagara Falls, in one of his early travel pieces, to select a random instance, he would take stock of Niagara's "unmitigated fluidity"; late, in his autobiography, on the death of Edgar Allan Poe, for another random example: "the extremity of personal absence had just overtaken him".[xvii] But now the language was more than ever self-conscious, and comic, as by the fact of its mediation it constantly implied an amused observer, not otherwise present.

As was recognized by at least some early readers of late James, the new difficulty of the language also was a kind of a tease which obscured an outrageousness. Thus Frank Moore Colby, in 1902, writing in *The Bookman,* in his opening paragraph:

> A year ago, when Henry James wrote an essay on women that brought to our cheek the hot, rebellious blush, we said nothing about it, thinking that perhaps, after all, the man's style was his sufficient fig-leaf, and that few would see how shocking he really was. And, indeed, it has been a long time since the public knew what Henry James was up to behind that verbal hedge of his, though half-suspecting that he meant no good, because a style like that seemed just the place for guilty secrets.

Colby went on to discuss James' new essay on George Sand. That earlier essay on women to which he referred was a piece by James on Matilde Serao, an Italian novelist who, for James, raised the question of what to do with the erotic in fiction—and, treat it comically, was what in effect he said.[xviii]

Colby, properly, was amused by the verbal hedge, but so, without doubt, was James himself amused, by his talent for what amounted to jaunty, terrifically intelligent persiflage. What on the other hand James now was really up to, however, on the other side of that hedge, was outrage only in the finest sense. With *The Portrait of a Lady* James had been a Victorian novelist, in the sense that he was about the business of proposing and resolving moral questions. Isabel Archer is a moral heroine. She renounces personal happiness for the sake of a greater good—like, indeed, Christopher Newman in *The American*, before her, to name the two most read of the earlier novels. Isabel will sacrifice herself in order to be a mother to her step-daughter. Newman will forego revenge by reason of his American sense of decency. And the same essential action of renunciation is in *The Bostonians* and *The Princess Cassimassima* as well, except that in fact in those novels the nature of what actually is the greater good is offered as being open to doubt.

James had addressed the matter in "The Art of Fiction," in 1884. In that essay he had asserted the novelist's freedom, in subject matter and form and finally as to the matter of "conscious moral purpose". (He was here quoting an essay by Walter Besant, to which his own essay was a response.) "Vagueness, in such a discussion, is fatal," said James, "and what is the meaning of your morality and your conscious moral purpose? Will you not define your terms and explain how (a novel being a picture) a picture can be either moral or immoral?" But of course he knew exactly what Mr. Besant and the many others like him had in mind. Besant was generally pleased with the current direction of English fiction. To the contrary, said James, it was a difficulty in contemporary English novels that they seemed to be addressed in large degree to "'young people,'" with the result of an unfortunate shyness. And a decade and a half later he was again saying the same, in another of his generalizing essays, "The Future of the Novel", observing "the demoralisation, the vulgarisation of literature in general, the increasing familiarity of all such methods of communication, the making itself supremely felt, as it were, of the presence of the ladies and children—by whom I mean, in other words, the reader irreflective and uncritical."[xix]

The remarks no doubt reflected an animus as well as a defensiveness directed against pietistic guardians of society and the arts. The impulse was, by just so much, not different from that of *The Yellow Book* and other contemporary proponents of art-for-art's sake, or from, on the other side, that of the new "naturalists" in France and America, like Zola and Frank Norris. But for James the rejection of prescriptive moral purpose in literature was not even a cause. He was not a signer of manifestoes. Both the art-for-art's-sake people (like Oscar Wilde, for prime instance) and the new naturalists might be seen to be moralists themselves just because the enemy had established the terms of the conflict. For James, now, the uses of fiction would not include accusations, one way or the other, nor appeal to ethical principle, either on one side or another. Nor, now, would there be a sorting-out of ethical dilemmas. In the novels of the nineties there are no grand renunciations. (Or, if Nanda Brookenham in *The Awkward Age* will renounce her lover, as discussed in pages following, the event goes to prove the point. The lover has already rejected her, and her plea is for a resumption of the adultery between her would-not-be-lover and her mother.) If, again, there are seeming large sacrifices as play of event in the "major-phase" novels coming next, it is the lesson of the nineties that those later actions might well be regarded skeptically.

For James, now, the routine society which provides his subject matter is a site where people do awful things to each other as is quite to be expected. Sex has a lot to do with it, and so the immorality is deep but is fathomable. James' language, meanwhile, delays and delays, and searches and considers possibilities, other problematics, until it releases a discovery, always provisional, the while it teases and distances.

All of this makes for singular adventure for the reader, but just as, so it would seem, it did for the author. The theater had led him to realize "the divine principle of the Scenario," so James several times said, and preparatory Notebook entries for the longer fictions of the second half of the decade are indeed detailed, sometimes elaborately detailed, as James worked out plot and character and, particularly, projected length of the whole of a work and of pieces of the whole. But the writing tended its own way. For one thing, except for *The Sacred Fount,* all of the novel-length fictions were composed in serial installments, against deadlines and sometimes overlappingly, and so deviations would have been likely to occur. There is a nice moment in the Notebooks when James takes sudden stock of a major turning-point in the plot of *The Spoils of Poynton,* when Owen falls in love with Fleda, and says that he really had not meant for that to happen, but now, because the serial of the novel was on-going, he was stuck with it. More revealingly, the careful projections of length–for *What Maisie Knew* twelve and a half pages about the parents, ten pages for the child's perceptions, etc.–never held. Similarly, characters projected for minor roles were discovered to offer rich possibilities for exploitation and emerged to the fore.

In the Preface to *What Maisie Knew,* looking back at what he said was another instance of an idea which had refused to remain humble, James would say of a fictive idea, that "Once 'out,' like a house-dog of a temper above confinement, it defies the mere whistle, it roams, it hunts; it seeks out and 'sees' life; it can be brought back but by hand and then only to take its futile thrashing." *The Awkward Age,* he said in the Preface, belonged to a group of productions which in each case asserted "an unforeseen principle of growth." The idea for the novel had started small, while the finished pages then before him emphasized "that truth of the vanity of the *a priori* test of what an *idée-mère* may have to give." "The truth is," he said, "that what a happy thought has to give depends immensely on the general turn of the mind capable of it, and on the fact that its loyal entertainer, cultivating fondly its possible relations and extensions, the bright efflorescence latent in it, but having to take other things in their order too, is terribly at the mercy of his mind."

That mind, as should be an obvious thing to say, did its work by way of fiction. W.B. Yeats would say that form, in poetry, was his plow. Just so, for James, fiction was the plow, perhaps throughout his career but most especially now when he was resolved to disallow authorial intrusion and to avoid "going behind".[xx] The negative side of the matter is worth remarking. The time of James' literary career encompassed the times of: Marx, Nietzsche, Freud, Husserl, Bergson, Herbert Spencer, then Bertrand Russell and Alfred North Whitehead. He had several times been in a room with Spencer, in 1877, at the Athenaeum Club, but said of him only, in a letter, that he seemed always to be asleep. Otherwise, none of these seemed at all to have figured for him, nor did any other of the other great or lesser names in philosophy and science of the nineteenth and early twentieth centuries, and certainly there is no evidence that in any of them he found any usefulness whatsoever. He had a mind so fine, as has been said, that no idea could violate it. To be sure, his father had been a philosopher of some note, and his brother came to be a psychologist, and philosopher, of very great note, but neither as a son nor a brother did he adopt any systems of thought from them.

It should be an obvious thing to say, that James' mind did its work by way of fiction, but, then, obviously it is not. James is an exciting writer, never more so than in this time in his career when he has made a deliberate break with past accomplishment and embarked upon uncertainties. The novel-length fictions in particular open up before their author, page by page coming upon unforeseen possibilities. For the reader this no doubt requires a special, unencumbered, participating kind of attentiveness, but James has become an especially distanced, marmorialized instance of a classic, not incidentally the more removed from experience by an accumulating academic criticism amounting often enough, in its self-sustaining self-referencing to a kind of collective autism. It is the case that it was even during his lifetime that he came to be The Master, consequently to be revered, or perhaps dreaded, or mildly mocked, but therefore to be forestalled from original, page by page apprehension. James succumbs to an adjective and becomes "Jamesian". The several plainly autobiographical stories about writers, of the early 1890s, might well be seen as attempts by James to rescue himself from the reputation by which he was already obscured.

It would seem to be rewarding to try to be present at the composition of the plays and the fictions, and also the essays—like that wonderfully privileged late secretary of his, Theodora Bosanquet (of whom more below)—as James formulated intentions and reconsidered and attended to realities of publishing and audience and lived a life, and succumbed (to echo his own metaphor for the process) to an imagination which was active, sly, witty, probing, exploratory, and (to extend the metaphor of the plow, and to refer to the exact sense of the word), profound.

—Which is what this book attempts to do. Following the writing it is "a reading of".

The three novels of the so-called Major Phase arrive immediately afterwards, 1902–1904. Different as are *The Wings of the Dove, The Ambassadors,* and *The Golden Bowl* from the short fictions of the 1890s, it would be odd were they to be found to be lacking the wit and the slyness and exploratory impulses of what James had just been doing–and in fact the Notebooks show that they are each already conceived and being pushed forward in the late 1890s. It is worth suggesting, in any event, that they be read by that light and not as being merely monumental. It is the purpose of the brief consideration which is given to them below to suggest just that.

Chapter One
The Mind of the Master

In his late years, 1907 to his death in 1916, it was no doubt his remarkable typist, Theodora Bosanquet, who knew James best. She had been poised to appreciate the nuances of the style. Preparing for the job, she had typed out paragraphs of *The Ambassadors,* like an actress preparing to take on a role. She had been present, taking dictation, as James converted thought into fictions. Moreover, she had a fine literary intelligence of her own. In her own later years she would write a study of Paul Valery. And she did have useful things to say about James' practice. He was well aware, she said, of his tendency to diffuseness. He more and more, she said, would prefigure his fictions as staged performances, arranged in acts and scenes. Importantly, she noted that he would often "talk out" his characters in a given situation so that when the passage was written, he would be aware of both their conscious motives and their concealments, with the consequence, further, that he created characters who told lies. "Most novelists," Miss Bosanquet wrote in a late memoir, "provide some clue to help their readers to distinguish truth from falsehood," but that was not necessarily the case with James.

Better than anyone else, Miss Bosanquet would also have known the very tenor of James' mind. Her recollections therefore have unusual authority, as when she would say of James that "When he walked out of the refuge of his study into the world and looked about him, he saw a place of torment, where creatures of prey perpetually thrust their claws into the quivering flesh of the doomed, defenceless children of light."[1]

But if so, James was not a man who himself quivered, either with sorrow or with wrath. Rather, and despite the elegance of manner, both personal and in his craft, James would seem to have been a man who hugely overbore—so that perhaps it is not unlikely that in the last moments of his life, in his dementia, he would think that he was Napoleon ordering new designs for the Louvre and the Tuilleries. The critic Stephen Donadio, particularly, drawing mostly from materials of James' later years, discovers the sheer strength of will of the man, as indeed confirmed by the very look of the man. "For all the apparently obsessive refinement and civility," Donadio writes, "no one who has ever looked into the unyielding eyes of the late portraits of The Master, or seen, in the photographs, just the faintest suggestion of the curled lip, or taken note of the unexpectedly massive hand gripping the end of a chair-arm, as if the novelist were established in the very seat of power, at home in some official residence considerably more worldly than the Palace of Art—no one whose consciousness has registered such details will doubt the reputedly withering power of James' personality."[2] And Miss Bosanquet, too, looking back to her first meeting with James, recalled that "He was much more massive than I had expected, much broader and stouter and stronger." She seems not to have observed the curled lip, but, she said, James might have been "some species of disguised cardinal, or even a Roman nobleman amusing himself by playing the part of a Sussex squire."

According to his own mid-1890s testimony in a letter to a friend, James had "the imagination of disaster" and said of himself that he saw "life indeed as ferocious and sinister."[3]

But if, once again, his imagination plumbed darknesses, he himself was not particularly vulnerable. He entertained his imagination. He peopled his fictions with characters who would do terrible, perverse things, but there was never any question, now, of evil, because the fictions were not moralized. Nor, by way of complement, is there any evidence at all that James had any fundamental belief in innocence. Thus, for instance, while there are children, they are equipped for dark (and sexual) deviousness, as the fictions go on to show. He wrote about children but, emphatically, not for children. His essay of 1899 "The Future of Fiction" is in fact largely a statement in behalf of a fiction which will not defer to the inexperience of the young, in either subject matter or form, but which will, rather, assault "delicacy" and the reading habits of "a community mainly devoted to traveling and shooting, to pushing trade and playing football." In what moreover is a repeated stratagem of James' writing, characters who seem to be perfectly nice and who, pointedly, seem to be ripe for sympathy, and are likely to be placed in pathetic circumstances, and with every reason to trust their author, will be exposed for the knaves or fools, or whatever, they helplessly are.

As has been often observed, in James' writing in the nineties there is a lot of sex. As of about 1896, as Edmund Wilson was the first to say, sex, for James, became even a kind of obsession, "in a queer and left-handed way". Furthermore, said Wilson, the theme of violation of innocence, now in "this relatively neurotic phase," secured a peculiarity wherein the effectiveness of the tales would derive not from the pathos of the sympathetic victim but "from the excitement of the violation," the victims often being children.[4]

But this misses the mark insofar as the statement implies any kind of a perverse sadistic delight, and misses the mark again by suggesting that the subject matter—sexual violation—was product, or symptom, of, peculiarly, the (relatively) neurotic phase of the nineties. (Wilson was writing before F.O. Matthiessen put forth "The Major Phase".)

The subject had been exploited by James from the beginning, blatantly in *Watch and Ward*, which had been serialized in 1871 when James was in his late twenties. In that novel James had told the story of a fellow, Roger, who raises and ripens a twelve-year-old girl, Nora, for his purposes. He will marry her when she grows up, but, we read, "Roger caught himself wondering whether, at the worst, a little precursory love-making would do any harm." "The ground," he says, "might be gently tickled to receive his own sowing; the petals of the young girl's nature, playfully forced apart, would leave the golden heart of the flower but the more accessible to his own vertical rays." Leon Edel in his introduction to the novel pointed to this and other examples of the book's "persistent erotic imagery" saying that they seem to have been set down with bland unconsciousness on the author's part, but the portrait of James we have from Edel's own great biography, as well as from countless other sources, indicates that James was a very ironical young man unlikely to be unconscious of a *double entendre*, certainly not one so persistently pressed, as in this example.[5] (In a letter of 1867 Alice describes the young Henry's elegant joshing at the James' dinner table, with "a good deal of eyebrow nostril and shoulder affectation."[6]) There was a wink here, as in similar other passages, and perhaps a snicker.

But the difference for James now in the nineties, after a career of exercise of imagination, was that he simply—or, rather, not simply—did not believe in innocence but found literary opportunity in the hypocrisy of innocence. Certainly he was not enraged. Rather, it was a portion of his opportunity that he could tease the sentimental biases of the typical reader. The critic Frank Moore Colby, in 1902, the year of the publication of *The Wings of the Dove,* was more accurate than Edmund Wilson in defining James' tone and, therefore, his presumed motives. Writing in *The Bookman* (in an essay entitled "The Queerness of Henry James," queerly enough) he observed that in a day of well-policed literature James was anomalous. "He is the only writer of the day whose moral notions do not seem to matter," he said. James' "dissolute and complicated Muse," he said, "may say just what she chooses," although it didn't really matter because nobody anyway could penetrate the prose, and also there were no graphic physical descriptions—"nobody sins," he said, "because nobody has anything to sin with." (But for James the physical descriptions would have been a distraction at best, as not for others. In a letter to Robert Louis Stevenson in 1893 he had complained that in Thomas Hardy's Tess "the pretence of 'sexuality' is only equaled by the absence of it.") Said Colby, James "has, in fact, written furiously against the proprieties for several years."[7]

Colby's "furiously" was also certainly an exaggeration. James was derisive, rather. He had to have been aware of the Anglo-Saxon restrictions, and was so, and was disdainful. In a letter to William Dean Howells, in the 1880s, he had remarked that he found French novelists to be admirable because despite "their handling of unclean things," they were "at least serious and honest". And he went on to say, wittily, that unlike the English writer who "wants to make sure, first of all, of your moral judgment, the French is willing, while it waits a little, to risk, for the sake of his subject and its interest, your spiritual salvation."[8] He was aware, moreover, of the need to disguise his own inventions. In a Notebook entry for *The Golden Bowl* he would caution himself that while the projected novel would be likely to satisfy the projected publisher, Harper, there might be a problem with "the adulterine element in the subject," but then quickly added, "But may it not be simply a question of *handling* that? For God's sake let me try: I want to plunge into it." And in the event, there would be elements in that novel a deal more improper than adultery, which he would handle.

If there was, anew, a lot of sex in James' writing in the nineties, it was there as in life, as a main provocation to human perversity, which latter was to be regarded as a subject matter. He was not angry. He did not titillate. Sex was of a piece with the dark comedy of human motives and relationships, which in turn were to be regarded steadily, implacably, distantly, and with amusement. That, and not the sex, was the subject. The gaze was satirical, dedicated to seeing what was going on behind and underneath.

A number of the short stories offer quick evidence, being the more unsparing because the more concentrated.

There was "Glasses," in 1896. Flora Saunt is one of James' needy young women, in need particularly of a wealthy husband. She has beautiful deep grey eyes, with which she will bewitch Lord Iffeld. But Flora is going blind—and here if anywhere would have been a case for an author's pity, as one might think, but James hurries elsewhere. Until she is safely married Flora will not wear the glasses which will save her sight. "Those wonderful eyes are good for nothing but to roll about like sugar-balls—which they greatly resemble—in a child's mouth," says an observer. When Lord Iffeld discovers the truth about Flora's infirmity, he cancels the engagement, for "The future in short assumed a new complexion for him when looked at through the grim glasses of a bride who, as he had said to some one, couldn't really, when you came to find out, see her hand before her face." "He had conducted himself like any other jockeyed customer—he had returned the animal as unsound." Flora does land safely, however. Another admirer, much less prepossessing in all ways except that he cares for her, does marry her.

And so much for the case of an upper-class bounder, except that James hangs on. Flora is poor Flora and Lord Iffeld is a cad, except that in fact the initial cruelty is only the beginning. Flora is not only desperate but is also desperately vain while except in the ways of flirtation, according to James' insistence, she is a young lady without any talents or accomplishments. She uses her lovely eyes, it is said, "to make fools of young men, but not to read or write, not to do any sort of work. She never opens a book, and her maid writes her notes." Moreover, she has "a scrappy little figure." It is said of her variously, with seeming authority, that she is an idiot and vulgar and incapable of telling the truth, and then the end of her story is grotesque. At the opera, after some passage of time, the narrator sees her without her glasses, seated in one of the receptacles of the grand tier, prettier than any of the other women, the object of interest and admiration from below. "Dressed in white, with diamonds in her hair and pearls on her neck, she had a pale radiance of beauty," so the narrator says, "which even at [a] distance made her a distinguished presence and, with the air that easily attaches to lonely loveliness in public places, an agreeable mystery." She casually moves her eyes over the house and, says the narrator, "I felt them brush me again like the wings of a dove." But the lovely lady is by this time totally blind. She mistakes the narrator for her husband when he comes to call. And: "Flora after a while again lifted the glass from the ledge of the box," so the narrator reports, "and elegantly swept the house with it. Then, by the mere instinct of her grace, a motion but half conscious, she inclined her head into the void with the sketch of a salute, producing, I could see, a perfect imitation of a response to some homage."

The narrator believes that Flora has now achieved happiness because "the question was now only of her beauty and her being seen and marvelled at: ...in life her activity was limited to that."

But then still again, and by way of an additional turn of the screw, the narrator is one of James' unreliable narrators, who in this case if he is not a liar or is not mistaken is also not a sympathetic witness. He is a portrait painter who presumably is a good judge of heads, and for the rest is judgmental, witty, and amused, given to a kind of self-congratulating brutality of judgment. Professing to like the young man whom Flora will eventually marry, he reports that he "stumbled into my room with awkward movements and equivocal sounds—a long, lean, confused, confusing young man, with a bad complexion and large, protrusive teeth," with, when he opened his mouth, "a remarkable revelation of gums." Coming upon Flora newly-equipped with glasses, he reports: "All I saw at first was the big gold bar crossing each of her lenses, over which something convex and grotesque, like the eyes of a large insect, something that now represented her whole personality, seemed, as out of the orifice of a prison, to strain forward and press. The face had shrunk away. . . ." Men perhaps do not make passes, but this narrator of this tale is a connoisseur of ugliness.

Again, "The Coxon Fund" of a couple of years earlier quite as determinedly if somewhat less brutally went about essentially the same business, sabotaging sympathy. The tale's Frank Saltram is a kind of celebrity intellectual who imposes himself on a family, the Mulvilles. He is fat and soft, is thick in the nose and has a hanging lip, and is unkempt. Much like Dostoevsky's bogus priest Foma Fomitch in *The Friend of the Family*, he rules his hosts by way of assumption of his due, is ungrateful as a matter of high principle, and drinks hugely. He is a great talker about uplifting things, especially when, as it is said, he is not "too enslaved for the hour to the superstition of sobriety." The Mulvilles meanwhile bask in the pride of having him in their very home for something more than four years, the while they are forced to make financial sacrifices in order to keep him. Nor does James make it easy either for them or for the reader because Saltram is not quite altogether a fraud. The narrator stands as guarantor of the fact that as a talker, when enabled, he repays attention, and he has published some papers. But he is mostly a fraud. Much of his production is in the form of prospectuses for undelivered lectures with such titles as "An Analysis of Primary Ideas". While, however, he is mostly a comic humbug, the Mulvilles are mostly fools, and it is to that harsher comedy that the tale goes. Their good will is as platitudinous as Saltram's prospectuses, and, after a manner, is just as suspect. When their dependent does finally depart, they will be "destitute" because, in all irony, as the narrator says, "They have no one to live on now."

It is to be seen that the ironies in this tale, too, moreover, reduplicate, to the point that everyone and everything is stripped. Beginning with the "Coxon Fund" itself. There had been a Lady Coxon, a thin transcendental Bostonian, who had been charged by her late husband to establish an "Endowment of Research"—the very idea of which, in itself, the narrator finds to be baffling—to be awarded to some earnest, disinterested, and financially needy seeker after Moral Truth. When Lady Coxon dies, it is given to her American niece to establish the fund and appoint its initial beneficiary, although, actually, not necessarily to offer it, because if no worthy candidate is to be found she can keep the money for herself, which in fact she needs. She is an attractive and clever young lady who is impelled by immoderate eleemosynary promptings, and so she gives the money to Frank Saltram, who promptly ceases to produce anything. She is Isabel Archer made foolish, beyond being duped.

And Frank Saltram has a wife, mother of his children, whom he has abandoned and who is an obvious candidate for charity except that her abandonment is itself her financial and social capital.

She was, says the narrator, "a deeply wronged, justly resentful, quite irreproachable and insufferable person" whose "personal fall had been a sort of social rise, for there had been a moment when, in our little conscientious circle, her desolation almost made her the fashion." "Her voice," he says, moreover, "was grating and her children were ugly."

Frank Saltram may have something of the looks and manners of a Doctor Johnson, minus at the very least the production, but in fact he had begun life as Coleridge, and what is to be inferred from the evolution of "The Coxon Fund" is particularly illuminating. James had been reading a biography of Coleridge. In the Notebook entry dated April 17th, 1894, he said that he had been "struck with the suggestiveness of S.T.C.'s figure—wonderful, admirable figure—for pictorial treatment," and in this first of two notations he developed his ideas at length in order to create a situation for the central figure. What James at this point had in mind, clearly, was a testament to the privileges due genius. The character was to be *young*, in italics, and "a wonder of *promise*." "Would not such a drama necessarily be the question of the acceptance by someone," James wrote, "of the general *responsibility* of rising to the height of accepting him for what he is, recognizing his rare, anomalous, magnificent, interesting, curious, tremendously suggestive character, vices and all, with all its imperfections on its head, and *not* being guilty of the pedantry, the stupidity, the want of imagination, of fighting him, deploring him in the details—failing to recognize that one *must* pay for him and that on the whole he is magnificently worth it." And he advised himself: "Live with it a little, *mon bon*, and the happy child will be born."

But the happy child, when born, soon afterwards, was happy enough but otherwise nothing like what had been projected, having undergone "a free rearrangement," as James would express the matter in the New York Edition Preface. The tale had become comic satire, everything having been turned around so that the great poet had become more-or-less a charlatan and for certain a moocher, and the poet's admiring attendants had become plural and fools. The second of the Notebook entries, written just a few days after the first, on April 25th, 1894, has to do mostly with questions of how to compress the story so as to meet the length restrictions of *The Yellow Book*, to which James was to send it, and that exercise might in itself have done something to drain the characters of demands of sympathy; James was now moving characters about, and seeing necessity for summarizing attributes rather than full presentation, and eliding character development and by that much distancing his characters and objectifying them.

But explanation for the extent of the shift in his perception of his characters is elsewhere. In a couple of passages in the second Notebook entry, where James was working out plot movements, he raised questions as to what the character who will become the American niece is to know, and when and how, and, as he does elsewhere in the Notebooks where he is working out developments of the tales, he conflates himself with the character who will be the narrator: "She must only hear about [Saltram] from me. I must have a little talk with her—to explain.... I *tell* the strange young lady—the pretty American girl—more or less about him," with more of the same. But then the narrator of the story to come will in fact emphatically not be James himself. Not only is the story not told in conventional third person, as James might have had in mind for the tale when he was writing these passages, but, as happens also elsewhere, the narrator-to-come is as satirically distanced as all of the other characters. Here he is witty, urbane, but also elegantly, universally condescending and dismissive. He it is who transforms the desires and humiliations of the others into a joke, and then again he is the arrangement by which James ultimately transformed Coleridge, the great poet who was a fine talker, into Frank Saltram, and transformed equally those initially projected superior persons who would sustain the poet whatever his vices.

Clearly the story changed on James as he submitted his characters to concentrated and probing process of imagination. Had the story gone as originally conceived, no doubt it would have been material for inspiration but it would have been an utterance entirely contrary to James' sense of things in these later years, and hostile to his indisposition to indulge embalmed prejudices.

Even such prejudices as had to do with the privileges of literary genius, and, then, even when, clearly, the genius was himself.

He wrote a number of stories in the nineties about unappreciated or mis-appreciated writers which, clearly, bore a personal burden, but even here, with just one exception, the tales tended to turn away from what was originally intended, and became satirical, leaving behind the one or the other fine novelist who had been projected to be at the center of the tale.

The exception was the first of them, "The Middle Years," published in 1893, just when James turned fifty. There would seem to be little doubt that in the momentous year James himself, like his hero Dencombe, would have been looking back over his career, exhaustedly, and contemplating an end to career, inevitably to life itself, while at the same time—he was now in the middle of his theater venture—hoping for what Dencombe calls "a second chance" and an "extension". "The Middle Years" is dolorously eloquent as it reflects on the life which has been dedicated to the art of fiction. "The infinite of life had gone," Dencombe observes, "and what was left of the dose was a small glass engraved like a thermometer by the apothecary." "He sat and stared at the sea," we read, "which appeared all surface and twinkle, far shallower than the spirit of man.

It was the abyss of human illusion that was the real, the tideless deep." And "It had taken too much of his life to produce too little of his art." The story nonetheless will lead him to recognition of what he has achieved, and to revelation of his range. "It *is* glory," he says, "to have been tested, to have had our little quality and cast our spell." To the young doctor with literary taste who has been ministering to him he says, "The thing is to have made somebody care"—and James' personal investment in the tale is the further confirmed by the quite audible homoerotic undertone in this passage. And then Dencombe proceeds to the high point of his eloquence: "We work in the dark—we do what we can—we give what we have. Our doubt is our passion and our passion is our task. The rest is the madness of art."

However, the next of the writer tales, "The Death of the Lion," published in early 1894, while it might well have gone the same way, carrying the same personal burden of sorrow and pride, in fact did not.

Neil Paraday, too, is in his middle years. He is fifty years old. He is a great but misunderstood novelist who has just completed his finest work. He has been sick and is likely to die, as in fact he will do and as the title has promised. Like Dencombe before him, he will be attended by a young man who is able to appreciate him, in this case the narrator. Unlike Dencombe, however, although almost entirely unread by the general public, he has become a celebrity, and will be slain by the lion hunters. That the subject was personal to James is obvious but is in any event confirmed by the Notebook entry, in which James says of his projected character that he will be a great man of letters who is tremendously made up to and *fêted* by persons not one of whom has acquaintance with his work, a situation which, he said, "would have the merit, at least, of corresponding to an immense reality—a reality that strikes me every day of my life." But even as he was planning the tale and then while he was composing it, he moved away from plaint and commiseration. "The whole intention of the tale," he suggested to himself, "should be admirably satiric, ironic"—adding in the next sentence that "The bewildered old hero is [to be] murdered by the reviewers," which event struck him, presumably, as being a comic irony.

The satire in fact moves away from this figure at the center and has to do instead, much more generally, with the sad, comic, and awful state of contemporary literature, together with the mechanisms of fame. The reviewer who has been primarily responsible for Neil Paraday's fame has never read a word of Paraday's fiction. The narrator, who is also a reviewer, although he retreats from the job, had been sent to interview Paraday by an editor, Mr. Pinhorn, who "had smelt the coming glory as an animal smells its prey." When Neil Paraday succumbs to his fate as a celebrity, his fate is represented particularly by Mrs. Weeks Wimbush, the brewer's wife "and proprietress of the universal menagerie." The primary metaphor—the celebrity as a lion—proliferates. The text is shot through with animal images. It's a jungle out there, and a circus. Two other quickly-forthcoming literary celebrities come upon the scene in order to chase Paraday from his hill. They are Guy Walsingham, the author of "Obsessions," and Dora Forbes, author of "The Other Way Round". Guy Walsingham is really a Miss Collop, "a pretty little girl who wore her hair in what used to be called a crop," and Dora Forbes is a florid, bald fellow with a big red moustache and showy knickerbockers. Guy Walsingham, although a young lady, is a proponent of "the larger latitude." Dora Forbes has taken a feminine pen-name because the ladies are such popular favorites. There are in the tale, as well, an Augusta Minch and a Mr. Rumble, as well as the sensitive and lovely young American girl who is named "Fanny Hurter" for no reason to be discovered in the development of the character, but which is fitting with the tone of the whole of the tale. If anything, Fanny is overly sensitive only spiritually, but the tale stands ready to mock all of its characters.

James not long before, commenting on the state of literary criticism, had remarked on "the deluge of doctrine suspended in the void".[9] Like Henry James before him, Paraday is invited to take part in "the periodical prattle about the future of fiction," as the narrator phrases the matter, and he dies.

"The Death of the Lion" was followed by "The Next Time" and "The Figure in the Carpet," both of them once again about misunderstood, unappreciated novelists. Considered as autobiography, as is virtually compulsory, what is astonishing about "The Next Time" is the amount by which the figure at the center is kept at a distance, permitted no Dencombe-like eloquence in his own behalf, and, although he does die at the end, as do all of these other novelists, he is much more the bearer of an irony than of a tragedy.

Needing money, Ray Limbert, the author of a series of exquisite failures, tries repeatedly, as he says, to "make a sow's ear of a silk purse," and, ever-hopeful, fails each time, the next and the next and the next. A few weeks prior to publication of the tale, reflecting on his failures in the theater, James was saying in a letter to his brother William that "you can't make a sow's ear out of a silk purse," and in correspondence the same day with Morton Fullerton he was saying the same, "You *can't*, after all, make a sow's ear out of a silk purse—which is what I have been too heroically trying."[10] The first Notebook entry for "The Next Time" is dated January 26th, 1895, following by just three days James' valiant reflection on, at once, the *Guy Domville* fiasco and the promise of the future: "It is now indeed that I may do the work of my life," he said, and as for his recent problems, "all that is of the ineffable—too deep and pure for any utterance. Shrouded in sacred silence, let it rest."

And now, having so vowed, and as was attested immediately by "The Next Time," he did enshroud the recent past, and something more: he entombed the pity of it. As he contemplated the story, the incident most present to him was an occurrence of twenty years before, at the beginning of his career, when he had agreed to write letters from Paris for the *New York Tribune*. The publisher had judged his letters to be insufficiently journalistic, which was to say not to the popular taste. And here he was again, except that by referring backwards he would be able to confront fresh wounds as though they were old ones.

The irony of Ray Lambert's perverse ambition is enhanced, moreover, by a perfect reversal. Lambert has a sister-in-law who is a popular novelist, who wishes for one exquisite failure in order to establish some artistic credentials, but she fails to fail. "It was not given to her not to please," says the narrator. "It was not that when she tried to be what she called subtle...her fond consumers, bless them, didn't suspect the trick nor show what they thought of it: they straightway rose on the contrary to the morsel she had hoped to hold too high, and, making but a big, cheerful bite of it, wagged their great collective tail artlessly for more." The narrator is himself a literary critic with elevated standards and tastes, whose praise is the kiss of death. There are, also, a Mr. Bousefield, and a lady humorist who writes screaming sketches and whose name is Minnie Meadows.

"The Figure in the Carpet" was not so rollicking as "The Next Time," but it too drifts away from what might have been the lyricism of a Dencombe, and into broad ironies. James would say in the Preface to the volume of the New York Edition in which the tale appears, that it had been his intention to reinstate the rights and dignities of analytic appreciation of literature, and indeed that is what, at least in its initial situation, the tale does seem to promise to do, before it goes elsewhere.[11] Once again, the narrator is a young reviewer. He will be told by the novelist Hugh Vereker (another of James' "supersubtle fry," as in the Preface James would describe all of these writers), that along with all of Vereker's supposed admirers, he had missed the essential, and obvious, "little point," the "little trick" of all his work, the figure in the carpet. That little trick is the "organ of life" of his work. It is as obvious, he says, "as concrete there as a bird in a cage, a bait on a hook, a piece of cheese in a mouse-trap," but it remains undetected by any of the critics. Nor, of course, as the story unfolds—or caroms, as in this case is the better word—is the thing, the "special beauty" as James referred to it in his Notebook entry, ever specified. The rest and the most of the tale consists, rather, of adventures connected with the guessing.

Especially in the years just following James' death, "The Figure in the Carpet" was taken to be a kind of an invitation to critical competition, inviting detection of the presumed figure in the great carpet of James' own prose, much as in the action of the tale itself—thereby wonderfully to extend the ironies of the tale. Like Hugh Vereker, who had died taking the presumed secret with him, so it was supposed that James had died taking the secret with him, intestate. In the first of the Notebook entries having to do with the story, seemingly by way of an afterthought, James had considered that the projected tale would provide a "lovely chance for fine irony" on the subject of "critics," in quotation marks; then the nicer, unspoken but certainly foreseeable irony was that he himself would become the mystery.

So in 1917 the critic Stuart Sherman would observe that "In that fascinating work *The Figure in the Carpet* [James] depicts, for criticism, what he would have called his own 'case,'" and went on to say, flatly and grandly, that "the thing which [James]... implored someone to observe and to declare is that he adored beauty." So in 1918, in an essay entitled "The Figure in the Carpet," the critic Joseph Warren Beach would observe that "The *ideal* of James is clearly a combination, or rather a *fusion*, of good taste with spiritual discernment." Ford Madox Ford, writing in 1932, would say, mostly on the basis of personal recollection, that the figure was "disillusionment". R.P. Blackmur, in 1943, would say, with a fine gesture of his own, that "The Figure in the Carpet" "would seem actually, as written, to mean no more than that there is a figure in the carpet if you can imagine it for yourself; it is not there to discover."[12] And thirty years later Maxwell Geismar, a determined but not a friendly critic, would say, enough, that "The Figure in the Carpet" is a "little parable of intellectual morbidity which hardly deserves, and was certainly never intended to gain, the solemn moralizing of the late James himself or the Jacobite cult"—which observation, if truculent, was not unintelligent.[13] While James Thurber had earlier come to essentially the same conclusion in "A Final Note on Chanda Bell," although narratively and with better grace. "You have found the figure, Thurber," says the baffling, exasperating novelist Chanda Bell, "but have you found the carpet?"

> This was accompanied by her shrewd, tiny smile. I could not determine whether she meant there was something to find that I had not found, or nothing to find at all, beneath the gleaming surface of her style. The devil of it was that I could not be sure of anything. I spent that night going over "The Huanted? Yatch" with a fine-tooth comb, searching for esoteric anagrams, feeling for what she had called "the carpet". I scrutinized, investigated, explored, took apart, and put back together again the entire fibre and fabric, uncertain of what shape and texture I was looking for. I read the thing backward,

> and I even tried to read it upside down and in the mirror of my bureau.

And he tries to read it sideways, again without luck.[14] Meanwhile, James' tale itself becomes a series of jokes, or, better, a piling on of jokes, pointedly at the expense of a series of literary small fry. The narrator, if baffled, is not, either, an especially shrewd reader of or even a devotee of the novels of Hugh Vereker. He is a young critic who is ambitious to make a reputation and earn some money. He has written a somewhat perceptive critical review of Vereker's most recent novel; Vereker attests to its general intelligence before telling the narrator that he has missed the essential point. The narrator thinks that Vereker is "awfully clever," as he says a couple of times. (The implication of that "awfully clever" becomes clearer, perhaps, in light of a remark by Theodora Bosanquet. She recalls James saying, "I rarely remember to have heard on English lips any other intellectual verdict, no matter under what provocation, than this broad synthesis 'so immensely clever'. What exasperates you is not that they can't say more but that they wouldn't if they could.")[15]

The narrator says that he has found Vereker's books to be "charming things". His friend and fellow critic, Corvick, is a better reader, who becomes a devoted searcher after the secret, and claims eventually (after a period of contemplation in India) to have found it. But then the discovery is not to be revealed because Corvick dies, tragically thrown from a dogcart while on an outing with his fiancee, and there is no further appeal to be made to Vereker himself because, first, Vereker has left for other places, and then, anyway, he dies, but it is possible that Corvick had entrusted the secret to his new wife, Gwendolen. Gwendolen is a novelist. At the age of nineteen she had published a novel in three volumes. The narrator, whose own style is characterized by a kind of snappy acuity, says of Gwendolen that "She had no sense of humor and, with her pretty way of holding her head to one side, was one of those persons whom you want, as the phrase is, to shake, but who have learnt Hungarian by themselves." Has she come into possession of Vereker's secret? Her next novel after Corvick's death is better than the earlier one, but then the one after that, so the narrator says, is not so good.

Gwendolen now remarries. Her second husband is also a critic, and, like her first husband, one who had reviewed her handsomely. Gwendolen dies, in childbirth, in a half a sentence. At the end, pressed by the narrator to reveal the secret, which Gwendolen surely would have told him, the second husband has no idea what the narrator is talking about.

It is to be added that there is an erotic element in all of this. At the beginning the narrator makes evident his jealousy of the more successful Corvick. As the tale unfolds, the subject of his probing comes to be the singular vital secret which, according to his supposition, is shared by a man and his wife. At the very end of the tale, the narrator is bent on informing the second husband that his wife had not told him everything, that she had kept something secret from him. Having planted suspicion, the narrator ends by saying that "The poor man's state is almost my consolation; there are really moments when I feel it to be quite my revenge."

"The Figure in the Carpet" figures itself, in fact, as a kind of prototype of much of James' writing in the nineties and beyond. The piling on of complications and reversals is a mark of the "Theatricals". The thematics of jealous probing after other people's intimate secrets, together with the whiff of erotic perversion, is in *The Turn of the Screw, In the Cage, The Spoils of Poynton, The Sacred Fount,* and each of the three of the novels of "The Major Phase". These several others differ from "The Figure in the Carpet" only most importantly in the fact that they treat of real secrets which are dirty little secrets, on the order of adultery, child molestation, and incest.

This is not of course to say that James had not from the beginning found amusement in darknesses and the grotesque. There had been *Watch and Ward* with its witty play within a situation of only slightly disguised child erotics in 1871. The first of James' ghost stories was "The Ghostly Rental," in 1876—a story which in a bit of dialogue incidentally provides a nice indication of James' procedure; the elderly gossip Miss Deborah, speaking of the goings-on at the nearby haunted house, says to the narrator, "Observe closely enough and it doesn't matter where you are. You may be in a pitch-dark closet. All you want is something to start with; one thing leads to another, and all things are mixed up. Shut me up in a dark closet and I will observe after a while, that some places are darker than others."

And in the novels and tales of the eighties there had been instances of an unexpected, offhand comic duskiness of imagination. Poor sacrificial Hyacinth Robinson, in *The Princess Cassimassima,* in 1886, is submitted to James' parody of Dickens' Jenny Wren, in the cheerful and intolerable cripple Rosie Muniment. In *The Bostonians,* also in 1886, Mrs. Farrinder is the public feminist who "at almost any time, had the air of being introduced by a few remarks," and who had a husband, whose name was Amariah. The heroic Miss Birdseye is "a confused, entangled, inconsequent, discursive old woman, whose charity began at home and ended nowhere." Quite beyond the occasional satires, moreover, while *The Bostonians* seriously engaged a serious public issue, it also reached for depravity. There at the beginning is the anticipation of Svengali in the mesmerist Mr. Tarrant, imagined to the point of intolerability by the fact that his subject is his daughter.

In the nineties, however, as not before, the satiric reach would become the rule, with the recurring subject of the fictions being the awful secrets in the lives of, on the whole, timid, vulnerable, ordinary, "desperately mundane" (as said André Gide), and very nice persons, often women, sometimes children, regarded and interrogated and probed with urbane wit and unforgiving tenacity.[16]

Chapter Two

Theatricals, The Other House, The Spoils of Poynton

In *The Other House* a little girl is murdered. Her name is Effie and it is her fourth birthday. She is drowned by Rose Armiger, a friend of the family. Rose is a vengeful person. She has been thwarted in love. *The Spoils of Poynton* ends with a fire; the house, Poynton, is burned, by random accident, which is to say by the author, resulting in the final thwarting of the lovesick maiden Fleda Vetch. The two novels were published in serial, in 1896, overlapping with each other, and were James' first since the *Guy Domville* episode of early January 1895, and followed upon his resolve to take up his "old pen" again, "the pen of all my old unforgettable efforts and sacred struggles."

He did not in fact pick up just exactly from where he had left off. The new novels were short, for one thing, and concentrated, allowing little room for authorial dilation, coming after the sprawl of the last novel previous, *The Tragic Muse* of 1890. Again, in the case of these two novels as in novels to come, James particularly attended to what he was now calling scenic method. Form, moreover and in the event, would both create and abet a difference in attitude toward character and plot; more than ever before these new novels would maintain character and action at an acutely observed but skeptical, detached, and unsympathetic distance, and in this deep sense, no matter what horrors might be allowed, the novels were now not only dramatic but theatrical and comic. Formally, tonally, thematically, and even morally, this is to say, the new novels were infused with the experience of the theater.

As for form, in the Notebooks in the months following the *Guy Domville* episode James repeatedly invoked what he took to be the primary salvageable lessons to be had from the theater years, namely composition by scene and scenario. In an entry dated February 14th, 1895, he asked himself, "Has a *part* of all this wasted passion and squandered time been simply the precious lesson, taught me in that roundabout and devious, that cruelly expensive, way, *of the singular value for a narrative plan too* of the (I don't know *what* adequately to call it) divine principle of the Scenario? If that *has* been one side of the moral of the whole unspeakable, the whole tragic experience, I almost bless the pangs and the pains and the miseries of it." If it were to be discovered, he went on, that the same principle might be a key to fit "the complicated chambers of *both* the dramatic and the narrative lock," then, so he said, "my little loss is converted into an almost infinite gain." Again, the following summer—August 11th, 1895—working at his idea for *The Spoils of Poynton,* he was suggesting to himself the necessity for knowing in advance "each of my steps, stages, tints, shades, every main joint and hinge" (albeit that in the execution, that was not what happened). "When I ask myself what there may have been to show for my long tribulation," he went on, "my wasted years and patience and pangs, of theatrical experiment, the answer, as I have already noted here, comes up as just possibly *this*: what I have gathered from it will perhaps have been exactly some such mystery of fundamental statement—of the art and secret of it, of expression, of the sacred mystery of structure."

But as is indicated by his own work in, as well as for, the

theater, the theater had been for him much more than, simply, a formal discipline. He had been intensely involved with actors and actresses and actor-managers and backstage machinations. He had attended rehearsals of his plays, and had brought lunches for the casts. It was towards the London theater and its people that he had written. With the one exception of *Guy Domville,* moreover (and disregarding his adaptations of *The American* and *Daisy Miller),* it was comedies that he had been writing—the subjects of which had been adultery and blackmail and bastardy and such other sordid human follies, if not quite murder, which subjects he had addressed wittily. And then the novels and tales to come would deal very largely with dark materials—murder, adultery, blackmail, and such—and would do so, largely, again wittily. If the theater yielded the divine principle of the Scenario (by which James seems to have meant, mostly, detailed planning for settings and for entrances and exits), and while the theater might yield lessons in scenic development and for compactness of structure, among whatever else, it also and more largely provided a perspective, and that perspective was equivalent to an idea.

Particularly as regards *The Other House* and *The Spoils of Poynton,* the relevance of the theatrical experience is direct. The initial Notebook entries for both of the novels are dated at a time just midpoint in James' engagement with the theater, within a couple of days of each other—and there is nice incidental confirmation of the essential theatricality of James' attitude towards the contemplated violence. He was apparently particularly serene as he set about imagining the ferocity to be written into these novels to come. They were begotten just at the moment of what seems to have been a very pleasant Christmas time. The first of the Notebook entries for *Poynton* is dated December 24th, 1893, and that for *The Other House* is the day after Christmas, December 26th, 1893.

The entry for *The Other House* begins: "I have been sitting here in the firelight—on this quiet afternoon of the empty London Christmastide, trying to catch hold of the tail of an idea, of a 'subject,'" following which and having caught his subject, James went on to develop his idea of what at this point was to be the attempted poisoning of a little girl, at length and in detail. Earlier in the month he had had a quarrel with one of the actor-managers on whom he had depended, but then within a few days and by the middle of the month he was telling another theater friend that the whole of the experience was "matter for a roaring Xmas fire," and at about the same time he had been writing to his actress friend Elizabeth Robins that he was looking forward to a session of play-reading with her, on the eighteenth following, and also that he had begun another play.[1] The general indication is of a mellowness of mood particularly as James imagined infanticide.

Again, when he would come to publish his unproduced plays of the period James would call them, not attempts at "drama," a word which he seems deliberately to have avoided, but "Theatricals," by which, although he did not say just that, surely he was indicating that the content of the plays was meant to be taken for entertainment, and (not that he had ever been without fondness for melodrama—of plot, of metaphor, of language), it was not unlikely that as he now conceived his fictions, he would contemplate the usefulness of overt theatrical effects. *The Other House*, in particular, might in fact have gone either way, to become a play or a narrative fiction, and in fact in the event it would be both. In the Notebook entry James had raised the question immediately. "Is there," he asked himself, "something for a tale, is there something for a play" in the projected plot materials, and he had answered himself, "It is the *play* that I am looking for, but," he added, "it is worth noting, all the same, for the *other* possibility." The play, as happened, did come first, in a sketch (which has been lost) intended for the actor-manager Edward Compton, and when the novel was published reviewers pointed out that essentially the novel remained a three-act play—perhaps in part because, reasonably, reviewers by this time considered that James was a primarily a playwright .[2]

Theatricals

The four comedies which James would call "theatricals" were: *Tenants, Disengaged, The Album,* and *The Reprobate,* all of them composed between late 1890 and early 1892 and published in two volumes in 1894 and 1895. They remain largely unread and, with an exception just now and then, remain unproduced, in part no doubt because James himself seems to have been embarrassed by them even as he published them, which was unfortunate both because they have their bearing on the fictions to come and because in themselves they offer surprises.

In his "Notes" for the published volumes, particularly the second of them, James apologized mostly for the fact that the plays had not been produced. He said that they had been "experiments in the line of comedy pure and simple." They practically, he said, "confess themselves exercises." They were designed, he said, so as to be "supremely susceptible of being played to audiences unaccustomed to beat about the bush for their amusement—audiences, to be perfectly honest, in country towns." Theatrical necessity had demanded that they be kept simple and, above all, as he said repeatedly and in various ways of complaining about the process, theatrical necessity had demanded that they be cut and trimmed and trimmed again, to the length of an entertainment of two and a half hours, or, so he said, the lesson most to be learned lay "in the periodical throwing overboard of the cargo to save the ship."

> The freight, the fittings, the ballast, the passengers, the provisions, the luggage, the crew, the whole thing must inexorably 'go,' and the vessel is not in proper trim till she is despoiled of everything that might have appeared to make her worth saving; till the last survivor in the last rag of the rigging has been consigned to the fishes, uttering that shriek of despair which lives on in the playwright's ear… —which shriek, however, so the lesson would turn out to be, was to become "sweet music" as the playwright might learn the trick of "that sole intensity which the theatre can produce."

He did after all publish the plays, however, and no doubt that whatever the source or sources of his embarrassment, in the writing of them James had not been engaged in anything he had taken at the time merely to be five-finger exercises. The plays had been intended for production by particular actor-managers, as he did say. Nor, despite the assertion in the "Notes", had he really composed them within the restricted ambition of trying to amuse the audiences in country towns. James had indeed been experimenting, but seriously. Whatever the dramatic and theatrical requirements to which he had endeavored to submit, the plays were, moreover and obviously, inventions which had appealed to his own imagination, the more so as he not only consented to but sought those intensities of effect which, as he said repeatedly, only the theater might produce, an intensity which, as he had said in some comments on Ibsen's "John Gabriel Borkman,"is the dramatist's great goal.[3]

The four plays were comedies, in their heft, to be seen now, as something between Congreve and Noel Coward. The dialogue sought witty, epigrammatic repartee. Mise-en-scène was for the most part the English country-house, peopled for the most part by a minor and belated aristocracy or squirearchy. In plot the comedies involved knotted intrigues requiring many entrances and exits as well as arbitrarinesses of development and revelation. Secondary characters were equipped with characterizing names, like "Captain Lurcher," and "Sir Montagu and Lady Brisket," not exactly to function as Humours or as labels but suggestive of Restoration conventions, which would in any event signal the fact that deep characterization was not to be expected. The plays candidly were artifices and did not invite sympathy beyond satisfaction in the mostly happy endings. Again, in a sense different from James' use of the term, the plays indeed implied experiment, not only as a matter of form, but by way of their cool and objective manipulation and testing of their basic issues, which, in all of the plays, had to do with the pursuit of love and money. Characters schemed and knew the way of the world, or were foolish and did not, and in either event possibilities issuing therefrom were put into the action. The plays were comedies and often joked and were funny and farcically intricate, and at the same time were not really light-hearted—which complexity of tone and implication might account for the fact that in their moment the plays failed to secure an audience and as well, in part, for the fact that they have invited very little comment since 1895, and that little, generally dismissive.[4]

Tenants is a play about adultery (reduplicated), bastardy, blackmail (reduplicated), and young love. Mildred Stanmore is the ward of Sir Frederick Byng of Beechingham Manor. She is eighteen, near to receiving her large inheritance (seven thousand a year; James was almost always specific with regard to money), and is in love with Sir Frederick's son Norman. Mrs. Vibert arrives from the Continent. She is a widow, has a twenty-year-old son named Claude, and has him in tow along with her son's tutor, Captain Lurcher. She wishes to rent the old lodge on the property of Beechingham, to be a tenant, but that is a ruse for in the old days, when she was married, she had been Sir Frederick's lover and Claude is the bastard son, unbeknownst to Claude himself. She and the tutor, who has also been her lover, have plotted to blackmail Sir Frederick to the end of his pressing Mildred with her seven thousand to marry Claude. There is also a Miss Dyer, a simple but frustrated person of a certain age who has been hired to be a female guardian for Mildred. Mildred will hold firm for Norman, who has been shuffled off to India but returns. Sir Frederick proposes marriage to Mrs. Vibert, which event prompts her to disengage from her plan except that the tutor won't allow her to do so and threatens to tell Claude who his father is. Mrs. Vibert, thus wrought upon, herself reveals the truth to Claude. Lurcher departs for places unknown, and so do Claude and his mother, leaving behind a plaintive Sir Frederick, a befuddled Miss Dyer, and Mildred and Norman who will soon be married.

James' first title for the play was "Mrs. Vibert," and plainly the play developed from his interest in the type: a worldly, clever, less-than-scrupulous, tainted woman, at once forceful and attractive, of the kind of Madame Merle in *Portrait of a Lady* but now forefronted and without woe. James would repeat the general type in subsequent plays. She offers opportunity for comedy by her introduction of secular realities, and thus of fresh air, into a place of, on the one hand, antique scrupulosities, and, on the other, simpering romance. She is in herself an acknowledgment of sex and greed, and is witty. Simply, she is not an innocent, and is of superior interest in being a woman with a past. Sir Frederick says to her, "You're not, perhaps, so young; and yet you're somehow—so new!," and she responds, "I've been revised and improved: I'm the latest edition! Let me reassure you—I'm better reading than I was."

Beyond her part in the plot, moreover, it is the kind of her knowledge that makes for most of the wit of the play. Only one character, Miss Dyer, is directly ridiculed. She is a mistress of propriety and is an old maid, and is at the same time, awkwardly, a coquette and a victim of her repressed desires, and she tries to flirt, and therefore, immediatedly, is ridiculous. But generally repartee in the play tends to undermining and reduction and swift rejection of evasive euphemism:

> MISS DYER: Chocolate creams? You know the way to a woman's heart.
> LURCHER: Not down her throat, surely!

> LURCHER: Mr. Byng's return *has* made a difference; but it's luckily all to my profit.
> MRS. VIBERT: You talk of your profit as a cannibal might talk of his diet!

> SIR FREDERICK: I've been at home two years.
> MRS. VIBERT: Yes, but you've been buried.
> SIR FREDERICK: And you're digging me up!

—this last put forth as a moment of courtship. As is the case in James' fiction generally, pressure is applied to metaphor, not infrequently so as to reveal the brutality concealed within.

James' first title for *Disengaged* was "Mrs. Jasper" and once again, plainly, the play developed from his interest in the actions of a clever woman, a younger widow this time, whose strength is a function at once of her wit and of her attractiveness to men as a young widow. All the men "make love" to her. "Her freedom," it is observed, "is the freedom of a woman who has lost her husband early," which observation in itself is to be taken as a comment on love and marriage. If there is no particular stain on this woman's past—the matter is not raised one way or another—nonetheless, young though she might be, she has a past. Her opposite in the play is Blandina Wigmore, a virginal young thing in need of a husband, who is defined by her lack of color.

Sir Montagu Brisket of Brisket Place flirts with Mrs. Jasper. Lady Brisket flirts with Percy Trafford, who flirts with both Lady Brisket and Mrs. Jasper. Mrs. Wigmore wishes to marry off her daughter Blandina to Captain Prime, a simple but noble young man who will be attracted to Mrs. Jasper. Mrs. Jasper is also pursued by Charles Coverley. Captain Prime is tricked into an engagement with Blandina. He is told that casual instances of propinquity with the young woman constitute an obligation which honor demands that he fulfill. Mrs. Jasper effects the disengagement and will herself marry Captain Prime, the other characters being variously paired off, except for Charles Coverley, who is left over.

With its many and facile flirtations and an amount of sexual punning, and with the implied comment on marriage, and given the pace of the action and the wit, this play directly hearkens to Restoration comedy. The actor-manager Augustin Daly proposed that James end the play with rhymed couplets. But the play also has its own peculiarity of tone. The central event of the plot, the gulling of Captain Prime, was taken by James from "The Solution," a story he had published approximately a year earlier. In the story the innocent is a young American diplomat stationed in Papal Rome of a century earlier. When he is tricked into honoring an obligation of which he had not been aware, to propose marriage to a young lady whom he can't stand, there is a strained but almost acceptable plausibility in the event. As a young American, so he is told, he does not know the customs of the country. The event is placed, moreover, in a romantic distance: it was long ago in a place which is no more. All turns out well, but the signal difference between the tale and the play is that in the tale the trick is cruel and is not treated comically. The trick as it is played in the play is the same trick, but the fact that the plausibility of it has been all but entirely removed makes the victim of it, a contemporary young Englishman and a soldier, much of a booby. He will do the honorable thing in an environment, moreover, in which everyone else knows that marriage is merely an arrangement. He is a "lamb," and as such is subject in James' way to literalization of the metaphor he bears:

> MRS. JASPER: The honour of a lamb—it's too lovely!
> COVERLEY: I feel as if I'd sent him to the butcher....
> MRS. JASPER: To be eaten with mint-sauce? He should be kept at least for mutton.

If, again, the Captain in his innocence is a target for comedy, Blandina, who is more of an innocent still, is entirely a subject for ridicule. The other characters mock her and so does the play. Mrs. Wigmore instructs her in flirtation, and she says "Yes, mamma." Take Captain Prime to the ruins, instructs Mrs. Wigmore, "One of the most celebrated sanctuaries of the Middle Ages; begun in the eleventh century, terminated in the fourteenth," and on cue Blandina speaks to Captain Prime of the ruins, "One of the most celebrated sanctuaries of the Middle Ages; begun in the eleventh century, terminated in the fourteenth." She is the single occasion for romantic love in the play, and is vapid.

In *The Album* Sir Ralph Damant deceives a dying man and robs a cousin of an inheritance (of four thousand a year), but is largely forgiven as the play moves forward, as he is hounded by venal women, who are ridiculed. Sir Ralph is next of kin to Mr. Bedford, who is dying upstairs, and is the sole heir unless his cousin Mark Bernal, who is missing and presumed dead, should turn up.

("He took to low courses," says Sir Ralph. "I believe he took to painting portraits. He wore queer clothes and knew queer people. He was wild—I'm convinced he was wicked. His tastes were vulgar; his abilities mean. He went to the bottom—he went to America.") Bernal does turn up, as is theatrically to be expected, and Sir Ralph conceals the fact. Then both Lady Basset and her ward, Maud Vanneck, whose mother is in Zanzibar, set forth to snare Sir Ralph. Sir Ralph will at the end give Mark Bernal the whole of the inheritance in order to be free of fortune-hunting women. Grace Jesmond, secretary to the now-late Mr. Bedford, is the fixer, like Mrs. Vibert and Mrs. Jasper before her, although for this once the character is straightforwardly poor-but-honest and is the daughter of a clergyman and is without either taint or ulteriority.

But the fun is in the other women. They are quarrelsome, rude, candidly mercenary, and most of all, comically pretentious. Maud has had "the Higher Education," so she says repeatedly.

> BERNAL: You're young, you're pretty, you're clever—
> MAUD: (*Interrupting, complacent.*) And I've had the Higher Education!

Whereas Miss Jesmond has not had the Higher Education and is, then, "not a trained intelligence." The plot brings both women to Bernal for training in art, saying separately but identically and repeatedly, "I feel I've a little gift that only requires direction."

The Album is the slightest of the four Theatricals. In a letter James would say that he had written it merely as a favor to the actor-manager Edward Compton who had found himself with a theater on his hands and nothing to produce, but even so, and no matter how casual the composition—if James is here to be believed—nonetheless the play had a content and bespoke an attitude, the more plainly perhaps just because of the slightness of the material. Sir Ralph, in the first instance, does a thing which in any decent melodrama would be dastardly without a doubt but which is here fixed in a context in which iniquity is only human and is to be fused into comic perspective. And as for the two women, they are comic according to the fact that they are allowed no sympathy at all.

In *The Reprobate,* as Jacques Barzun has said, all the dramatis personae are jokes, "not the sardonic jokes whom James knows how to keep half descriptive, half damnatory, but thoroughly laughable jokes."[5] The "reprobate" is Paul Doubleday, a young man with a past, although a brief one. His late mother, "alas," it is said, "was—indelicate." Pending his delayed inheritance he is being kept safe from temptation by the ministrations of his stepmother, the second and inflexible Mrs. Doubleday, and by Mr. Bonson, a friend of his late father. Paul will be saved by and for the heroine, Blanche Amber. Meanwhile, for this plot has numerous filaments: Blanche is pursued by Pitt Brunt, M.P. for Blackport on the Smutt; Mrs. Doubleday, who has five thousand a year, is pursued by Captain Chanter; and Mrs. Freshville, a chanteuse returned from Paris, "fresh and showy, with hair conspicuously golden," according to the stage directions, has designs on both Captain Chanter, with whom she has had a past, and on Paul, with whom she has also had a past, suggestive but in this case chaste. Paul will marry Blanche; Captain Chanter will marry Mrs. Doubleday; and Mrs. Freshville goes off boating with the Member from Blackport on the Smutt.

The characters are jokes and the plot rushes forward—or, rather, around—at the speed of farce, sweeping up improbabilities as it goes, but at the center of it there is an issue, of vitalism versus moralism, exaggerated, as it is explored, and made farcically blatant. The tainted Mrs. Freshville is a breath of fresh air. Paul is thirty years old and, until he breaks forth, is kept from: tobacco, cards, wine, women, and the novels of Emile Zola. Mrs. Doubleday keeps Paul under lock and key, literally, locking him in a room. On the other side, the Member from Blackport speechifies.

But here, too, unexpected intensities break forth, carried by the very artificiality of character and plot. There is very little nuance here, but once again metaphor—of language and of action—is pressured. If Paul is to be kept from temptations, the play does demand that he be kept in a separate room literally under lock and key, and that being the case, he becomes a caged animal, wherefore the idea of vitalism becomes virtually feral—and, indeed, at the end the play retreats when Paul discovers that now that he is free he is not after all tempted.

Paul, it is said, is "vicious." "One would think," so the butler observes, that Paul "was a domestic animal." When years ago Paul had been in Paris, "steeped to his lips in vice," his father and stepmother had pursued him, says Mrs. Doubleday: "We had a hunt! And, after unspeakable anxieties and incredible efforts, we finally ran him to earth." When Paul leaves his room it is said that he has "escaped". Paul thinks of himself as being "a kind of moral leper, with a warning cowbell round my neck," if not a "freak of nature or melancholy monster: the pig-faced lady or the piebald man!" It follows, moreover, and despite the fact of Paul's retreat at the end, towards domesticity, that the idea of joy will be the less sweet as it is the more brutishly instinctual. Blanche Amber, the heroine and the liberator, says to Pitt Brunt in an initial encounter, "I detest exemplary women.... And also exemplary men!" When Paul at the end says that after all he is "as good as most men," Blanche wants more. Disgustedly (according to stage directions) she says, "That's far *too* good!" In an encounter with the Member from Blackport on the Smutt she says:

BLANCHE (*With slight irony*): Yes—you're faultless.
BRUNT: (*Much gratified*): Delighted to hear it from *you,* Miss Amber!
BLANCHE: You wouldn't be if you knew—
BRUNT: If I knew what?
BLANCHE: That I can enter into—every aberration!

This is saucy exaggeration. Or perhaps is not. The assertion is modified by the fact that Blanche is the young heroine in a comedy, but, after all, is modified not at all entirely. Some quantity of literalization remains just because the play need not have gone so far as it does, beyond expectations and conventions of romantic comedy.

Guy Domville, composed in 1893 and produced in 1895, is the one non-comedy, and in that commonplace sense it is the one serious play of the period of James' concentrated involvement in the theater. Despite the opening-night disaster, or quite conceivably because of it, the play was much praised by the "cultivated" critics, so named by the young drama critic George Bernard Shaw, and his criticism was more or less echoed by other young critics in the audience, including Arnold Bennett and H.G. Wells. It was the task of the dramatic critic to educate the dunces, said Shaw, particularly "the handful of rowdies" who had brawled at James on the occasion of the opening. But then the particular terms of Shaw's own list of the merits of the play were so general and finally so abstract as to suggest that his purpose was to defend a distinguished and wounded writer rather than to salvage the play itself. The play, said Shaw, had "a rare charm of speech." "I am speaking," he said, "of the delicate inflexions of feeling conveyed by the cadences of the line, inflexions and cadences which ... are as grateful to my ear as the music of Mozart's "Entführung aus dem Serail" would be after a year of "Ernani" and "Il Trovatore." (Shaw was also a music critic.)

And *Guy Domville,* moreover, contained a story of "fine sentiment and delicate manners."[6]

But for all of the sentiment and manners, the story part of the play was in fact distinctly related to *The Reprobate* of two or three years earlier. In both plays a sequestered young man is to be brought into confrontation with worldliness.

In *Guy Domville* the year of the action is 1780. Guy is a young man who is about to leave England in order to enter a Benedictine monastery in France. (There is suggestion of the difficulties of a Catholic minority in England at the end of the Eighteenth Century, but then the play does not after all develop in that direction.) An emissary of the family Domville persuades him to abandon his religious ambition because it has befallen that Guy is the last male of the line of the Domvilles, an ancient family, wherefore, in order to preserve the line, he must take up his family position and also marry a certain person. The certain person, Mary Brasier, is, however, in love with someone else, and, besides, there are schemes afoot. In Act III Guy delivers the lady to her lover, presents another lady, a young widow, whose affections he does possess, to a would-be rival, altogether abandons his new worldliness, and will take off for France.

The howling of the rowdies occurred in Act II when, taking up his supposed duties to family, Guy the former petitioner to Mother Church, breaks character, woos Mary Brasier, dresses, and sometimes speaks, foppishly, plays cards, and in the central episode of the Act, engages in a drinking contest. "There's scarcely a rule [of the Church] I haven't utterly abjured," he says, "there's scarcely a vow I haven't scrupulously broken!"—In Act II, this is to see, Guy is in the state of vice that Paul Doubleday had inhabited prior to his Act I and toward which he again aspires in his Act II. The two are engaged in essentially the same progress: from restraints

Paul proceeds toward libertinism and ends in moral convention. Guy begins in piety, tastes the liquor, and then ends in the stricter constraints of the monastery. In both instances both sets of transformations are abrupt, due in good part, no doubt, to the rule of the two-and-a-half hours of the theater, but in fact accommodated much more readily in farce. For that matter, the central conflict in the play has a kind of made-up quality.

In *Guy Domville*, moreover, as in the comedies, the plot engages some matters of bastardy and of mercenary scheming, and those matters, significantly, are maintained at a secondary level of importance—significantly because even in this instance of serious drama matters which might appall or horrify or secure disgust, or in any event secure one or another kind of excited moral response, again take their place as mere tropes. Even in this serious drama, this is to say, the perspective is that of comedy. Vice and crime are background buzz. This is what people do.

James' drama criticism, dating back to the 1870s in Paris, has to do mostly with actors and acting and less with playwrights. Ibsen, however, was to be the notable exception. James seems first to have become aware of the playwright in early 1889.[7] Early in 1891, near the beginning of his own engagement with the theater, he met Elizabeth Robins, the American actress who would become his friend and who was introducing Ibsen to the London stage. James gave her a Norse grammar because, so she said, her own knowledge of Norwegian was meager.[8] He saw the Ibsen plays when they were produced and wrote about both the plays and the productions, particularly praising Robins' performance. His expressed appreciation of Ibsen, this is to say, was very much bound up with his own involvement in and desire for success in the theater.

And Ibsen's plays had bearing for James' own writing, which is not, however, quite to say that he was influenced by Ibsen. His appreciation of Ibsen proceeded through reluctances and negatives, and then, despite all superficial seeming, Ibsen's bleakness of vision was, for all of the Norwegian difference, not alien to his own. Ibsen offered James confirmation of his own irony, which might be more frigid in Ibsen than in the comedies he was just now writing but not more so than in novels to come.

Oddly, perhaps, but significantly for his own work, James began by looking to Ibsen for a sense of the comic, which, at least in any ordinary sense and as he was immediately to discover, he was not likely to find. If Ibsen did not have the comic spirit in any usual or ordinary sense, that was to be explained, at least in part, so James said in an essay of 1891 on *Hedda Gabler,* because "his people" were "of inexpressive race," living "in a world in which selection has no great range."

> This is perhaps one reason why they none of them, neither the creator nor the creatures, appear to feel much impulse to *play* with the things of life. This impulse, when it breaks out, is humour, and in the scenic genius it usually breaks out in one place or another. We get the feeling, in Ibsen's plays, that such whims are too ultimate, too much a matter of luxury and leisure for the stage of feeling at which his characters have arrived. They are all too busy learning to live—humour will come in later, when they know how.

Ibsen's great gift, said James, seemed to be "made up of negatives." Ibsen lacked not only humor but, additionally, the quality of free imagination, and he also lacked style. He had no charm. He was "massively common and 'middle-class.'" But the gift, said James, was a great one nonetheless. Neither Ibsen's spirit nor his manner was small; he was never trivial and never cheap. "He holds us," James said, "without bribing us." He admired Ibsen's characters, furthermore, for their frequent "certain angular irony"—*Hedda Gabler* in particular he found to be "a play indeed suffused with irrepressible irony," and where Ibsen's portraits were satirical (as in the case of the husband, Tesman, in *Hedda Gabler*), there was "ridicule without the smile, ... a sort of sarcasm that is nearer to tears than to laughter."[9]

Hedda Gabler was the product, James said, of "the artistic exercise of a mind saturated with the vision of human infirmities," but it was something other than a simple and undeviating grimness that he found in Ibsen. The "miracle" of Ibsen, as James expressed the matter in a later essay, on Ibsen's *John Gabriel Borkman,* was "a result of so dry a view of life, so indifferent a vision of the comedy of things"—and while there would be no question of direct influence, that dryness and ferocity and, exactly, "so indifferent a vision of the comedy of things" which James found in Ibsen, would indeed mark the fictions following the playwriting years.

Especially in Ibsen's *The Wild Duck* James discovered a "pervasive air of small interests and standards, the sign of limited local life," and it would happen more often than not in the fictions of the nineties that James' protagonists were to be confined and limited by circumstance—Rose Armiger, Fleda Vetch, a telegraph girl, the poor young woman who becomes a lonely governess, a child—and when not so explicitly limited by circumstance they will all of them be frustrated from achieving a larger and more vital life. Meanwhile, as James also discovered in Ibsen, there will be explosive energies beneath. When at the end of the play Hedda Gabler shoots herself, the would-be lover, Brack, says "But, merciful God! One doesn't *do* that kind of thing." But James knew that, to the contrary, one indeed *does.*

The Other House

Rose Armiger drowns the little girl Effie. She does so—although she miscalculates—in order to remove impediments to marriage with Effie's father, Tony Bream. Tony's wife, Julia, who had died shortly after the birth of the child, had demanded a promise from Tony that he would not remarry during the child's lifetime. The promise constitutes one of two impediments for Rose. The other is the presence of a second woman, Jean, who is a rival for Tony. In his Notebook entry James had projected a "Bad Heroine" and a "Good Heroine." The "Bad Heroine," Rose, tries so to arrange the murder that suspicion will fall on Jean. Tony, in order to protect first Jean and then Rose, himself confesses to the murder, but not convincingly. At the end, Tony will marry Jean, although not immediately, and Rose is taken off—to China—by a previous lover, Dennis Vidal. The family doctor, Doctor Ramage, so arranges matters that it will be believed that the child has died of a sickness which, conveniently, she has had. There is also a next-door neighbor, Mrs. Beever, who wants to marry off her son Paul, to Jean.

The Other House is the one of James' novels that is most often overlooked, excepting perhaps for *The Outcry*, of 1911, and, when not, then it is almost always dismissed as a sport, on grounds at once structural, intellectual, and moral. For Leon Edel it was "one of James' most unpleasant novels: a piece of subtle mechanical play-tinkering with powerful stuff of the emotions which [James] does not seem to understand or to command: an outburst of primitive rage." Generally, if not universally, when accounted for at all, the novel is noted and dismissed as mere melodrama, an inept thriller in which the villain is not even punished, without roundness of characters, to be accounted for mostly by the circumstances of its initial, serial publication, for money, in a popular paper, the

Illustrated London News.[10] Even James himself seemed to have concurred, at least initially. In his negotiations with the editor of the paper, Clement Shorter, he had guardedly not risen above the commercial. "I should be very glad," he wrote to Shorter, "to write you a story energetically designed to meet your requirement of a 'love-story' ...but the sum you name is less than I am in the habit of receiving." Nonetheless, he said, he wanted "to capture the public of the *Illustrated News*" and, in a following letter added, "I shall endeavour to be thrilling." When the novel was published, by Heinemann, it in fact received generally favorable reviews, which event, if proof that he had succeeded and that the audience was generally thrilled, seemed after all not to thrill James. "*The Other House,*" he wrote to brother William, "shows symptoms of being the most successful thing I have put forth for a long time. If *that's* what idiots want, I can give them a bellyful."[11] A dozen years later, however, he did retrieve the novel in order to reconstitute it into a play and then again, in 1910, in a Notebook entry having to do with the plotting of a tale he was then writing, he would invoke the model he felt that had accomplished in *The Other House*. "Oh, blest *Other House*," he wrote to himself, "which gives me thus at every step a precedent, a support, a divine little light to walk by," with the time of the writing of the novel remembered as "the old enchanted months!"

In his initial consideration, as recorded in the Notebook entry of 1893, thinking at first that *The Other House* was more likely to work out as a play rather than as a fiction, James saw it as being developed in three discrete Acts, which he outlined in considerable detail. Sometime shortly after the date of the Notebook entry he wrote the lost play scenario, and then, three years later, the novel, in which the three Acts of the play became three Books, each with a single setting, each carefully described, with forward development relying largely on dialogue, and with plotted entrances and exits along with directions for the actors: "Tony had gathered the loose net of the hammock into a single strand, and, while he smoked, had lowered himself upon it, sideways, in a posture which made him sit as in a swing;" "'I don't mind telling you frankly,' said Dennis, while with two fingers softly playing upon her lower lip, she...."

When the play was imposed on the novel, consequences followed. Perspective was altered. The author was now watching the narrative, as it were on the other side of the proscenium, with effect on his attitude toward characters and story. "Dramatise, dramatise!" so said James that he had said to himself, writing in the Preface to "Daisy Miller," and this time he had done it. The actors in the novel perform. The author who has composed them, having made a situation for them and having created them with certain looks and certain conditions of character, is otherwise remote, neither sympathetic nor judgmental, nor—as a paramount matter—does he explain, and the result is a work which is in fact at once more compact, dense, and is darker than any of James' previous ten novels.

The kind of James' involvement, or, rather, his non-involvement, in this tale which is to be about infanticide, begins with jokes on names and with related amusing grace-notes of characterization. Mrs. Beever, the next-door neighbor, and Tony Bream, are partners in a small-town bank, "Beever and Bream," she by way of widowhood and he by way of inheritance. The slightly fishy, or in any event aquatic implications of the names go no further, but, to the point, are funny just in themselves—although there is a stream lying between the two houses, in which little Effie will be drowned, and so the characters do have some non-fiduciary relationship to liquidity. Not that James will exactly mock his characters, but he refuses them the dignity which, considering what they are about to go through, should be their due in any proper romance. These two are, exactly, two generations of small-town bankers, not ridiculous as such but defined by their lack of glamor. Mrs. Beever, the elder of the two, is "short and solid," and so "early Victorian," as a character remarks, "as to be almost prehistoric," but for all of that, she has eyes which are very small, is shrewd, calculating, unlikely to be taken in, and she keeps very good accounts which are neatly pigeonholed. Tony Bream is boyish, wonderfully sociable, with an orchid in his lapel. He is the public face of the bank. There is something, it is said, "exaggerated" about him, meaning "a certain quality of passive excess which was the note of the whole man and which, for an attentive eye, began with his neckties and ended with his intonations."

> To look at him was immediately to see that he was a collection of gifts, which presented themselves as such precisely by having in each case slightly overflowed the measure. He could do things—this was all he knew about them; and he was ready-made, as it were—he had not had to put himself together. His dress was just too fine, his color just too high, his mustache just too long, his voice just too loud, his smile just too gay. His movement, his manner, his tone were respectively just too free, too easy, and too familiar; his being a very handsome, happy, clever, active, ambitiously local young man was in short just too obvious. But the result of it all was a presence that was in itself a close contact, the air of immediate, unconscious, unstinted life, and of his doing what he liked and liking to please.

The scenes of the action are settings, composed by way of further typifying the characters. Given the structure of the novel—Book I takes place in Tony's house, called "Bounds", and Books II and III in Mrs. Beever's garden and then in her house, called "Eastmead"—it is not at all clear which of the two houses in *The Other*

House is the "other", but they are nonetheless appropriately distinct and respectively suitable. Tony's Bounds is "quite violently" new, in the view of Mrs. Beever, and although elegant, is provincially so. Her own Eastmead, on the other hand, has a lovely established garden, and old-fashioned mahogany is to be found within.

As with Tony and Mrs. Beever, so for the others. James is ironic and amused, in a way to imply objectivity strictly without sympathetic bias. Dennis Vidal will do a hero's part in the novel, by taking Rose away with him, but he is "a short, meager young man" with a small head and dry, thin lips. Paul Beever, intended by his mother for Jean, is tall and fat, with his mother's small eyes and a deep fold of flesh around his young neck. "He promised to become massive early in life," it is said, "and even to attain a remarkable girth." In a moment of sorrow he is observed "working it clumsily, one of his little eyes with the base of one of his big thumbs." Dr. Ramage has "a face so candid and circular that it suggested a large white pill." Even young Jean, the designated artless innocent, is denied any authorial pity. She is eighteen years old at the beginning—her age is specified in the later, play version of the novel—and she is still younger than her years. Tony will remark on her "extreme juvenility". Mrs. Beever refers to her casually as a child, and one as yet wanting sense. The dominant character in the novel is Rose Armiger, and much in the plotting issues from her ability to fascinate men: Tony, Paul, and Dennis. Her appeal is candidly sexual while her beauty is, explicitly, blemished. Her eyes are of an extremely light gray, "so strange as to be ugly." She has a wide, full-lipped mouth which, when she smiles, reveals "a flash of small square white teeth," although then, in a flash, she will be strikingly handsome. She has "a peculiar way of looking at a person before speaking."

James appraises these characters even as he invents them, and then, after applying some pressure, allows for dark and hidden probabilities to emerge—a process, it may be added, which largely defines each of the other of James' novels of the nineties.

First and primarily in *The Other House* there is Rose. Her story, which is the same thing as to say the pressure which is put upon her, is: frustrated passion, abetted by jealousy, will lead her to commit the murder, by which she intends to implicate her rival, Jean—except that her part of the novel really is about the progressive revelation of character which will make the horrific part of the story to be credible, the plot part of it being merely useful. Rose is not merely passionate, not merely sensualized, in the way, for instance, of Hedda Gabler She is very much an actress. (With her large pale eyes and wide mouth, she indeed looks like Elizabeth Robins as is to be seen in some of that actress's published photographs.[12]) Rose is, as is said, "ardent and subtle." She has the actress's gift for duplicity. "Again there came into the girl's face," it is said, "her strange alternative look—the look of being made by her passion so acquainted with pain that even in the midst of it she could flower into charity." She works upon others. "Her abasement," we read, "had brought tears into Tony's eyes. She saw them there as she looked at him once more, and she measured the effect she produced upon him." Thus, into the small world of these provincial bankers she brings possibilities of perversity. She is disturbing and exciting.

Rose is made credible, moreover, by being provided with multiple, sometimes straightforward but also sometimes deviant urgencies. Among the straightforward motives is a financial one. Tony will be a good catch, minus the obstacles, not only because he is charming but also because he is a banker, unlike Dennis, who is someone's employee. Rose is a poor girl without family, dependent on a small inheritance. She lives in a London flat. Marriage to Tony will give her a place, an "anchorage," as she says. But then marriage to Tony, beyond that matter, will also give her the place previously occupied by Julia, with whom she had shared an unpleasant childhood. They had been less than blood sisters but more than chums, united, as she says, by "the tie of a common aversion," namely the lady who had raised the two of them. The degree of their union, in Rose's idea of it, is hinted near the very beginning in colloquy between Rose and Mrs. Beever while Julia is upstairs, dying. "You must remember," Rose says to Mrs. Beever, "that I'm Julia's oldest friend.... I'm the one thing of her own that dear Julia has ever had." "Don't you count her husband?" asks Mrs. Beever, and Rose says, "I count Tony immensely, but in another way." The wicked aunt and stepmother had, says Rose, almost made us sisters, "with the delightful position for me of the elder, the protecting one." She has been staying on at Bounds, she says, because "Julia's the one thing I have of my own," to which Mrs. Beever with her conventional understanding, or perhaps her unconventional shrewdness, replies, "You make light of our husbands and lovers!" In a climactic confrontation with Jean, when Jean has been forced to admit that she loves the little girl Effie because she is in love with the unobtainable Tony, Rose challenges her: "Because you adore him—and she's his?" Jean says that that is the case, and Rose says: "*I* want her for another reason.... I adored her poor mother—and she's hers." The previous men in her life are dismissed as cowardly or effeminate. Her uncle, she says, had died of horror of his wife, while Julia's father is afraid of his wife and is a "muff". Befittingly and explicitly, moreover, she does not like babies.

The promise which is at the heart of the plot—James' working title was "The Promise"—will amount to a death sentence, but the version of the promise to which everyone assents, so far as we can know, is not really what the dying Julia had demanded. James is as sly here as he will be in novels and tales hereafter. Tony says to Rose only that Julia had asked him not to take a second wife. After a moment, Rose interprets. It must be Julia's wish, she says, that little newborn Effie not have a stepmother. "If you had known, as I knew it, Julia's girlhood," she says to Tony, "you would do justice to the force of that horror. It possesses her whole being—she would prefer that the child should die." And it is Rose, at just this point, who adds the codicil to the vow. It must really be Julia's idea, she says, that Tony is not to take a new wife while his daughter lives. "If you would lose Effie," she says, "the reason would fail." And she urges Tony so to put the matter to Julia "because she'll be more convinced if you strike her as really looking at what you subscribe to."

Julia is apparently not convinced. Rose, as oldest friend, has regularly visited at Julia's sickbed, and we have indication of Julia's actual motives when we hear, from Tony, that she is doing what she can by way of furthering Rose's engagement to Dennis Vidal. The last person, then, to attend upon Julia is Effie's nurse, who, embarrassed to have been charged with the announcement of Julia's last wishes, tells the others that Julia has told her that Tony, in order to gratify her, had assured her that in the event of her death he would not again marry. Only and absolutely that. Nonetheless the others, the doctor and Mrs. Beever, who have not been privy to the exchange between husband and wife, add and endorse the fatal clause: after the nurse's announcement, "In the lifetime of her daughter, that is," the doctor hastens to add. Mrs. Beever echoes the statement, and then so does Tony, and so the ground is set for Rose at once to take the place of her adored Julia, and as well, as happens, to annul the facts both of Julia's marriage and her motherhood.

Given James' non-intervention, more and more is allowed. Tony confesses to the murder which he did not commit, not convincingly but plausibly all the same in this novel which does not strictly so much create complications as refuse to cancel possibilities. ("As one grows older," James was writing to a correspondent just in the moment when he was composing the novel, "one's manner inevitably becomes more complicated—one's reach, or embrace, ampler."[13]) Tony likes pretty girls, naturally and frankly, and does not discourage the interest he inspires including that of his wife's oldest friend. Between Books One and Two, Rose has returned to London, where Tony has visited her. His involvement with Rose has evidently been not more than so much as that, but in his ease with himself he is slow to acknowledge what he knows—what it is that with his actions and with his charm he has suggested, and the pleasure of it. In Book Two, as they walk in the garden at Eastmead, Rose asks him why he no longer calls her by her first name, and Tony suddenly sees "a circumstance of which he had already had glimpses; but for some reason or other it was now written with a largeness that made it resemble a printed poster on a wall." He is momentarily confused, but then—for his charm is irrepressible—his face is composed in kindness and Rose is thus the more encouraged. At the end we are to know that he has known and might have acted. "She loves me!" he says. "My silence is a part of the crime and the cruelty." "I knew it—I always knew it," he says to Jean. "And I made her come." "You were kind to her—as you're always kind," says Jean, and Tony responds, "No, I was more than that. And I should have been less." "I liked it," he adds, "while I was safe. Then I grew afraid." "Afraid of what?" Jean asks, and he replies, "Afraid of everything. You don't know—but we're abysses. At least *I'm* one!" And he says, mysteriously, "There are other things. They go back far," but we are not to know what those other things are and the matter is dropped, because that is as far as the presented character can go.

Nor, for that matter, is young Jean, the designated innocent, entirely innocent. She is guilty by the amount that she has used little Effie for her own purposes, acting as more than helpmate for the father, and has done so from the beginning, following the mother's death. "It was just because she was yours that she was mine," she says to Tony, finally, and, "What could I do, you see? To you I couldn't be kind," in a context in which the quality of "kindness" has already become ambiguous. "Didn't I try not to think of you?" she says. "But the child was a beautiful part of you—the child I could take and keep." By mothering the child she has, moreover and reasonably, made little Effie into the appropriate device for Rose's doubling vengeance, against both Tony and herself. Nor is Mrs. Beever, the meddling next-door neighbor, entirely innocent. Jean now has an income of three thousand. Wishing to save her for her son, banker that she is, it was she who had invited Rose to Eastmead in the first place, for Tony. Rose is fascinating. Tony, says Mrs. Beever, "must think of that sort of thing." But surely Tony won't break his vow and marry her, says Doctor Ramage, but Mrs. Beever, with her small eyes, calculates the better. "I don't care whether they marry or not," she says, leaving Doctor Ramage to wonder—appreciatively, it seems—about her morality. It is Jean she wants. "I protect *my* girl," says Mrs. Beever, leaving one to wonder what she means by protection.

And there is the dying Julia herself, who, whether or not she had agreed to the fatal loophole, had nonetheless imposed a lifetime sentence upon her husband—the more exacting in fact, if the promise not to marry was not to be limited to the lifetime of their daughter. In either event, it is the fact of the promise that has made for the tension of unfulfilled desires. And there is Dennis Vidal, the meager young man to whom everyone is indebted for his whisking Rose away to China, but it is not after all civic consciousness that moves him. Rose has treated him poorly, but Rose is fascinating.

"You often failed of old," he says to her, "to give me what I really wanted from you, and yet it never prevented the success of your effect on—what shall I call it? ... On God knows what baser, obscurer part of me!" But now, after the murder, he *has* her. And there is Doctor Ramage, who will make it known that little Effie died of an illness. In the early Notebook entry James was to have him along with Mrs. Beever figure as "the *public,* the judging, wondering, horrified world." And so in a way he does figure, although ironically and although the world has shrunk to the society of the two provincial houses. Since everyone is more or less suspect—excluding perhaps only fat Paul and a couple of servants—it is in the public interest that the prior complacent hypocrisy of the order of things should be restored.

Which leaves only little Effie's nurse, named Gorham. She will know that while Effie might have been sick, she was not after all sick to death. But Gorham will after all not be a problem because, first, the doctor knows that doctors are despots and can impose their truths, and secondly and pointedly, she will not be a problem because she too is "tremendously devoted" to Tony and will "do anything." No one, in fact, will question Tony because everyone likes him too much, and, on that note, the novel ends.[14]

The Spoils of Poynton
Or
The Palpitating Girl

The Spoils of Poynton, like *The Other House,* and of the same moment, presented itself to James first of all as at least something much like a play. In the Notebook entry dated December 24th, 1893 he recorded the seminal anecdote, something someone had said at a dinner party. Coming back to the anecdote, in the Notebook entry dated May 13th, 1895, at a time when he had just begun once again to address himself to fiction primarily, he was reminding himself that "every thing of this kind I do must be a complete and perfect little drama," and two days later he was writing: "I seem to see the thing in three chapters, like 3 little acts," which he then proceeded to elaborate. And then once again, two months after that, once more taking up the material for the novel, he remarked on the "wasted years and patience and pangs, of theatrical experiment" which might yet, however, he said to himself, provide him with lessons for narrative structures, leading him in the next instant to his renewed planning for the novel in a series of "acts". And then still once again, in February, 1896, when he was well into his struggles with details of plot—the first installments of the serial were to appear in April—James was once more invoking the wished-for yield of "the long years and pains, the acquired mastery of scenic presentation."

Writing in the Notebooks, James worried and elaborated his ideas for this novel in greater detail and at greater length than for any other of his novels or tales previous or to come, but then the great reach of the eventual short novel is directly related to the fact that it was not structure that in the end triumphed in *The Spoils of Poynton,* despite the amount of the labor for neat joints and clear scenic structure. The lesson of the Notebook entries—seven of them—is, rather, the trouble James was having in keeping his story under control. Nina Baym has pointed to the successive shifts and adjustments in James' thinking and planning as he composed the Notebook entries (made the more necessary as the serial publication proceeded) and the discrepancies between plot ideas as set forth in the Notebooks and what was happening in the novel itself.[15] One of the nicely revealing passages in the Notebooks occurs in the entry for October 15th, 1895, when James was already far into his composition, where he discovers to his surprise that his hero (so-to-speak), Owen Gereth, has fallen in love with his heroine, Fleda Vetch. "I had not intended to represent a feeling of this kind on Owen's part," he wrote. "Now, however," he said, "I have done so; in my last little go at the thing…it inevitably took that turn and I must accept the idea and work it out." Nor, it happens, does what James would have to say about the novel in the Preface to the late New York Edition have any necessary authority of bearing. As Professor Baym has also pointed out, the Preface reflects some of James' preoccupations at a later time in his career, particularly with centers of consciousness, and does not really describe the novel at hand, while at the same time the Preface actually contradicts the record of composition which is in the Notebooks, which James presumably had at hand as he was writing his Preface.

The individual chapters of the novel are in fact largely although not consistently obedient to the wish for "scenic presentation" and are "scenic" in the sense that each is set in a single certain place with an action consisting of a confrontation between two or sometimes three persons. The controlling and signifying eventuality of the stated ambition, however, to write a complete and perfect little drama, is once again not in the efficiency or neatness nor at all in the structure of the thing but in perspective, in the apartness and thus the neutrality of an author whose prose will be transfigured by his characters, on a stage where meanings will be created, admitted, and entertained. Having composed an initial situation for a discrete number of characters, James will allow them both to perform and, in the favored Jamesian term, to "bristle". There is consequence for tone in the fact that once again the author is not sympathetic. Irony is inherent in the perspective. As happens in *The Other House,* the author watches, having made himself to be remote and bemused.

The original anecdote, recorded by James on Christmas Eve of 1893, concerned a young Scottish laird who by the death of his father had inherited a large house filled with valuable things. The mother was thereby dispossessed although allowed the use of a small dower-house; the son married and he and his wife took possession of the house, whereupon the mother removed things that she wanted. The son and daughter resisted. There was a scandal and the mother ended by declaring that the young laird was not the son of his supposed father.

"It is all rather sordid and fearfully ugly," James wrote, "but there is surely a story in it," and the story which he at this point projected focused on the plight of the mother, who, he considered, would be a proud person of fine taste—"with a knowledge and adoration of artistic beauty, the tastes, the habits of a collector". She would be victimized by "the ugly custom" of inheritance in England. The son's chosen wife would be the product of a house the very opposite of hers: "the kind of house the very walls and furniture of which constitute a kind of *anguish* for such a woman" as she. (James had already once and not long before contemplated the ugly English custom of inheritance. It had figured in the plotting of his 1889 novel *A London Life,* although there without attributions of anguish. Of the mother in that novel, a Mrs. Berrington, it is said that "it was a sort of fascination to wonder how she could have such abysses of placidity.")[16] The mother in *Spoils* would fix upon another young woman for her son to marry, with tastes, "exquisite tastes" like her own, but the son, stupidly and perversely from the mother's point of view, would persist in his own choice.

But there was more to the story inherently, and in the eventuality, as in that of *The Other House* and of fictions to come, James did not so much create complications—the basic situation with its vectors of conflict stayed put—as, once again, refuse to cancel possibilities.

When Mrs. Gereth first meets Fleda Vetch, within the first couple of paragraphs of *The Spoils of Poynton,* that central matter of "taste," which is to be their bond, is already made to yield to James' dispassion. The two women have been visiting Waterbath, family home of the wife-to-be, Mona Brigstock. Mrs. Gereth responds to the house and by extension to the family in language which is aesthetic and urgent. She finds herself driven from "the aesthetic misery of the big commodious house" to a garden, although she knows that "the flowers at Waterbath would probably go wrong in color and the nightingales sing out of tune." She had this morning dressed herself with care even though, as she reflects, "It was hard for her to believe that a woman could look presentable who had been kept awake for hours by the wall-paper in her room."[17] Insofar, moreover, as Mrs. Gereth is defined by her taste and, more to the point, defines herself by taste—for furnishings, objects, *bibelots*—she has been entered into an area of moral ambiguity which had been much pondered by James. In *The Princess Cassimassima* little Hyacinth Robinson had died for taste, maybe all to the good. But Gilbert Osmond in *Portrait of a Lady* had made taste to be a metaphor for a kind of absolute of inhumanity, as to some moderated extent it had been also earlier for Roderick Hudson, later for Gaston-Pachert in *The Reverberator,* and Gabriel Nash in *The Tragic Muse*. Mrs. Gereth remains the victim of the ugly English custom, but her self-justification on the grounds of superior taste makes her both less and more than a case of plight.

And as for Mrs. Gereth, so for Fleda Vetch, upon whom Mrs. Gereth will fix. The very fact in itself of that aesthetic appreciation which she is to share with Mrs. Gereth will make her a subject, a case, inviting ironic scrutiny, and, contrary to plan, she emerges almost immediately as the more interesting character because her situation, inherently, is more complicated. James does equip her with some circumstances, but almost by subtraction. She is explicitly—within the second paragraph of text—not beautiful. In his first notation for the novel James had thought that the young woman would have grown up surrounded by lovely things, but Fleda, in the event, comes from a poor home, where in fact she is no longer welcome, where she had been surrounded by her father's collection of "old brandy-flasks and match-boxes, old calendars and handbooks, intermixed with an assortment of pen-wipers and ash-trays" gathered from penny bazaars. She has been to Paris to study for a year with an impressionist painter, but (the fact of James' own distaste for Impressionism aside) she is not very original. Her sister is about to get married, and does, leaving her behind. She is a person without place to live, without a place in the world, and her name is Fleda Vetch—a name, no matter how James himself might have pronounced it, which it would have been impossible to utter mellifluously. (There had been the character named "Anastasius Vetch" in *The Princess Cassimassima,* the caustic old fiddler who befriends Hyacinth, but whatever James' intention in that instance, it was something else to present the name to a heroine up for marriage.)

The "things" in themselves have, in fact, very little presence in the novel, a matter which James acknowledged in the Preface. The real center of the novel, he said, "would have been the felt beauty and value of... the Things, always the splendid Things, placed in the middle light, figured and constituted, with each identity made vivid"—except that the novel did not allow room for that kind of elaboration. As the novel works itself out, there is very little description of the things, in themselves, and what there is, is generalized, with the single exception of the description of one certain object, the so-called Maltese cross, which will figure in the plot. There are "brasses that Louis Quinze might have thumbed," and Venetian velvet hanging over cases of enamels, and "rare French furniture and Oriental china"; there are "old golds and brasses, old ivories and bronzes, the fresh old tapestries and deep old damasks," but none of them really, discretely, seen. The value of the splendid Things for the fiction would seem in fact to have diminished for James as he contemplated the novel. His working title was *The House Beautiful*. Then in a letter to his editor he said that he thought of calling the novel *The Great House*.[18] It appeared in serial, however, under the title *The Old Things*, without the beauty or the greatness, and then, finally, the Things took on their identity as *Spoils*, as of a battle, a something to signify a victory.

But having little inherence, they, or more particularly, the idea of them, was nonetheless terrific. They are surrogate. In spite of James' specific announced intentions, the novel went its own way. Desire—sexual desire—is its pulse. The Things, in Fred See's nice phrase, come to constitute an alibi of desire.[19]

Mrs. Gereth, having, as it is said, a "passion for the exquisite," has been dispossessed fundamentally. She is recently widowed. She is about to be replaced in her home by her son's choice of another woman, a young and pretty and romping Mona Brigstock. What plainly and fundamentally she must and does want is once again to be the woman of her house. Her scheme, to find a substitute for the usurping Mona Brigstock who will be just like herself only younger (and also plainer), to take her place in her home and to marry her son—that will add charge and all but an explicitness to a situation which in the nature of things already has a sexual repleteness. Her investment of Fleda will be for the purpose of a seduction at near second hand, plainly and coarsely enough. Of her son, come to a point of exasperation when Fleda hangs back, she will say that he must have "the ordinary feelings of a man," a point which is meant not at all to be ambiguous. "Only let yourself go, darling—only let yourself go!", she says to Fleda—as, she later presumes, Mona has. That passion for bric-a-brac which in this situation has been elevated to being an aesthetic ideal and by which the interchangeability of the two women is established, is a refuge for desire and is also an instrument of allure, of a kind which Mona has not.

There is a great deal of kissing and embracing in this novel, but between Mrs. Gereth and Fleda. Mrs. Gereth needs Fleda. Fleda is almost necessarily susceptible, because needy. Mrs. Gereth offers her a place to stay, sometimes in a flat in London, sometimes at the dower-house, whatever the outcome of the suit for Poynton, and maybe there will be a husband thrown in. But the relationship, given the stakes, is by the terms of James' perception more than one of mutual accommodation. When they first meet at Waterbath, as Anne Coon has pointed out, their behavior is like that of shy lovers.[20] Fleda has risen from a bench in the garden. Mrs. Gereth pulls her down again and "for a minute," it is said, "as they sat together, their eyes met and sent out mutual soundings. 'Are you safe? Can I utter it?' each of them said to the other." The immediate subject of their mutual recognition is the decor of Waterbath, leading to their sharing little jokes at the expense of the Brigstocks, and innuendoes of malice: "When, as criticism deepened, Fleda dropped the suggestion that some people would perhaps see something in Mona, Mrs. Gereth caught her up with a groan of protest, a smothered familiar cry of 'Oh, my dear!'" Mrs. Gereth, it is said, has been "struck with the acuteness of the little girl who had already put a finger on her hidden spring." And it is within this initial scene, moreover, that Mrs. Gereth arranges for the basic and underlying vectors of plot. Mona and Owen appear. The two couples go for a stroll. Mrs. Gereth so manages things that the lovers will be separated so that first she and Owen will be paired together, and then, by way of an invisible intervention, Owen and Fleda.

Owen is handsome and heavy. Mrs. Gereth has acted very warmly. Poor Fleda has suddenly been doubly eroticized, and acts appropriately when on her first visit she is confronted by—it is all very passive—the beauties of Poynton's things.

> They went at last, the wiseheads, down to Poynton, where the palpitating girl had the full revelation. "*Now* do you know how I feel?" Mrs. Gereth asked when in the wonderful hall, three minutes after their arrival, her pretty associate dropped on a seat with a soft gasp and a roll of dilated eyes. The answer came clearly enough, and in the rapture of that first walk through the house Fleda took a prodigious span. She perfectly understood how Mrs. Gereth felt—she had understood but meagerly before; and the two women embraced with tears over the tightening of their bond.

Mona wants the Spoils and will not marry Owen without them. Mrs. Gereth removes the Spoils to her dower-house and will send them back only on condition that Owen breaks with Mona and marries Fleda. Fleda, the palpitating girl, is in this arithmetic at once a virgin offering, a dandy new collectible ("one of my best finds," Mrs. Gereth will later say), something of a leech, an aroused lover, and a mother surrogate. Her further adventures consist of her trying to be the one thing and another.

Owen is one of James' amiable oafs, like, most recently, Captain Prime in *Disengaged*. "Poor Owen," it is said, "went through life with a frank dread of people's minds." He too is measured by his collectibles, in his case eighteen rifles and forty whips, and Fleda, frankly, as is said, "had come to rejoice in his manly magnificence more even than [she] rejoiced in the royal cabinets of the red saloon." Perhaps to her surprise and certainly, as noted, to James', Owen does fall in love with her, while she, from the beginning and then to the end, wants to protect Owen. "His blunders," she reflects at the beginning, "his innocence, only added to the appeal he made to her. She would cover him, she would protect him," and so to the end when she considers that she will have done just that, and Mona is certainly right when she tells Owen that Fleda would be a nice old Mummy for him, like his Mummy. On the other hand, there is Owen's manly magnificence. He is earthy. "In the country, heated with the chase and splashed with the mire," he reminds Fleda of a peasant in national costume, of "all nature in one pair of boots," and he has for her "a tremendous pull" which, perversely enough, is also somewhat filial. One of the few overtly erotic gestures in James occurs when the two of them are alone and Owen declares his love, at which point, tea having been served, Fleda nibbles on a biscuit. Mona's mother barges in a moment later and, seeing that bit of a nibbled biscuit, supposes more or less accurately that she has caught the two of them *in flagrante*. "I don't know what girls may do," Fleda will eventually say to Mrs. Gereth, "but if he doesn't know that there isn't an inch of me that isn't his—!"

The crucial action of the novel is, then, Fleda's prolonged refusal of Owen. As a matter of very high, indeed exquisite, indeed tortured principle, she renounces. Having engaged himself to Mona, he must honor his word, she says, and honor demands that only Mona might end the engagement—which in fact she might do if she does not have a guarantee of receiving the household goods, which event Fleda is in a position to effect. But Fleda will not take so easy a way out. Principled renunciation would of course have been familiar territory for James, dating from Christopher Newman in *The American*, to the moral eloquence of Isabel Archer in *Portrait of a Lady*. Here, however, the renunciation is manifestly unreasonable, suspiciously insistent, and artfully prolonged. (It is a likelihood in the novel that Mona is not madly in love with

Owen, and Owen says to Fleda directly that she, Fleda, is forcing him to marry someone he does not love. The first intimation that Fleda will protect Owen, morally, as she thinks that she thinks, by refusing him, occurs in Chapter III, shortly after she has first been introduced to him, and so to near the end in their various meetings and her much tergiversating.) With all of its ethical delicacy, Fleda's renunciation, in this novel of surrogates and fetishes and displacements, is in fact suffused with a vocabulary of desire. Coming to visit her in London, Owen is suggestively unwilling to leave. "He stood there," it is said, "with his hand on the knob and smiled at her strangely. Clearer than he could have spoken it was the sense of those seconds of silence," but for an excited Fleda "her one thought was not to hear, to keep the act uncommitted." By refusing to respond to Owen's clear overtures she will force him first of all to break with Mona and therefore to be more "manly". "She could easily see," it is said, "how wrong everything must be when a man so made to be manly was wanting in courage." In the same moment, "in the ardor of her meditation," she pictures to herself a likely scene in which Owen's "strong arms must have clasped a remarkably handsome girl," Mona, "as close as she had permitted," whereas, she reflects, her own stony stares, no doubt in her thinking the more intense, "had been the more triumphant, albeit that she herself had no beauty."

The other side of this coin is Fleda's swooning despair as fulfillment is offered. When the candid consummation of desire occurs, as nearly as is to be allowed, it is sorrow that is invited. In the meeting of the two in which all is revealed, "He clasped her, and she gave herself," so we are told. "The surrender was short, but the relief was long: she felt his lips upon her face and his arms tighten.... they were together without a veil. She had not a shred of a secret left"—and the end of this is "the strangest thing of all," namely her (prematurely postcoital) "momentary sense of desolation." For Fleda, renunciation is as much intimacy as she can stand, and reasonably so because any alternative would plunge her back into the confusion of her many roles and desires.

Nonetheless, the manly Owen beckons one more time. Having married Mona, he perhaps has been entertaining some regrets and in any event invites Fleda, in his absence from Poynton, to come to the place and take away a memento. "What I want you to take from me, and to choose for yourself," he writes, "is the thing in the whole house that's most beautiful and precious. I mean the 'gem of the collection,'" which is a small ivory crucifix from Malta. "Would she act upon this offer?" Fleda asks herself, and answers, "She would act with secret rapture." She hesitates, however, as she is used to doing, this time for a month, but this time with very good reason. She has been invited, so in effect she knows, to commit trespass into the home of the newlyweds and to come away with, as it were, the family jewels.

She takes the train to Poynton, third-class, this palpitating girl and nice old mummy, in order, in this final tremor of ardor, to come closer to the fire than ever before she has dared, and at the end of her journey she comes upon a Poynton which, all ironically and appropriately, is in flames. The proximate cause is the clumsiness of the new servants. Mrs. Gereth had had her early fears about that. But it is the author who sets the blaze by way of demonstration and rescue. Fleda will return to Mrs. Gereth to take her place in a place prior to that near miss. "I'll go back," she says, as well she might.

Chapter Three

In the Cage, The Turn of the Screw

In the Cage

Food for Thought

The unnamed telegraph girl in *In the Cage,* of 1898, is one of a quick trio of lettered but indigent very young Jamesian women who, constrained by their poverty, are teased, just once, by the beckoning of a greater world, by which at the end they will of course be rejected. Each is imprisoned, one way and another, while just beyond, just beyond reach, is the soliciting glamor which in turn for each of them is intricate with sexual desire. Their story is their frustration, expressed more or less violently. The telegraph girl's immediate predecessor, Fleda Vetch in *The Spoils of Poynton,* in 1896–1897, with her refined taste, had been led to the fire but finally had got nowhere other than where she had started. The unnamed governess in *The Turn of the Screw,* also of 1898, is equipped with the learning which enables her to be a governess, and she goes crazy. In *In the Cage* the base metaphor is literalized, in a tale of complex implication which is at once comic (with its sprinkle of funny names, to speak only of that) and vicious, and once again is greatly distanced and is peculiarly threatening.

Class division, for one thing, is here a constant of implication, at once funny and ominous. *In the Cage* is a city novel, not only in milieu but in emphasis, like only *The Princess Cassimassima* of a dozen years earlier. It was particularly, said James, the everyday fact of the neighborhood telegraph office—likely, in this time in London, to be installed, with its clerks, in the nearby grocery store—that provided him with his occasion. "The postal-telegraph office in general," he said in the Preface to the New York Edition, "and above all the small local office of one's immediate neighborhood ... had, to my sense, so much of London to give out, so much of its huge perpetual story to tell, that any momentary wait there seemed to take place in a strong social draught, the stiffest possible breeze of the human comedy." And so had grown for speculation, he said, "the question of what it might 'mean,' wherever the admirable service was installed, for confined and cramped and yet considerably tutored young officials of either sex to be made so free, intellectually, of a range of experience otherwise quite closed to them."[1]

As between the sexes, he of course chose female, as he would for all but one of his novels of the nineties. In her cage in a corner of a Mayfair grocery, the telegraph girl is an anonymous receiver of messages meant for others, and the tale that is told of her is that, particularly, she reads and interprets the covert exchanges composed by two of her customers, a man and a woman who seemingly are involved in an illicit, therefore exciting relationship. She "wonders," as James says in the Preface, and divines and imagines, and finally projects herself into her customers' lives, when it is her job only to count the words and charge accordingly.

Like Fleda Vetch, the telegraph girl is a palpitating kind of a girl, but now the screw has been turned more tightly. Literally confined as she is, and not only by class and poverty, the gain for James is in severity, and therefore, it followed, in candor of imagination for both the author and his heroine. Imaginatively, they could go the limit, given the degree of the provocation.

Within her frame of wood and wire, the telegraph girl has the life really (as she herself knows, for in fact she has been considerably tutored) of a guinea-pig or a magpie—not only for the matter of her being on display because in fact she is mostly looked at without being seen, but as well as a matter of what amounts to devolution of species. She is the small thing in the corner, just not quite an insect. Her life behind the network of wire is both confined and unremittingly dull, to the point that dullness becomes an agent in itself. She is tortured by ceaseless noise and is oppressed by the permanent grocery-store stench.

The first paragraph of the little novel is uncharacteristically swift. "Her function," it is said of the girl,

> was to sit there with two young men—the other telegraphist and the counter-clerk; to mind the "sounder," which was always going, to dole out stamps and postal-orders, weigh letters, answer stupid questions, give difficult change and, more than anything else, count words as numberless as the sands of the sea, the words of the telegrams thrust, from morning to night, through the gap left in the high lattice, across the encumbered shelf that her forearm ached with rubbing. This transparent screen fenced out or fenced in, according to the side of the narrow counter on which the human lot was cast, the duskiest corner of a shop pervaded not a little, in winter, by the poison of perpetual gas, and at all times by the presence of hams, cheese, dried fish, soap, varnish, paraffin and other solids and fluids that she came to know perfectly by their smells without consenting to know them by their names

—that swift reduction to "solids and fluids" going to define both her environment and, virtually, the condition of her being. Meanwhile, the counter-clerk is sympathetic to the point of insistency, while the other telegraphist, Mr. Buckton, is hostile; his elbow freely enters the girl's right side while "the counter-clerk's breathing—he had something the matter with his nose—pervade(s) her left ear." On their side, all three of the captives in the cage, in the quiet time when their upper-class customers are at their luncheon, refer to the moment as the time when the animals out there are feeding—meaning the other animals, perhaps beyond their own appreciation of the irony but not beyond James'; when the summer holidays were to come, he writes, they "were holidays for almost every one but the animals in the cage."

In nothing previous to this had James ever indeed been so emphatic about the unlovely sheer creaturely being of any of his characters. Millicent Henning in *The Princess Cassimassima,* by way of convenient comparison, while her social condition is lowlier still, is a jolly and remarkably free young lady, while in the same novel Rosy Muniment, that terrifying parody of Jenny Wren, is pure will. Here in this little novel all of the characters, both low and high and on either side of the cage, are in one way or another animals and furthermore are in one way or another predators, of one size or another.

Class conflict was in the nature of the case, as James explicitly understood, but more to the point for him was nature within character, which was to say innate brutishness, merely exacerbated by the divisions of society. "You may starve in London," James would say in the Preface, "without discovering a use for any theory of the more equal division of victuals—which is moreover exactly what it would appear that thousands of the non-speculative do," but for the artist with, as he put it, his morbid imagination, the matter came back to his "irrepressible and insatiable, his extravagant and immoral, interest in personal character and in the 'nature' of a mind," with "'nature' of a mind" becoming a field for cool skepticism.

For the telegraph girl, envy, hatred, and longing are also in the nature of the case, aggravated further by the fact that, as James made her, she is a person who can and does know the arbitrariness of social position. Her family has fallen low from a higher place. Hence her being one of the "considerably tutored". She, her mother, and her elder sister, we are to know, had recently been "ladies", until suddenly and in some way unspecified they had slipped. Her elder sister has at this point "succumbed to all but absolute want" while her mother smells much of the time of whiskey. The telegraph girl's case is the more complicated, moreover, by the fact that she now finds herself to be not so bad off as her sister and her mother, but then in a way to complicate the matter still the more, here in this cage, to which in a manner she has rebounded from recent wretchedness, she is something of a snob just for the reason that not long ago she had known better estate. She is pleased that the cage, while it imprisons, also provides her with social and professional separation from the grocery clerks here at Cocker's in Mayfair, whom she scarcely deigns to recognize. And then still once again, her social situation, beyond the fact of her physical situation, is the more intolerable because to this extent it is indeterminate. She has known social mobility, mostly downwards but, by way of a prick to her discontent, there has been the little motion back up.

She is currently engaged to Mr. Mudge, a grocer with ambition, who currently, happily, has removed himself by taking a position at another grocery store while the telegraph girl remains at Cocker's. Marriage to Mudge will be a grocery marriage. The telegraph girl has often asked herself "what it was marriage would be able to add to a familiarity that seemed already to have scraped the platter so clean." Here at Cocker's in Mayfair the clientele is select and is food for fancy. Often, in free moments, by way of further nourishment, the girl reads lending-library books all about fine folks, at ha' penny a day, her situation incidentally being subtly but exactly marked by the fact that those books are published in fine print and are very greasy.

Confined and frustrated and yearning and anonymous, and thus pressed, "her quite definitely winged intelligence," as James puts it in the Preface, takes over. She fantasizes, much along the lines provided by her ha' penny novels but to the point where fantasy is insufficient and demands performance. Particularly, she will come to be privy to the hole-in-corner liaisons of Lady Bradeen and Captain Everard. These two send coded telegrams to each other. Divining fiercely, the telegraph girl breaks the code. She guesses at troubles between the two. Next she offers comfort or services or whatever she can to the handsome Captain Everard, having more-or less—for she is unable fully to admit her motives to herself—managed an accidental meeting with him one evening outside his flat. At the crisis, having to do with a mistake in one of the messages and presumably involving the suspicions of the cuckolded Lord Bradeen, the telegraph girl will save the lovers by correcting the mistake, for she has broken the code and has also memorized dates and places. She has divined fiercely and has concentrated no less.

But then, poor girl: The crisis past, the lovers barely acknowledge either the services of the telegraph girl and her existence even less, and so, after all, she will marry Mr. Mudge thus to mark the final confounding of her desperation to escape and to be seen. The door to the cage has always really been locked shut. The one name James has used for her throughout other than "the telegraph girl" has been "the betrothed of Mr. Mudge."

There are intensities here, however, which both go beyond and frustrate what clearly should be pity for this poor girl.

Because the love affair into which she has intruded herself is an adulterous one, a forbidden one, in the exciting mode as is to be presumed of the ha'penny literature which is background to her imagination, her sympathy for Captain Everard is the more candidly sexualized, first as a matter of imagination and then in action. She prowls. She stalks Captain Everard in his neighborhood. He is alluring because he is a rake and an adulterer. The sum of what Captain Everard is, for the girl as for the reader, is to be known by his name. For that matter, "Cocker's" as the place of the girl's employment already has a redolence, and would have had for late Victorian readers. From the beginning, when Everard first enters the grocery store, the girl admires his way with a cigarette. He is tall and fair and good-humoured. Her pursuit of him is accompanied by her denials of any impropriety on her own part, of thought or character or deed, but these are merely lies, both necessary and transparent. Her fantasies will involve a betrayal of Mr. Mudge but she tells herself that gullible, dull, cautious, unimaginative Mr. Mudge believes in her, "believed in her with a belief—!," although she is then quick to add that he has reason, for "if there was a thing in the world no one could charge her with it was being the kind of low barmaid person who rinsed tumblers and bandied slang." As she contemplates the incredible possibility of a rendezvous with Captain Everard, "with the web of revelation that was woven between them," she quite thrills herself "with thinking what, with such a lot of material, a bad girl would do. It would be a scene better than many in her ha'penny novels, this going to him in the dusk of the evening." But she is a good girl.

When the rendezvous does in fact take place—that is, when at dusk Everard comes upon her at his doorway—the scene vibrates with innuendo. Everard will take the girl on a stroll through a park where other young women are on the stroll and where lovers are to be found on the benches. Nothing of an overtness does take place, but the milieu is redolent, something could happen, and the girl reflects on what, were it to happen, that might mean for Everard's connection to Lady Bradeen, which in turn leads her to reflect on what kind of a girl her social class either makes her or, perhaps, better, allows her to be. She says to herself: "This was one of the questions he was to leave her to deal with—the question whether people of his sort still asked girls up to their rooms when they were so awfully in love with other women. Could people of his sort do that without what people of *her* sort would call being 'false to their love'? She had already," we read, "a vision of how the true answer was that people of her sort didn't, in such cases, matter"—didn't count as infidelity, but "counted only as something else"—and James adds, "she might have been curious, since it came to that, to see exactly as what." The language itself, of class resentment, this is to say, enhances sexual curiosity and excitement. She is a good girl, but, so we are to know, sitting on the park bench with Everard, the girl feels a strange emotion, "indeed excitement within excitement; above all a conscious joy in testing him with chances he didn't take."

On the stroll she says to her Everard companion, "But I've walked so much out of my way with you only just to show you... that anything you may have thought is perfectly true," and at the climax of the scene, and after many cross-purposes and ellipses of communication, she exclaims beseechingly: "I'd do anything for you. I'd do anything for you." Nor does she not at least half realize just what she has said. "Didn't the place, the associations and circumstances," so she reflects, "perfectly make [her statement] sound what it wasn't? And wasn't that exactly the beauty?" It was as though, she reflects, she had been seated with the Captain on a satin sofa in a boudoir, albeit she had never seen a boudoir.[2] And in any event her realization of the sexual explicitness of what she has said seems to be clear when later she tells Mr. Mudge about her evening in the park. "What do you mean by 'anything'?" asks Mr.

Mudge, and she says, "Everything."

But at the same time, and for another and darker matter, the girl's reflections become threat. Given "the web of revelation" which she supposes to exist between herself and Everard, and reflecting what with such a lot of material a bad girl might do, she contemplates blackmail, nothing less.[3] She considers "letting him at last have it," as to say to him, "'I know too much about a certain person now not to put it to you—excuse my being so lurid—that it's quite worth your while to buy me off. Come therefore: buy me!'" But the kind of her interest in the Captain is not strictly mercenary and therefore the nature of "the purchasing medium," as James puts it, is left open. It will not be "anything so gross as money". She wants something else.

She has prowled and she leaps, and she is frightening. The Captain, on his side a predator by nature, knows more than a little about rapacity in the wild, and in his London way tries to escape. He has reason to be frightened by the girl's elliptical suggestions of her knowledge of his secret affairs. When she tells him that she has remained at Cocker's only for him, the statement has ominous implication. When the girl asks him if he has ever spoken about her to anyone else, that too is cause for alarm. At the end of the scene in the park the girl cries out, "I won't give you up," and then once again, with passion, "I won't give you up!", and that is cause for terror. So when subsequently he comes back to the telegraph office, he peculiarly lingers, and when he places a telegram with the girl, he puts down "redundant money," while also, as the girl deduces, he begins to take his telegrams elsewhere.

And still again for the poor telegraph girl, and beyond the pity which in all obviousness she deserves, much like the grocers although in a medium other than exchange of cheese for money, it is the case that she too feeds upon the rich. She is pitiful and resentful, and resentful and vengeful, and therein is nice complication for dispassionate reflection. The girl's situation presents her with vivid evidence of the inequality of the division of victuals in English society, and she reads the evidence both appropriately and passionately. She is aware of "the immense disparity, the difference and contrast, from class to class." "What twisted the knife in her vitals," it is said, "was the way the profligate rich scattered about them, in extravagant chatter over their extravagant pleasures and sins, an amount of money that would have held the stricken household of her frightened childhood, her poor pinched mother and tormented father and lost brother and starved sister, together for a lifetime." She hates the rich, as she bluntly says. She thinks vengeance, and James' knowledge of her resentment secures a rare directness. "There were," he writes, "the brazen women, as she called them, of the higher and the lower fashion, whose squanderings and graspings, whose struggles and secrets and love-affairs and lies, she tracked and stored up against them till she had at moments, in private, a triumphant vicious feeling of mastery and ease, a sense of carrying their silly guilty secrets in her pocket, her small retentive brain, and thereby knowing so much more about them than they suspected or would care to think."

She will not go out to shoot an aristocrat, like Hyacinth Robinson before her, but that is because James imposes a greater frustration upon her and thus provides her with a more intricate and a more devious complexity. Vengeance as a constant idea in itself, as a rhythm of being, is for the telegraph girl fine satisfaction. Her anger will itself pleasure her, as—by way of further complexity—she herself realizes. To her friend Mrs. Jordan the girl will say that she knows all the little games and secrets and vices of the rich, and while her knowledge doesn't lead to anything, as she admits, she nonetheless has her hatred. "I hate them," she says, and "There's that charm!" More plainly albeit that she is distraught, in the scene in the park she says to Everard that she stays on at Cocker's because all of the people of his set come there and because, as she says, "I like all the horrors.... Your extravagance, your selfishness, your immorality, your crimes." "I like them," she says, "I revel in them," albeit, as she adds, "for all I get out of it is the harmless pleasure of knowing." Despite which, the customers of Cocker's ought to have reason to fear.

At the end the telegraph girl will prove to have been in fact harmless in the direct sense that no one has been physically hurt or scandalized or anything of the sort, and society, at the termination of this novel, has in all irony been reprieved. The girl certainly has not been merely "touchingly curious," as has sometimes been said.[4] She has breached the social bounds, she is a threat to the existing order, and more to the point of James' evident realization, she has enjoyed herself. This is to see that it is not merely the unfairness in itself of the existing order that is finally at issue, nor simple envy, nor suspicion of a conspiracy there down below. The vision is now deeper and much more bleak. There is appetite here. For this girl the fine folk are delightful and are her prey. The affair of Captain Everard and Lady Bradeen has provided the telegraph girl with, as it were, food for thought.

And in this she is after all properly the betrothed of Mr. Mudge despite the superficial seeming that he is a lower version of a Tessler to the girl's Hedda Gabler. Mr. Mudge, with his very white apron and very clustering curls and his too-present *h's*, and the chuckle in his Dickensian name, is a grocer with a dream. He has plans, and his plans naturally are contingent on his ability to exploit the appetites of such fine folk as go to Cocker's. He is a grocer's grocer and for that reason in the eye of the telegraph girl he after all does have his beauty. He is professionally oleaginous and at the same time happily primitive. There had been an occasion, as the telegraph girl recalls, when at Cocker's he had collared a drunken soldier, a big violent man, and had "shaken the delinquent in his skin." Had Mr. Mudge and she not already been affianced, she recalls, at that moment he would have conquered her resistance. His charm is essential and alimentary. The girl resents him for his seeming smug ignorance of what she knows to be the immense difference between the two of them, with, as she will barely recognize, the one point they have in common being that they were both "practically human," but that point in this novel about a girl in a cage is a large point indeed. He is not bothered by his affianced's somewhat infidelity except for the fact that in his way of accounting she has got nothing out of it. Not that he himself knows nothing of the sex game and more particularly how a human being might be masterful in it. In a nice moment after the girl has confessed, he draws from his pocket a packet of chocolate-creams. "Have another?—" he says to the girl, "*that* one." (But she takes a different one.) Like the girl, in any event, Mr. Mudge stands ready to enjoy the rich most especially for the fact of their immoralities, or "the exuberance," as is stated, "of the aristocracy." The rich for him, it is said, proposed "a class that Providence had raised up to be the blessing of grocers.... The more flirtations, as he might roughly express it," it is said, "the more cheese and pickles. He had even in his own small way been dimly struck with the linked sweetness connecting the tender passion with cheap champagne, or perhaps the other way round."

The rich, meanwhile, in the nature of things, feed upon the poor, and in this vision of the way things are, also devour each other. As happens and as will eventually become known to the telegraph girl, the intrigues of the very young and beautiful and insolent Lady Bradeen and the handsome Captain Everard are not after all purely, loftily adulterous. The girl's friend Mrs. Jordan has received knowledge from her betrothed, Mr. Drake, recently engaged as butler to Lady Bradeen. The something she has learned lacks detail but suggests a sordidness and, beyond that, a viciousness in the direction of criminality. We learn that Captain Everard had had debts, and that Lady Bradeen had been compromised. "Something was lost—something was found," says Mrs. Jordan. It is thought that Lady Bradeen had stolen something in order to help her lover, at that point forcing Lord Bradeen to act except that he had conveniently died, wherefore now Lady Bradeen has been able to force the reluctant Captain Everard to marry her. "She just nailed him," says Mrs. Jordan, and so much for true love. Mrs. Jordan's Mr. Drake, a handsome man and six foot two, a man-sized drake, will moreover provide incidental confirming evidence pertaining to the matter of true love. He has just been dismissed from the service of the bachelor Lord Rye, either although or because, as Mrs. Jordan says, he was "A great and trusted friend. Almost—I may say—a loved friend." The telegraph girl reflects passingly on the oddity of that "almost". Mr. Drake had wished to "sleep out" now that he was to marry, but Lord Rye had objected.[5]

When James sent a copy of the novel to his friend Paul Bourget, more particularly to Bourget's wife, it was with the remark that the thing was "a poor little pot-boiling study of nothing at all, qui ne tire pas à conséquence… a monument to my fatal technical passion, which prevents my ever giving up anything I have begun."[6] No other reference to the novel appears in any other of James' published letters nor is there any mention of it in the Notebooks, and this observation to the Bourgets certainly is not to be taken as serious self-criticism. The tone in fact of many of James' many letters to Bourget is one of a peculiarly deliberated offhandedness, but on the other hand James' polite shrug here does have a suggestiveness.

Something akin to an ironic dismissiveness is undertone throughout the novel itself.

Clearly, in any event, James' intentions had not been ideological in any usual sense. The poor little caged telegraph girl is always to be pitied despite everything. She is victimized by: the social system, by romantic fiction, and the by meaningless routine of her telegraph cage in the age of mechanical transcription. But for all of that, she seethes and is dangerous. The characters who collectively are called "the rich" are on the other hand something more than contemptible, worse than is accounted for in any of the telegraph girl's accusations in those passages in which she does become accusatory, while nonetheless and in a way of vertiginous irony, they secure from the telegraph girl, and from her friend Mrs. Jordan, an admiration which is so warm as to be erotic. Characters and characterizations are complex and contrary, as might be expected, but it is also to be seen that now once again that while the sheer attentiveness is fierce, James' sympathies on either or any side of the social division are in fact conspicuously unengaged.

Thus at any moment, as is also to be seen, and by way of reinforcing the bleakness of the idea of humanity within a society, the general grimness now and again gives over to jokes and other comedy, not by way of relief. (About Maupassant James had written some ten years before, "M. De Maupassant sees human life as a terribly ugly business relieved by the comical, but even the comedy is for the most part the comedy of misery, of avidity, of ignorance, helplessness, and grossness.")[7] In this grim novel there are funny and suggestive names: the Dickensian "Mr. Mudge," and, slyly, Captain Everard (although it is raised as a possibility that that is not his real name, in which case the name becomes the more characterizing), and Cocker's. In the immediate neighborhood of Cocker's are "the dearest furnished apartments" which provide custom, named Simpkin's, Ladle's, and Thupp's, and there is a customer named Mrs. Bubb.

Again, it is in the novel's penultimate scene that the telegraph girl learns from her friend Mrs. Jordan the more sordid truths of the affair of Everard and Lady Bradeen, and that scene is one of a high comedy of misunderstandings and verbal miscues. Mrs. Jordan with her own passion for the rich and titled has agreed to marry Mr. Drake, the loved friend of Lord Rye, who will open doors to the rich and titled. Mr. Drake has been a member of his lordship's circle, so the telegraph girl has been led, ambiguously, to believe, and now, so Mrs. Jordan tells her, he will be "going" to the beautiful Lady Bradeen, who has "engaged him." "And was Lord Rye engaged?" the telegraph girl wants to know, until it comes to her that Mr. Drake is one of those who, "majestic, middle-aged, erect, flanked on either side by a footman and taking the name of a visitor," in literal fact opened doors.

Mrs. Jordan herself, nearsighted and with extraordinarily protrusive teeth, meanwhile reduplicates the telegraph girl's own adventure but more flagrantly, thus to provide another perspective beyond endearing sympathy. She too, as the widow of a clergyman, has fallen low from a higher estate. She has made a business for herself of flower-arranging for the rich, which requires her being in and out of their houses, which fact, in turn, provides spring to her vision, no doubt to James' amusement. Mrs. Jordan felt, it is said, "that a single step more would transform her whole social position." "On its being asked of her then," it is said, "if she circulated only in a sort of tropical solitude, with the upper servants for picturesque natives, and on her having to assent to this glance at her limitations, she had found a reply to the girl's invidious question. 'You've no imagination, my dear!'" she says. She knows that "a door more than half open to the higher life couldn't be called anything but a thin partition," and Mrs. Jordan's imagination, it is said, "quite did away with the thickness."

But Mrs. Jordan settles for Mr. Drake because, as she must finally admit, it is better not to starve. The telegraph girl, seated with Mrs. Jordan in the latter's "damp dusky shabby little room," perceives in her hostess's compromise the fact of her own dreams and delusions and her own return to reality. She will in fact be a little better off than Mrs. Jordan who still, foolishly, clings to the idea that in some manner she is marrying into "society", even though her husband will need permission to sleep with her. The betrothed of Mr. Mudge will at least have her own house. She will hurry the marriage. She determines. She reflects. She is filled with her own thoughts. At the very end of the tale, at the end of her afternoon with Mrs. Jordan, she walks across the bridge over the Paddington canal and is enveloped, appropriately and with all of the drear ambiguity of her situation retained, in the brown gloom of a London fog.

The Turn of the Screw

Convention and Chaos

I

Like the heroine of *In the Cage*, the governess is anonymous and is a function of her employment. The story is the story of a governess, whose name is "the governess," as *In the Cage* is the story of a telegraph girl. She is a subject matter and along similar lines. Following upon arousal, so brief as in her case has been the encouragement to desire, like the heroine of *In the Cage* (and for that matter like Paul Doubleday in James' comedy *The Reprobate*), the governess is effectively imprisoned, now in a remote country house, circumstances having been invented for her so that communication with London will be precluded. She is of course considerably tutored, like, as James had supposed, those telegraph workers whom he had observed, and as well like Fleda Vetch, and, confined as she is, the governess will have intellectual experience of an extraordinary sort, as was promised to the telegraph girl, which is to say that her mind will be affected. Once again, moreover, like both the telegraph girl and like Fleda Vetch, the governess is a palpitating young girl (and like Fleda, as she is a governess, is cast impossibly, preposterously, in the role of a nice old mummy). In the time of the story she is twenty years old, all but technically a teenager, come up from the country to the haunted house. And like Rose Armiger, two years earlier, she will murder a child, perhaps for love.

The Turn of the Screw is in a line with other novels and tales of the moment, this is to say, but is another reach forward—rather a light-hearted one—in the direction of the darkness. Very nice persons in all of the major items of the moment, virginal young girls, exactly (who will be still younger in other fictions of the moment), are given their rope and are thereby made available to adventure ranging all the way to horror.[8]

Ten years later, in the 1908 Preface to the New York Edition, James would be insisting once again as he had been saying from the beginning, that *The Turn of the Screw* was not more than a little *amusette,* readers having seemed one way and another to be taking it seriously. So the ten years earlier, writing to various correspondents, he had been protesting that like particularly *In the Cage,* this tale had been composed for the popular market and for the money. And of course James was right, he would have known. The tale had been serialized in a popular magazine, *Collier's Weekly*. But that there was something disturbingly more to it, that within this amusement of a well-turned little ghost tale there were underlying, and eruptive, and unaccounted-for surplus energies—that both in the moment of publication and ever since everyone has seemed to know, maybe but not certainly James to the contrary. That there is deep instability within, that the story doesn't really fully contain itself, that it presses for explanation, not to say relief.

Few other fictions in English, if any, in any event, in modern times, of similar modesty (with respect to the manner in which it offers itself, and with respect to its length), have solicited any greater amount of speculation and scrutiny and unearthing of clues, commentary laid upon commentary upon excursus, so that by now *The Turn of the Screw* is a kind of continuously aggregating palimpsest of itself.[9] And that is the case although almost all of the criticism since the early 1930s has been raised on either one of just two premises of interpretation: whether or not the ghosts are "real" or are, rather, the invention of the sexually-repressed governess. If "real," then the story is either simply a ghost story, meant to frighten, or is a moralizing one in which the governess seeks to protect Innocence, that of the children, against a predatory Evil, that of the ghosts.[10] On the other side, the single significant objection to the "Freudian" reading, as it is usually called, rests on an otherwise seemingly inexplicable twist of the plot, much grappled with in the history of the criticism. After the governess sees her first ghost, namely the red-headed stranger standing on the tower, she describes him for the housekeeper, Mrs. Grose, and Mrs. Grose immediately identifies him as the valet Peter Quint, deceased. If Mrs. Grose is able to identify this stranger, who is dead and who therefore must be a ghost, then it must be the case that the governess has not hallucinated and that at least one of the two ghosts is "real," and it is then likely that so is the other one, that of the governess' predecessor, Miss Jessel. But this is to become unnecessarily entangled in what is actually a plot at a secondary remove, as James constructed the tale. The governess' story consists of a reading of a recovered manuscript. It occurs as first-person narrative. As James constructed the tale, the governess has had reason to propose confirmation of the reality of her ghosts especially as there might be reason to suspect that they were not real, and James' characters do tell lies, whether or not they know that they do. James' late heroines do frequently fantasize, moreover, as in the cases of Fleda and the telegraph girl and of Milly Theale to come, and if the governess now hallucinates, that amounts only to a single further flight of the winged imagination and at the same time, nicely, amounts to just one more turn of the screw. Moreover, and as will be seen, there are deliberate clues enough in the short novel that what for the reader is to be taken as the givens of plot is for the governess a field for self-serving and obsessed invention.

For all the immense weight of interpretation that has been put upon the little novel—"Freudian," "Lacanian," Marxist, gendered, moral, religious, *et alia*—James' own insistencies obviously retain prior importance.

What James chiefly recalled when he came to write his Preface to the tale for the New York Edition, was the freedom he had experienced in the composition, particularly as he remembered his problems with *The Aspern Papers*. Unlike *The Aspern Papers,* with its basis in an actuality, the search for some letters of Lord Byron, *The Turn of the Screw* had raised no questions for him or possible objections on the grounds of historical or cultural realities. It was in this sense that, as he said, *The Turn of the Screw* was a "perfectly independent and irresponsible little fiction" which for its strength and ease had "a perfect homogeneity." There had been no necessity for considering any kind of outside linkage. He had not found himself responsible even to "ghosts" as in any reality they might be according to—clearly he was skeptical—"the today so copious psychical record of cases of apparitions." And as for that, these "recorded and attested 'ghosts'" he had found to be too little expressive to be useful to a fiction, "as little expressive, as little responsive, as is consistent with their taking the trouble—and an immense trouble they find it, we gather—to appear at all." Real ghosts were boring. They didn't seem actually to do anything. "I had to decide in fine," said James, "between having my apparitions correct and having my story 'good'".

"The thing had for me," said James, further, "the immense merit of allowing the imagination absolute freedom of hand," leading to "my impression of the dreadful, my designed horror." He was insistent that what he had made was "a piece of ingenuity pure and simple, of cold artistic calculation, an *amusette* to catch those not easily caught," particularly, considering that it was a ghost story, to catch those who were "the jaded, the disillusioned, the fastidious".[11] In the several recorded letters touching on *The Turn of the Screw* following publication, moreover, James had likewise and repeatedly been insistent that his intentions had been those of an artist, strictly. "I am only afraid," he was writing to one of his correspondents, "that my conscious intention strikes you as having been larger than I deserve it should be thought.... As regards a presentation of things so fantastic as in that wanton little Tale, I can only rather blush to see real substance read into them." (The correspondent, Dr. Louis Waldstein, whose letter is not preserved, seems to have been concerned for the preservation of the innocence of the children, Miles and Flora.) To H.G. Wells James was writing that "the thing is essentially a pot-boiler and a *jeu d'esprit*." The same day, to another correspondent, Frederic Myers, who seems to have been concerned for the amount of the reality of the ghosts and the details of the kind of their communication, James was saying that "The

T. of the S. is a very mechanical matter... a merely *pictorial* subject & rather a shameless pot-boiler," in which he had "evoked the worst I could, & only feel tempted to say, as in French: 'Excusez du peu!'"[12]

While, however, the tale had allowed James freedom from linkages to history, society, culture, and, as well, from the "copious psychical record of cases of apparitions," there were other and deliberately invoked constraints which did clearly figure for him.

Several pages of the Preface are given to distinction between ghost stories and fairy tales and then to distinctions between types of fairy tales. Peter Quint and Miss Jessel were not "ghosts" at all "as we now know the ghost," James said, but goblins, elves, imps, of the sort of "fairies of the legendary order." As for types of fairy tales, *The Turn of the Screw* was an adjustment between the orders of Cinderella and Blue-Beard on the one hand and the Arabian Nights on the other. Cinderella and Blue-Beard and their like were marked by their compactness of anecdote, while the tales of the Arabian Nights were long and loose and copious and endless. In *The Turn of the Screw* James had aimed, so he said, at the free working of imagination but within bounds so as to achieve an "absolute singleness, clearness and roundness," and he considered that he had succeeded. The tale, he said, "is an excursion into chaos while remaining, like Blue-Beard and Cinderella, but an anecdote."

All of this was to say, by way as it were of ground rules, that *The Turn of the Screw* alluded to conventions of story-telling, that it invoked certain and ancient genres, in which the author had found a field for play. Against the accepted conventions, or, better, against accepted conventions of reading, James had made a fairy tale not for children, and, what amounted to the same thing, a ghost story intended to capture "the jaded, the disillusioned, the fastidious." (All of "the good, the really effective and heart-shaking ghost-stories... appeared all to have been told," so James also said in the

Preface.) Blue-Beard and Cinderella are perhaps also replete with sexual innuendo and otherwise propose horrors, so he might also have said, but not (perhaps paradoxically) for the jaded.

And James was writing as well, with conscious intent, within a tradition of the gothic, with his ghosts and the remote locale of the action, and Bly with its crenellated structures and battlements and the cawing of the rooks, and the mystery and the fear. After the first of her encounters with the red-headed stranger, the governess wonders, "Was there a 'secret' at Bly—a mystery of Udolpho?" Furthermore, being, as she is, considerably tutored, the governess wonders if perhaps there was at Bly "an unmentionable relative kept in unsuspected confinement?" for of a certainty she will have read *Jane Eyre*. Writing, moreover, within the conventions—or, better, continuously alluding to the conventions—of ghost stories and fairy tales and the gothic, James, as Millicent Bell pointed out, was also composing a version of what since the 1840s had been called the "governess novel". For the governess in actuality, said Bell, "her respectability and her obligation to uphold the purity of the nursery often meant celibacy; the world of courtship and marriage was closed to her.... Yet she was often shut off from the rest of the world as well. Loneliness was the common complaint of governesses." Such being the case, the governess was ready made for fiction, and thus James' governess as an instance of an actual occupation was also a stock figure in a literature.[13]

And still once again as a matter of literary conventions, the secluded country estate was, as Steven Marcus has pointed out and as James had to know, a typical locale in nineteenth-century pornographic literature.[14]

II

So much—that the governess' tale is put forth as being just that, an instance of traditional artifice, a story in a line of story-telling—is clearly implied, indeed clearly stated, by James' elaborate preparations for the presentation of the tale, excepting only that the reader is to be prepared to know that when it comes, the governess' tale will be "beyond everything." James' initial scene is itself so deliberately a standard device, so much a convention of fiction as to be parodic, as it establishes an audience for what is a story-telling contest. The scene is one of coziness. It had been on a Christmas Eve. A number of us, it is said, had been gathered round the fire listening to a story recited by one, Griffin, which, if gruesome, was "gruesome, as on Christmas Eve in an old house a strange tale should essentially be," which is to say that if gruesome, the tale was also and appropriately a Christmas Eve entertainment. And then James has someone tell a second tale and does so because the scene is one of story-telling and is not otherwise an introduction to an action. That second tale for itself is dismissed—it was "not particularly effective," it is said—with the effect, again, of confirming the scene in itself. And then there will be the main event, the third story, which, it is promised, will be one better than the first, Griffin's, because while the first had been about the appearance of a ghost to a child, this third story, says the new contender, Douglas, will be about *two* children, with "the effect of another turn of the screw."

Douglas, moreover, who will bring forth the governess' manuscript and read from it, is a story-teller of superior cunning. It is observed that Douglas had not been following the telling of that second story, with the effect thereby of his claiming attention to himself. ("This I took for a sign," says the narrator, "that he had himself something to produce and that we should only have to wait.") Douglas, risen and with back to the fire and hands in his pockets, looks down upon his audience and promises something really new and never before heard, and, we read, "our friend, with quiet art, prepared his triumph by turning his eyes over the rest of us and going on: 'It's beyond everything.'" He passes his hand over his eyes, making a little wincing grimace, and promises that his tale will surpass everything "'for dreadful—dreadfulness!'" whereupon one of the women in his audience, speaking no doubt for them all, cries out, "Oh how delicious!," but Douglas, master of the situation as he is, takes no notice of her. Douglas now makes his audience wait an additional four nights, when he will read from the ancient and hitherto secret manuscript. Numbers of the ladies have meanwhile departed owing to previous arrangements but have departed "in a rage of curiosity, as they professed, produced by the touches with which [Douglas] had already worked us up"—with the result that the remaining audience was the more compact and select, seated round the hearth, "subject to a common thrill."

It is to be seen that the elaborate preparatory scene is just that, and is not a frame. James had presented himself with a variety of interrelated stock materials, both subject and form: ghosts and ghost story, and fairy tale, and the furniture of the gothic, and the governess, and little children, all of it insistently identified by the mechanism of the initial scene as material for an entertainment, a direction as to the spirit in which what follows is to be read. This story will be just what James claimed, namely an *amusette,* an entertainment, which *as such,* as comedy, in the way typical of James' fictions in the nineties, would offer fine opportunities for discovery of genuine human dreadfulness.

More particularly, he had here presented himself with opportunity for exploration and radicalization of the potentialities of character of the governess-as-trope. So, according to the likelihood of a governess newly arrived, this governess will be young, frightened, lonely, "privately bred" and therefore uncertain (the governess' tale hints at the fact that she is not a good teacher, that she does not know enough) and sexually susceptible. As in the likelihood of a new governess, this governess will be thrust into an established household which has, inevitably, a history which the other servants (for she is a servant herself) are to be presumed to know. As a servant she will be nominally superior to the other servants but as a practical matter, not. As a governess, moreover and most urgently, she will be confronted with necessity to assert authority over young children who are her social superiors, whom she serves. She has reason to fear them. She will have to take control in a situation of complex and contrary challenges, in which as a practical matter she controls very little. Her one available tactic as a practical matter, is to make others like her, which is to say, to charm, to seduce—failing which, however, and almost as a necessary matter, she will be able to fabricate her own narrative of events.

A few "facts" are established in the introduction to the governess' tale—that is to say, some elements of the story to come are established which, being outside of the story to come, have an authority prior to what is related in the first-person narrative to come. There had been a governess, the youngest daughter of a poor country parson, who at the age of twenty, not having had any previous experience and seeking employment, had been interviewed by the handsome bachelor in Harley Street, who had had children to dispose of, his orphaned little nephew and niece. It is a matter of considerable emphasis in these introductory pages that in all probability the governess had succumbed to the seductive charms of the splendid bachelor, which charms also are emphasized, and, it is said, the governess' passion had probably been sharpened by the fact that she was to have seen him only twice. We are to know that it was a stipulation of her employment that the governess was never to trouble the bachelor of Harley Street. In residence at Bly, to which the governess is to be dispatched, there had been the housekeeper, Mrs. Grose, an excellent woman, and—a matter of some importance—several other servants: a cook, a housemaid, a dairywoman, an old groom (for an old pony), and an old gardener. Previously, there had been the governess' predecessor, a most respectable person who had done beautifully till her death. There is no mention of a valet.

In the same way that James puts these few facts into play, so then in a manner does the governess, but from her position within the facts. Like Fleda Vetch and like the telegraph girl in *In the Cage*, and for that matter like a line of James' heroines going back to Catherine Sloper in *Washington Square*, the governess is a vulnerable young girl who is susceptible to her own fancies. As is not the case with those others, however, we have the governess in first person, like an actress left to her own inventions, on her own, without mediation, without authorial interpretation. And she is much more fiercely creative than any of her predecessors.

The famous ambiguity (and the density) of *The Turn of the Screw* is entirely a function of the fact that the governess is herself the author of her tale. Virginia Woolf commented on the silence of *The Turn of the Screw*, where everything—the twitter of the birds at dawn, the far-away cries of children, faint footsteps in the distance—goes to make for an accumulation of quietness.[15] But it is the governess who suppresses the background. Bly does come equipped with a staff of servants, so Douglas has told us, and the governess does refer now and again to the presence of maids and particularly of a servant named Luke, but except for the housekeeper, Mrs. Grose, these others have scarcely any presence in the action of the tale—except possibly in one instance, and in that instance they figure as a negation. Near the end of the tale, after Mrs. Grose has left with Flora, the governess protests to Miles that after all they are not alone, "We've the others," but Miles points out correctly that "Yet even though we have them…they don't much count," which altogether is to say that fortuitousness and distractions are thus canceled, as the governess seeks to impose an absolute of her own presence.

Her tale then describes an adventure in exorcism, meaning not only the getting-rid of her own ghosts but as well the elimination of all impediments to a controlling consciousness. Everything is to go, all intrusions upon her creativity. Bly in her telling is indeed remarkably still. The governess prepares for the appearance of Peter Quint by invoking a complete silence: "I can hear again, as I write, the intense hush in which the sounds of evening dropped. The rooks stopped cawing in the golden sky and the friendly hour lost for the unspeakable minute all its voice." The servants, throughout the action, are present only so sufficiently as to mark their absence. The governess begins in separation first from her family and then from her employer, the handsome bachelor, and resists requests from both Mrs. Grose and Miles to be in touch with him. That leaves the principals, but as the governess comes to her climax, first Mrs. Grose and Flora are forced by her to remove themselves, and then Miles dies, leaving the governess alone—climax indeed—with a dead boy in her arms.

There can after all be little doubt that the governess invents both her ghosts and their story. She is a palpitating young girl placed by her author in a situation which will invite romantic imaginings with erotic content, which the ghosts will enact. Since the related tale is a first-person account of those imaginings, it does however become a nice question as to what other than the ghosts is imaginary and whether anything, any action not previously vouchsafed in the introductory chapter of *The Turn of the Screw,* is "real," as in the ordinary conventions of fiction. And to press that question is indeed to discover post-modernist vertigo, of a sort which is indeed fully anticipated in James' fiction, here and elsewhere. The question will become demanding in *The Sacred Fount* and *The Sense of the Past.* But it is not yet here quite so demanding. We can find slippages and fractures in the governess' attempts to make her story, and then it is exactly her imposition upon resisting realities, with consequences, that is the story of *The Turn of the Screw.*

The governess is nothing if not self-absorbed, and that becomes the matter of crucial information about her. We do, that is to say, despite something James says in the Preface, overhear her in "her relation to her own nature." (James' point seems to be that she does not see herself from the outside, but in fact she does, only not objectively.) Arriving at Bly and delighted by the unaccustomed luxury of her new surroundings, in her second paragraph the governess records her looking into the long mirrors and seeing herself, for the first time ever, head to foot, and what follows is in good part an elaboration of the instance. "I was wonderful," she will observe of herself on the occasion when she is first confronted with the problem of what to do about Miles' dismissal from school, and "oh I was grand" she says when, near the end, she lies to Miles about Flora's disappearance from Bly, with many self-approving expressions of her performance in between. At the same time she is a virtuoso valetudinarian, persistently recording her ups and downs. In the first sentence of her tale she confides, "I remember the whole beginning as a succession of flights and drops, a little see-saw of the right throbs and the wrong," and what follows is a transcription of the same; that succession of flights and drops is the rhythm of her tale. She is also a persisting insomniac, right from the time of her arrival at Bly and quite prior to the coming of Peter Quint, and that too is a part of her record of herself.

This "suppositious author," as James calls her in the Preface, is created to say, as we can know, both less and more than the truth of her encounters, which truth however we can also know. For one very large matter we can know the truth of Mrs. Grose's estimation of the governess, apart from the matter of whether or not she believes in the governess' ghosts, and we can know the truth exactly by the amount that the governess' account of Mrs. Grose's affection, by James' doing, is patently misleading. From the beginning, in her first meeting with Mrs. Grose, the governess is wonderfully pleased to realize that Mrs. Grose likes her, except that her expression itself of the ascribed pleasure undermines the flat statement. "I felt within half an hour," she says, "that [Mrs. Grose] was so glad—stout simple plain clean wholesome woman—as to be positively on her guard against showing it too much. I wondered even then a little why she should wish *not* to show it," a reflection which, as she goes on to say, might have made her uneasy, but the matter is dropped. The overt irony, or at least the sense of it, is then repeated throughout the tale. "Please, Miss," says Mrs. Grose, "I must get to my work," and the governess writes, "Her thus turning her back on me was fortunately not, for my just preoccupations, a snub that could check the growth of our mutual esteem." Dialogue between the two consists as frequently as not of the governess interrupting Mrs. Grose mid-sentence, for the sake of preventing dialogue, which would thwart her creativity. So she takes control:

> "Would you mind, Miss, if I used the freedom—."
> "To kiss me? No!" I took the good creature in my arms....
>
> She visibly tried to hold herself. "But he *is* handsome?"

> I saw the way to help her. "Remarkably!"
> "And dressed—?"
> "In somebody's clothes. They're smart, but they're not his own."
>
> She was still vague. "And what *is* your remedy?"
> "Your loyalty, to begin with. And then Miles."
> She looked at me hard. "Do you think he—?"
> "Won't, if he has the chance, turn on me? Yes, I venture still to think it."

As with Mrs. Grose, so with Flora and Miles. "I felt quite sure she would presently like me," the governess says at her first meeting with Flora, and by the second day at Bly is asserting "the affection she had conceived for my person." (Flora, on that first occasion, faced with the prospect of sleeping in the governess' bedroom, had been "timid," according to the governess, which would be to say that she had been afraid, and "in the oddest way in the world, had been perfectly frank and brave" about it.) Both children, she says, were "extravagantly and preternaturally fond of me," at the time when she has begun to watch them for signs of their being secretly engaged with ghosts. She does say that she wonders that the children do not guess that she is thinking strange things about them and that they are not disturbed by her suddenly now and again, in little outbreaks of passion, catching them up and pressing them to her heart—and it is a matter of clear implication that indeed they would be, and are, indeed, disturbed. Here and in actions to follow the children clearly are engaged in humoring the governess, just as she says that she suspects, but for motives entirely explicable by her strangeness, and it is testimony to the completeness of her self-engagement that even as she suspects, she takes comfort in what she insists is the affection Miles and Flora have for her. During schoolroom hours, even as she is on the watch for their guile, the children, the governess says, "had a delightful endless appetite for passages in my own history to which I again and again treated them," and, she says, "it was in any case over *my* life, *my* past, and *my* friends alone that we could take anything like our ease," which is to say that ease comes upon her—she cannot speak for the children—when she talks about herself.

All of her estimations are clearly extravagant when not fantastic. Flora "was the most beautiful child I had ever seen." Miles was "incredibly beautiful" and from the first, like his sister, he had emitted a "fragrance of purity." If Peter Quint and Miss Jessel are also immoderately described, that of course has an aptness—Quint the satyr, with his close-curling red hair and queer red whiskers, Jessel dark as midnight in her black dress, with her haggard beauty and her unutterable woe. Given ghosts, they will be gothic, extreme, ravaging or ravaged.[16] The governess' ghosts are derivative and literary. "Real" ghosts, as James was to suggest, would have been boring, and they would have been useless as well.

Clearly the governess does have use for her ghosts. She makes them so as to enact an illicit love affair in her behalf and so at the same time as to make it frightening. The ghost who will be Peter Quint is summoned for the first time (as Edmund Wilson first pointed out) just as she is thinking about the handsome bachelor of Harley Street, who subsequently will be known as "the Master". Miss Jessel, her predecessor who has died, clearly is in line to be her surrogate and it is likely that a Quint had indeed been free with Miss Jessel. "He did what he wished," says Mrs. Grose, says the governess, to which the governess says with abrupt and revealing candor, "It must have been also what *she* wished."

But the governess is much more richly inventive than all of that just as the potentialities of her character, for her author, are more far-reaching. Peter Quint stands in for the Master, but so also then, clearly, does "the little gentleman" "Master Miles", as he is called, whom Peter Quint seeks to possess, which is to say, to corrupt, which certainly means to sexualize, while Miss Jessel stands in for the governess herself the while she seeks to possess, which is to say corrupt, which is to say to sexualize little Flora, who then in this comic arithmetic also stands in for the governess. The ghosts have no designs on herself but only on the children, so the governess early on determines (by way only of a sudden "shock of certitude"), but with the consequence that there will be a play of indirection which in turn will permit the governess to regard her little charges as being sexually charged, with implied permission for the kind of her relationship to them—the while, however, that she is attempting to be surrogate herself for the children by offering herself, as she says, to be "expiatory victim" of the ghosts. The governess is soon certain that the children carry on secret correspondence not only with the ghosts but with each other, and thus it becomes her purpose, necessarily beyond her knowing except in hidden ways, to replace Flora with herself—thereby in effect to resolve, to bring clarity to the erotic confusion she has created.

Or, to do so insofar as possible. The Master remains unavailable but the little Master is on the premises. Flora and Mrs. Grose are to be removed. The governess has frightened them and off they go. There are the other servants at Bly but, again, as Miles says, they don't much count. Conditions for romance have been concocted. And at the end there will be *liebestod*.

The governess' "dreadful liability" to ghostly impressions, as she puts it, is a constant. Insomniac that she is, she hears, or believes that she hears, ghostly presences her first night at Bly, quite prior to Quint. "There had been a moment," she says, "when I believed I recognised, faint and far, the cry of a child; there had been another when I found myself just consciously starting as at the passage, before my door, of a light footstep." Her own perception that she might also be crazy is also a constant, discernible in the chinks of her own expressions of fear. It takes her three days to tell Mrs. Grose about the apparition on the tower (which in itself is cause for speculation); she says, "It wasn't so much yet that I was more nervous than I could bear to be as that I was remarkably afraid of becoming so." The children, she says, had only her to stand between them and the ghosts, and so she "began to watch them in a stifled suspense, a disguised tension, that might well, had it continued too long, have turned to something like madness," and of course it does continue. The children, she says to Mrs. Grose, are talking about their correspondence with the ghosts. "They're talking of *them*—they're talking horrors!" she says. "I go on, I know, as if I were crazy; and it's a wonder I'm not."

The narrator of the tale unknowingly reveals secret truth about herself, of course by design of her author. Given the figure of the governess both in fact and fiction, nice and amusing and startling possibilities are there to be explored, which is what most of all takes place in *The Turn of the Screw*.

James' exploration does, however, go further. The schoolboy who is there for the purposes of the governess is another figure for exploitation, virtually a trope. It is not a great mystery as to why Miles has been expelled from his school. The governess herself certainly seems to have a reasonable idea of the truth of the matter. As much as she protests his angelic innocence, she wants him to be "bad," a matter which in this context will mean something other than playing tricks on Aunt Polly. Prior to the first meeting with Miles but after she has knowledge of the expulsion, she will tell Mrs. Grose that she likes boys "with the spirit to be naughty," adding the significantly unsolicited proviso, "But not to the degree to contaminate . . . ." She will soon be certain that Miles has been expelled "For wickedness. For what else—when he's so clever and beautiful and perfect? Is he untidy? Is he infirm? Is he ill-natured? He's exquisite—so it can be only *that*."

At the end, forced to confess the reasons for his expulsion, Miles will say only that he "said things" and those things to only a few, "Those I liked." Which is as a literal matter to leave everything undefined: naughtiness and badness and wickedness and the nature of the "things". With respect particularly to the corruption to be imputed to the ghosts, James would say in the Preface, "Only make the reader's general vision of evil intense enough . . . and his own experience, his own imagination, his own sympathy (with the children) and horror (of their false friends) will supply him quite sufficiently with all the particulars." Specification would weaken the case. And so it is, by implication, for Miles' own and inherent wickedness, except that one—the reader, the governess—would be likely to know what would be the particular of the wickedness to be suspected of school-boy friendships in Victorian public schools.

There is nice suggestiveness in the fact that James' source for the story was an anecdote told him one evening in 1895 by his friend the Archbishop of Canterbury, Edward White Benson. Prior to his becoming Archbishop, Benson had been a public-school headmaster who was famously zealous for trying to protect boys from bad habits, of which he was aware. He had opposed cubicles and had encouraged flogging. As Archbishop he was engaged particularly in efforts to promote sexual morality in national life, as surely James would have been aware. The telling in itself of the anecdote, this is to say, would have had associations of an illicit sexual sort. In any event, the suspicion of homosexual practices within the public schools was currently widespread, especially as between older boys and younger pretty ones.[17] And Miles is both young and pretty.

The governess, however unwittingly, reveals her purpose to possess Miles. She is excited early on by the prospect of dealing "with a boy whose education for the world was all on the point of beginning," but in fact, as she knows from the beginning, Miles' education has already advanced, he is only somewhat virginal. This is to say that Miles offers his own possibilities for narrative exploitation. The governess terrifies him. Unable to leave Bly, as he wishes to do (and as he cannot do because the governess has imprisoned him), he placates the governess and does so, as the climax gathers, in the way not only that she clearly wishes but, to the point, in the way he knows. He flirts. He acts the cavalier. He proffers sexual innuendo.

"You know, my dear," he says to the governess, "that for a fellow to be with a lady *always*—!" and she reflects, "His 'my dear' was constantly on his lips for me, and nothing could have expressed more the exact shade of the sentiment with which I desired to inspire my pupils than its fond familiarity." That "my dear", this is to say, is not here simply a convention of address.

The governess visits Miles' bed at night, at first standing over him with her candle, then moving to sit down on the edge of the bed and taking hold of his hand. "Then you weren't asleep?" she asks, and "What is it ... that you think of?", to which Miles replies, "What in the world, my dear, but *you*?" He thinks also, he says, of "this queer business of ours .... the way you bring me up. And all the rest!" What, asks the governess, does he mean by "all the rest," and he answers, "Oh you know, you know," the while she continues to hold his hand and while their eyes meet, until she throws herself upon him. "Dear little Miles, dear little Miles," she says, and kisses him, and again, "Dear little Miles, dear little Miles, if you *knew* how I want to help you"—and he answers appropriately, by blowing out the candle.

On an evening after dinner Miles plays at the piano for the governess. Again of an evening he comes to sit with her before the fire in the darkened schoolroom and after two hours, so the governess tells Mrs. Grose, we kissed goodnight. At the dining table after Mrs. Grose has left with Flora, alone except for the maid, the two are silent, "as silent," so the governess muses, "as some young couple who, on their wedding-journey, at the inn, feel shy in the presence of the waiter," but Miles is equally attuned. "Well—so we're alone!" he says when the maid finally leaves. "Don't you remember," says the governess, "how I told you, when I came and sat on your bed the night of the storm, that there was nothing in the world I wouldn't do for you?," and "Yes, yes!" Miles says, "Only that, I think, was to get me to do something for *you*!" What finally he does do, at least prior to submitting to the governess' fatal embrace, is to confess that at school he "said things" to those he liked, which things it is evident that the governess very much wants to hear for herself. The governess in this final scene of the tale has in effect been pressing Miles to say something bad.

III

The intention, James was to say, in the Preface, was "to catch those not easily caught…the jaded, the disillusioned, the fastidious," which was to say that this seeming ghost story was to draw belief from readers who were not likely to believe in ghosts. In fact, however, there is very little of the ghosts in the tale. When present—the exactly eight times that they are—they are there very briefly and the most that they do is to stare and mostly less than that. They do not squeak and gibber. The story is about a governess who reports seeing ghosts, and the question of belief resolves into a question of whether or not a governess—pretty much a typical governess—might be so much more radical a case of loneliness, frustration, entrapment, desire, than the cases of, for instance, Rose Armiger, Fleda Vetch or the telegraph girl, that she might see ghosts, and why.

One of James' readers, H.G. Wells, seems to have objected that James had failed to elucidate the governess' own "subjective complications," and in the Preface James would refer to a reproach made by one of his readers, perhaps Wells, that he had not "sufficiently 'characterized'" his young woman, to which he might have replied that the tale is one of characterization entirely.[18] Characterization is what is done to Miles, offered as a more-or-less typical Victorian schoolboy, but, that, as another turn of the screw. James was not solicited by the charms of children. The governess, sequestered as she is in her circumstances and virtually immured as she is in her own mind, is a character so manifestly present as to be a horror. James goes on in the Preface to protest that in the governess "we have surely as much of her own nature as we can swallow in watching it reflect her anxieties and inductions." Which is the case. The snare for that fastidious reader for whom the tale was designed is in the fact that what is offered explicitly as being just a story created from a stock of story conventions, has become indeed, as according to James' own judgment, "an excursion into chaos." Hers, this governess', is so extreme a case of loneliness, frustration, entrapment, and desire, that this typical governess sees ghosts. It could happen. Might very well. Except perhaps for the extremity, almost inevitable that it would. That's where the credibility is.

And it has been a trick, and that's where the amusement is, but there is more, a leftover terror. The governess has been at the business of imposing a form upon her anxieties and inductions.

She has composed her hallucinations into a story, a ghost story, by which her horrors are to be contained, but she has been only almost successful in doing that, and because there have been chinks in her tale allowing the madness to peep out even as it has been beckoned, which is to say that because we can know now that we have been seduced into participation in insanity, the abyss opens anew.

Chapter Four

What Maisie Knew

The heroine of 'Moods' is a fitful, wayward, and withal most amiable young person, named Sylvia. We regret to say that Miss Alcott takes her up in her childhood. We are utterly weary of stories about precocious little girls.

North American Review, July 1865

I had never been in an English workhouse before, and this one transported me, with the aid of memory, to the early pages of *Oliver Twist*.... Here entered to us some hundred and fifty little children of charity, who had been making a copious [holiday] dinner, and who brought with them an atmosphere of hunger memorably satisfied—together with other traces of the occasion upon their pinafores and their small red faces. I have said that the place reminded me of *Oliver Twist*, and I glanced through this little herd for an infant figure that should look as if it were cut out for romantic adventures. But they were all very prosaic little mortals. They were made of very common clay indeed, and a certain number of them were idiotic.

An English New Year, 1879

I

Maisie has been: "a picture of childish innocence, preserved in the midst of glaring evil," but then again a demonstration not of innocence preserved but of "the gradual emergence in the child of a moral sense," also a high-spirited Victorian social comedy, a dark Jacobean comedy, a testimony (with reference to the episode of Beale Farange's almost-black American "Countess") to the racial basis of American literature, an account of divorce as it affects the children, and, more comprehensively, a study in cognitive psychology. For Frances ("Fluffy") Hodgson Burnett, who had a kind of jurisdiction in these matters, *What Maisie Knew* was a children's book, appropriate for children. She presented a copy of the novel to a little girl of her acquaintance, the daughter of some American friends. More recently *Maisie* has been a triumphant acknowledgment of the corruption of innocence with interesting correspondences to mainstream child pornography. At the end we find Maisie offering up her virginity to her step-father; we are meant to enjoy the repeated exposures followed by violations of Maisie's innocence, while she repeatedly and miraculously survives violation, like the heroine of *The Story of O,* says Sally Sears, and all of those other girls who "bounce back restored and unfaltering after an evening of rape, mutilation, and scourging."[1]

No other of James' novels has been read more contrarily than *What Maisie Knew,* not because of any fundamental ambiguity or obscurity, but because no other of James' novels is so unsettling as *Maisie*. It is James' most devious novel and is so in good part, perversely enough, because of its diligence, which is to say the sheer straightforward persistence with which it probes, behind and below. It is said of little Maisie that early on she had come to know that everything had something behind it, and James certainly thought the same, as always but especially in this novel. The suspicion drives the novel. In *What Maisie Knew*, as Marius Bewley has said, "the trap-doors are more yawning... than in any other of James' novels,"[2] and of course it was James who discovered the trapdoors and opened them and gazed.

Particularly, the novel shocks and confounds at the same time that it jokes and invigorates, by its resolute progressive unraveling of its initiating literary and cultural clichés.

Beginning with genre, as James surely knew. With its little heroine, forefronted by the giving of her nice name to the title, the novel promises to be an episode in what was the currently immensely popular mode of children's literature. But then also, alternatively, or, rather, at the same time, the situation which makes the novel go—divorce, adultery—was stock theatrical commodity which without doubt James considered to be just that, although of course this was not at all to say that the stock situation itself was without its underlying, animating urgency—sex, primarily—which might be material for amusement and exploration, both at once. Moreover, all of the five major characters who surround Maisie are, in this rich novel, literary or theatrical clichés, as for that matter is each of the few other minor characters, while for James they await revelation of their confounding potentialities of character and motive.

It did not need James' immediate reviewers to tell him that with this novel he had solicited particular generic assumptions. At the center of the novel is the presumably sweet, peculiarly precocious, assuredly victimized little Maisie, six years old when the novel begins, unwanted by either of her parents in the late years of the nineteenth century in England, in a time and a place of child-worship and in the moment of the golden age of children's literature.

The germ of the novel had been presented to James as a poignant case. At a dinner table, the venue of the large number of James' sources, James Bryce's sister-in-law, Mrs. Ashton, had told James of a child being *divided* (James' italics in his Notebook entry) between divorced parents, each subsequently remarried, with the child being shuffled between the two households, consisting, each of them, of parent-plus-step-parent. There is no knowing how James, at table, had responded to Mrs. Ashton's story, but the first of the Notebook entries, composed two days later, shows plainly that it was not the pathos that moved him. He did not remember whether the child had been a boy or a girl but on the whole thought, immediately as he wrote, that a little girl would be better—besides, in *The Pupil* he had already done the case of a little boy—and that something might be done with the anecdote particularly having to do with the relation of the child to the step-parents. Mostly, for James, the situation was exploitable.

Certainly for Mrs. Ashton as for almost anyone else, it would have been the pathos that would have been the point, and—as James well knew—it would have been the pity of it that would have been the charm of it for such of his contemporaries as: Kenneth Grahame, author of *The Golden Age* and *Dream Days*, or James Barrie, author of *Sentimental Tommy: The Story of His Boyhood* and *The Little Minister*, or Margaret Deland, author of *The Story of a Child*, or Fluffy Burnett, or his frequent editor Thomas Bailey Aldrich, author of *The Story of a Bad Boy*, or, for that matter, in all likelihood, Mark Twain, whose appeal, James had said, was to rudimentary minds.

James' response to real, living children, near relations aside, seems throughout his life to have ranged from stern calculation to awkwardness to indifference, but when it came to the literature of the worship of children he was constant. Early on, something—

that utter weariness which he said had been provoked by little-girl precocity in Louisa May Alcott's novel *Moods*—is no doubt to be attributed to the self-consciousness of a young man (in 1865 scarcely beyond his twentieth birthday) who had been entrusted with book reviewing and consequent presumption of authority in the matter of literature. Louisa May, moreover, was the daughter of a family friend and so perhaps would have been counted upon to understand both the affectation and the joke of it, as seemingly she did.[3] But James had nonetheless so early as this hit upon principle. His reflections on Louisa May were pleasing to him. He immediately repeated the basic sentiment in a review of 1865 of a novel by Miss Adeline Dutton Whitney (*The Gayworthys: A Story of Threads and Thrums*). Regarding an episode of courtship in that novel he observed that the novel's "radical defect is the degradation of sentiment by making children responsible for it," a practice which, James said, was becoming the bane of our novels. "If we desire to learn the various circumstances under which love-making may be conducted," he advised, "let us not repair to the nursery and the school-room." And then once again, in the same year, now reviewing some novels by Mrs. Elizabeth Rundle Charles, he discovered a pernicious contemporary school of fiction, of vast proportion, which provided books "which grown women may read...to children without either party being bored," followed a year later by a review of another novel, by Mrs. Charles, *Winifred Bertram*, in which James noticed, regarding the little girl in the novel, that "She walks through these pages shedding light and bounty, counsel and comfort; preaching, prescribing, and chiding. She makes as pretty a figure as you could wish; but...as a member of this working-day world she is almost ridiculous."[4]

Thus perhaps the supercilious young man, but in "The Future of the Novel" in 1899, almost a quarter of a century later and two years after the serial publication of *What Maisie Knew*, James was saying much the same thing, with similar disdain and now in the accents of acknowledged authority. The contemporary novel, he said, had been degraded by the circumstance that writers and publishers pandered to an audience of boys and girls—including "girls," he added, in the later stages of their lives. Great fortunes were to be made, he said, by writing "the literature, as it may be called for convenience, of children"—at this point quite probably particularly having in mind Francis Hodgson Burnett, his country neighbor—and the novel had accordingly become flaccid, cowardly, and trivial.[5] Now, after the decline of the great day of Richardson and Fielding, he wrote, "there came into being a mistrust of any but the most guarded treatment of the great relation between men and women," and nowadays and according to the current fashion, "whatever the prose picture of life was prepared to take upon itself, it was not prepared to take upon itself not to be superficial." "We need not, after all," James suggested, "be more royalist than the king or more childish than the children."

That great contemporary dominance of the literature of children did immediately overwhelm the reading of James' novel of childhood at the moment of its publication. Reviewers generally were uneasy about the fact that this little girl had been exposed to moral squalor, or "evil," as was sometimes said, but if *Maisie* was not a children's book proper, nonetheless, so the general reading went, the plot happily had been so turned that childhood had been rescued and thereby, as according to governing convention, had been asserted.

And it is one of the meanings as well as one of the ironies attending *What Maisie Knew* that, as *The Turn of the Screw* would be a version of the governess story, so *What Maisie Knew* is a version of the Victorian-child story, but inevitably a parodic version and then, given what we will eventually know that Maisie knows, a subversive version. There will be other more involuted novels to come, but the tone of *What Maisie Knew* is complicated beyond anything else James ever wrote or was to write, and a chief element of the tone of it is just there, in the animus of parody. Little Maisie is of a type. Her literary contemporaries are present in the novel as implied shades. Maisie, however, sheds neither light nor bounty and also is not ridiculous. She is a victim of the great relation between men and women but is also, as is to be discovered, a product of it in more ways than one.

This Victorian child performs, moreover, within a context of other available established, particularly theatrical tropes—and it is to be noted that James' first Notebook entry for *What Maisie Knew* is dated 1892, at a time when he was all-but-fully engaged with the theater. Adultery was popular, as was divorce. These were standard adventures and, more often than not, subjects for comedy.[6] In each of his own "Theatricals" James had himself dealt with "The Marriage Question" in one way and another and in each instance as standard comic material. Now in the novel he constructed a pattern of couplings and uncouplings and re-couplings—the four characters consisting of the parents and the step-parents who criss-cross and redouble—which, if not quite in itself farce, at least alluded to farce. Even his title for the novel, moreover, had its distinct farcical evocation—not quite pornography but of a French-maid kind of naughtiness, as to say that the little girl, with a wink and a grin, knows some secrets, as to say, "Oh, What Maisie Knew!" And then again even her name implies something of the same conjoined as it is with knowingness. A knowing Maisie offers a promise which, for instance, a knowledgeable Fleda Vetch, the heroine of *The Spoils of Poynton*, could not.

Maisie will be subjected to comic allusion multiplied, and to characters who at least initially—before, as will be seen, the novel took hold of James—are stock figures who also, just by so much, are ripe for caricature.

So Sir Claude, Maisie's step-father to be, is the handsome young man who sets hearts aflutter and is always getting into complications, and, whether or not he is married, is a gay bachelor, in the several senses, and is otherwise a shallow young Englishman. He might well be a character in Oscar Wilde.

Maisie's governess and then stepmother-to-be, pretty Miss Overmore, seduces. That is her defining occupation and dominant humour. She is also, as might be noted, a more broadly and comically sketched version of the governess in *The Turn of the Screw.* She is very poor, with seven sisters at home, is said repeatedly to be very pretty, and if not considerably tutored, nonetheless, with all calculation, is adept at graces. When she eats she holds her fork with the little finger curled out. It's classy. It is peculiarly to the point that components of her prettiness are not offered; she is by so much the less individualized. She has fine eyes, which she can roll, but otherwise and generally it is her role, as James had suggested to himself in a passage in the Notebooks, to be "a type". She flirts, she insinuates, she calculates, she supplants Maisie's mother, Ida, by marrying Beale, and becomes, like Ida, "a woman of fashion". And then she sets forth to have Sir Claude, who is younger and who is Ida's second husband.

The succeeding governess, Mrs. Wix, with her "straighteners" and the braid on the top of her head of "a turbid sallow unvenerable white," who should be a device for the plot and not integral to it, is odd and fussy and is a loving and loveable old person who presumably is outside of the sex roundelays, and is straight out of Dickens. Precocious Maisie perceives almost immediately that in the eyes of the world she is a figure mainly to laugh at—which is to say that

James, who made her, laughs.

James was amused most of all, manifestly, by the vile parents, Ida and Beale Farange, especially by Ida. In early entries in the Notebook James had named the parents "Hurter". That the name struck him as being comic, rather than being entirely dire, would be evidenced by his use of it in "The Death of the Lion" in 1894, into which he had inserted the minor comic character "Fanny Hurter". He had abandoned "Hurter" perhaps because in this context he found the name to be overly restrictive, overly simplifying, or with emphasis unfortunately falling on the grimness, when he wanted another pitch. In any event, when he came to the writing he discovered in Ida and Beale opportunity for high satire quite beyond their plot function. The Faranges are awfully good-looking. Together they make up "some twelve feet three of stature". Ida is a champion billiards player, an odd fact which has something but after all very little to do with the making of the plot of the novel—at a point in the novel it is supposed that she is off to a billiards match when really she is engaged in one of her liaisons—but which swiftly characterizes her. She breaks balls. She is flat-chested, appropriately given the kind of mother she is. And James has a fine time with her:

> Notwithstanding some very long lines everything about her that might have been large and that in many women profited by the licence was, with a single exception, admired and cited for its smallness. The exception was her eyes, which might have been of mere regulation size, but which overstepped the modesty of nature; her mouth, on the other hand, was barely perceptible, and odds were freely taken as to the measurement of her waist. She was a person who, when she was out—and she was always out—produced everywhere a sense of having been seen often, the sense indeed of a kind of abuse of visibility.

When as might sometimes happen she presses her small daughter to her bosom, it is to a bosom cut low: "She was always in a fearful hurry, and the lower the bosom was cut the more it was to be gathered she was wanted elsewhere."

As for Beale, he is predominantly beard and teeth without necessity of other occupation, which in any event he has not: "Beale Farange had natural decorations," it is said, "a kind of costume in his vast fair beard, burnished like a gold breastplate, and in the eternal glitter of the teeth that his long moustache had been trained not to hide and that gave him, in every possible situation, the look of the joy of life." The beautiful teeth fetch Miss Overmore, soon to be Mrs. Beale, and along with the beard, Maisie, too, when she is older.

Having no reverence for the sentimentalized child, James submitted his figure of a victimized little girl to a milieu of comic allusions—and that process had now in turn the startling effect that Maisie was to be seen in critical perspective, not entirely stripped of pity but not embalmed in sweetness either. James' affections for Maisie are, if in play at all, not notable but, rather, give way to—a very different matter—the intensity of his interest in the girl.

For that matter, the very tone of James' telling of Maisie's story goes to deprive Maisie of facile pity the while it sustains critical perspective. Sentences coil in on themselves and invert their own meanings. In the Notebooks James had said to himself that his line was to be "the consciousness, the dim, sweet, sacred, wondering, clinging perception of the child," but, as he would observe after the event, in the Preface to the New York Edition, that attempt had been doomed to failure and it had become authorial necessity to attend to and constantly to amplify Maisie's various conclusions—and in the event Maisie's story is told by a narrator who is superior to the action and who typically is witty, quick with a paradox, and is frequently arch—and this is the case not only as applied to Maisie's own and personal story; this narrator is available for observation and interpretation of all of the characters, to see which is to note that the novel as a whole is controlled by the narrator and not by Maisie. It is the narrator who says that Maisie "had achieved a hollowness beyond her years." And again: "Mrs. Wix suffered her wound to bleed and resentment to gush." Ida "directed to him the face that was like an illuminated garden, turnstile and all, for the frequentation of which [her latest friend] had his season ticket." Moreover, the characteristic syntactical density of James' mature style reaches here now and again to the point of burlesque of itself: "while they sat together, there was an extraordinary mute passage between her vision of this vision of his, his vision of her vision, and her vision of his vision of her vision." (That James would have been aware of and have intended the comedy of the notorious passage is the more likely because we know that he was dictating the part of the novel in which it appears to his frustratingly imperturbable first amanuensis, William MacAlpine). "If [Mrs. Wix] was not to be seen that day, however, the evening was marked by an apparition before which, none the less, overstrained suspense folded on the spot its wings."

The medium of the novel is irony. The wit together with the extravagance of metaphor together with the intricacy of the syntax—self-conscious, without a doubt—is so pervasive in the text of *What Maisie Knew* as virtually to disappear except for the crucial fact that it everywhere keeps Maisie at a distance, and the constant effect is ironical because the plot of the novel, were it to be left to itself, would want everywhere to go its own other way, towards feeling and charm and sentiment and pathos. The novel is unsettling in very great part because, once again, it works to disallow the promise which in the first place it has solicited. We are offered poor little unwanted Maisie seemingly for purposes of commiseration but the work of the governing perspective of the novel directs that instead we will follow the author in his surmise of the probabilities of Maisie's response to the givens of her situation, that rather than surrender to sentiment.

Mrs. Wix might have stepped out of Dickens, but this is not a Dickens landscape. Maisie's world is entirely middle-class. Maisie has no safe haven of a home and is moved back and forth, but she is moved back and forth into very nice houses, with servants. Throughout the novel there is a current of reference to the cost of things—in the hard, non-metaphorical terms of money—but poverty is not an issue, or, rather, is not an experience. Nor certainly is this a Dostoevsky world. Archetypal crime for Dostoevsky, as Quentin Anderson pointed out, included assault on a five-year-old girl "who—awful and inescapable fact—had a vagina," while for the kind of James' controlling consciousness there can be no possibility of a social entity in which a Maisie might actually be raped. But, Anderson to the contrary, in *What Maisie Knew* as elsewhere, James did look well into the abyss.[7]

II

As happened typically but especially with the novels of the late 1890s, material got away from James. *What Maisie Knew* had been planned as a ten thousand word story—"a *real* 10,000" James had said to himself, plaintively, in one of the Notebook entries. The various Notebook entries, almost as extensive as those for *The Spoils of Poynton* and more detailed, give us a James who is striving for control and is constantly losing. As he began the writing of the novel he was projecting a first chapter of exactly 12 ½ pages, about the parents, to be followed by a second chapter of 10 pages, and so on.[8] But the project would not remain so humble, as he himself was to say, retrospectively, in the Preface. "Once 'out,'" so he would say of the theme of this novel as of others, "like a housedog of a temper above confinement, it defies the mere whistle, it roams, it hunts, it seeks out and 'sees' life; it can be brought back but by hand and then only to take its futile thrashing."

Ruth Yeazell has noticed James' fascination, to be remarked especially in the late prose, with concealed meanings lurking in well-worn phrases, and to the same effect "with dramatic plots which suddenly emerge from cliché metaphors."[9] It is to be added that just as James probed and prodded commonplaces of language for hidden and vitalizing meanings, so did he with clichés of fiction generally, with the result—fascination typically getting the best of him—that even his parodies of the clichés were themselves likely to yield more and more meaning.

It is thus that within the comedy and the satire of *What Maisie Knew* is contained this novel's peculiar and unsettling intensity. James bore down. Of Maisie it is said that she had developed "a sharpened sense for latent meanings," and so with the novel, with consequence that the amusing ironies—of language, of character, of situation—while amusing also glitter with darkness. And the little girl grows up.

The wit is always there but metaphors also turn violent both within the text and, even more informatively, in James' recorded thinking about the novel. James speaks in the Preface not about the end of Maisie's childhood but about "the death of her childhood," and of her childish intelligence as a repository "of objects embalmed in her wonder". In the text itself, Maisie's recollection of her nurse Moddle becomes "an image faintly embalmed in the remembrance of hungry disappearances." "Poor little monkey!", uttered at the beginning of the novel by an unidentified good lady, becomes "an epitaph for the tomb of Maisie's childhood." Maisie is to become a vessel for the bitterness of her parents, "a deep little porcelain cup in which biting acids could be mixed." A lesson awaits Maisie when Sir Claude fails to return to Boulogne as expected: "She was yet to learn what it could be to recognize in some lapse of a sequence the proof of an extinction, and therefore remained unaware that this momentary pang was a foretaste of the experience of death." For Mrs. Wix, as Maisie observes, separation strikes a nerve: "Embedded in Mrs. Wix's nature as her tooth had been socketed in her gum, the operation of extracting her would really have been a case for chloroform." (James goes to some trouble in order to make this metaphor. Quite superfluously so far as plot is concerned, at the beginning of Chapter Five he sends Maisie to the dentist accompanied by Mrs. Wix. The obvious aim was to make the pain indisputable and visceral. Given his own history of dental problems, he knew where to find pain.) Or the metaphors turn grotesque. Beale's teeth become fangs. Contending for Maisie against Sir Claude, Mrs. Wix concludes "with an unparalleled neigh of battle," following upon an earlier instance when Mrs. Wix's laughter had sounded to Maisie like "an unsuccessful imitation of a neigh." When Mrs. Wix agrees to remain behind in Boulogne with Maisie while Sir Claude returns to England, Maisie senses "a faint fragrance of depraved concession." One smells a rotting corpse.[10]

Once again, it is a portion of the peculiarly harsh irony of the novel that Maisie's victimizers are in the first instance not quite real but are stock figures, so considered by their author, and ripe for caricature. The nice little girl thus is to be found to be trapped by characters who are clearly fictional. But nonetheless, and with these other characters as well as with Maisie herself, James presses and presses forward and is unable to resist the pursuit; the other characters do change and do take on depth, some less, some more, but entirely with the double consequence, first that, in this novel about Maisie, the other characters do begin to take on lives of their own so that the novel expands beyond what can be Maisie's experience, and secondly that Maisie will be not only abused but will also be challenged.

Thus the awful Ida, having been so elaborately and so spiritedly abused by her author, is finally a frantic, bereft, lonely, aging person, who is awfully ill—or says that she is, but there is no reason not to believe her, and if she is not, that would be to make her the more frantic. Having moved from man to man, she is out of men. She is at the end of the line, about to take a boat to a place the name of which she cannot recall except that it is in South Africa. In the final interview, explaining herself to Maisie, Ida is profuse and prolonged but "not exhaustively lucid." She rambles. She is inconsequent. She is clearly distraught while, in a remarkable insight which James presents to Maisie, it is said that she gathers support from what Maisie now suddenly knows has been the chief and necessary means of her support all the while, namely her very selfishness and "habit of brutality". James knows at this ending, and will have Maisie know, that for this character, whom he has ridiculed, imperiousness and selfishness have been strategies of self-preservation. That does not make her to be amiable but it makes her, here at the end, suddenly, much less a caricature; it testifies to vulnerabilities; we can now know, retrospectively, that Ida's failings have after all been human, not only moral, and by so much it is not allowed to Maisie to respond merely to Ida's abandonment of her. Learning that with one of her suitors, the character named the Captain, her mother has forfeited still another and seemingly a fine loyalty, "there was literally an instant in which Maisie saw—saw madness and desolation, saw ruin and darkness and death."

And with Beale, something of the same, with the difference that it has been swagger rather than calculated brutality that has been his stratagem for self-preservation. In his youth he had been destined for diplomacy, James says, and attached, without salary, to a legation, which enabled him often to say, "In *my* time in the East," but contemporary history had passed him by. Now at the end that swagger which has been his way with the world and which has been matter for comedy, has become plaintive bravado of masculine prerogative. In the Countess' drawing room, he opens a box of chocolates for Maisie, with six rows of bonbons, and says, "I can do what I like with these for I don't mind telling you that I gave 'em to [the Countess] myself," and that squeaking contention constitutes what in itself would be utter revelation—both the grasping for pride and the effort, after everything, to impress his daughter—except that there is one further revelation to be had, when James and we and Maisie come to know that the Countess gives him money.

And something of the same, once again, with Miss Overmore-become-Mrs. Beale. She enacts the governess story by marrying the master; she enacts her role as seductress. Like everyone else in the novel, she has made Maisie into a utility for her convenience, but the motives of this very poor girl with her seven sisters at home have from the beginning been so comprehensible as to solicit sympathy, and, besides, she has fallen in with a bad crowd. At the end, moreover, she is a desperate woman who will be found to muddle that "marked type" which James had planned for her to be. At the end she finds that her prey, Sir Claude, is elusive, and comes then to know that she will have to wrest him from the sexual attractions of a child. The pretty woman who has made the most of her charms is entangled in unexpected, startling reaches of sexual fact, while for Maisie she has become the other woman.

But clearly it was the two afterthoughts of characters, Sir Claude and Mrs. Wix, who proved most to solicit further and more extensive possibilities.

To follow the Notebook entries is to see both James' uncertainty about Sir Claude and also his lesser interest in him. At first the as yet unnamed character was to be Ida's new husband, merely, whom Maisie will like better than Beale. Later he was to be the Captain, "simple, good, mild chap, bullied, hustled by his wife," with the interesting idea attached that he wants to have a child of his own with Ida, and when that child dies he is to foregather with Maisie "who is as 'lonely' as himself—*délaissée* in a way that touches him"—which at this point would have made him to be reinforcement of a governing idea of loneliness, loss, and abandonment. The entry is of late 1895, when James was making detailed plans for the novel. At this point all of the women were to have suffered the loss of children: Ida (who was to have had a miscarriage), Mrs. Wix, and Miss Overmore as well who, after two years of marriage, has "been confined and lost her little girl." But the idea of loss itself got lost. A few months later, when James was well into the composition, he was perceiving that while Sir Claude adores Maisie, as does Mrs. Wix, and while he is "very nice, very charming to Maisie... he must get a little tired of her." The simple, good, mild chap now has a "pretty, pleasant, weak, bullied" nature, and is disgusted with Ida.

As he comes into the novel itself, Sir Claude, if weak, is by no means so essentially passive and harmless as the planning would have had him to be. He becomes, in brief, a womanizer, with an eye for random pretty women, who is afraid of women, and that is why he seduces—for clearly it amounts to that—the little female child whom, in another contrary of passion, he continuously addresses as though she were a boy, and whom he rejects when it becomes clear that, indeed, as the critic Quentin Anderson would have had it, awful and inescapable fact, she has a vagina. Maisie is "old boy" and "old chap" and "old fellow" and "old man" and "dear man" and "Maisie boy" and "dear old man". The character who was to have wanted to have a child of his own is discernible in Sir Claude as he comes to be, but mixed with or undermined by his other confused and complicating kinds of desire, lending another meaning to his wanting to have a child of his own. Flirting with the new Mrs. Beale he says, "The truth about me is simply that I'm the most unappreciated of—what do you call the fellows?—'family men.' Yes, I'm a family-man; upon my honour I am!", but then a moment later, by way of implicitly defining for himself what the strange hyphenation really means, he says, "I'm an old grandmother.... I like babies—I always did." He likes to romp, as Maisie, the plausible baby, perceives.

The character who was to foregather with Maisie because of a commonality of loneliness will now foregather with her because he is afraid of her mother, and then, soon hereafter, because he is also afraid of her new stepmother, while Maisie herself presents not exactly no sexual challenge but of a kind so sufficiently ambiguous as to be deniable. The dark matter becomes entirely explicit just before the midpoint of the novel when Sir Claude tells Maisie that he had married her mother in the first place just because he was afraid of her, that now he is afraid of Mrs. Beale, and when Maisie asks him if she herself does not make him afraid, says "I *should* be in fear if you were older." But this conversation in itself first of all conveys a sense of calculated, suggestive indiscretion, and secondly directly suggests, to Maisie, as it is meant to, if not with entire forethought, not really that she is too young for amorous possibilities, but that her turn is to come, and then not only that, but that it has arrived. It is to say, "How old *are* you, anyway? Maybe old enough." Not much later Sir Claude will be kissing her gently and speaking to her of her "fatal gift of beauty." Mrs. Beale is present at this latter juncture and knows exactly what is happening because she interrupts by saying to Maisie, "He isn't speaking of personal loveliness—you've not *that* vulgar beauty, my dear, at all!"

Sir Claude issues erotic charge wherever he goes and, particularly, there is sexual implication in almost all of his passages with Maisie. He inspires, as it is said, a sentiment. Maisie is smitten from the first by the photograph of the man who will be her stepfather, with his fair smooth face and regular features and amiable air and the "general glossiness and smartness" of his appearance, which goes to promise that when he enters the novel he will be something other than and more than a family man. In their first encounters Sir Claude enrolls Maisie in an amorous conspiracy, to keep the secret of his romping with Mrs. Beale. Sir Claude begins regularly to visit Maisie in her domestic schoolroom, where it is said, in one of the oddest passages in the novel, "he had plainly begun to recognize that if he was to have the credit of perverting the innocent child he might also at least have the amusement"—the perversion referring seemingly to his having made Maisie a witness to his alliance with Mrs. Beale, but which if it is something much less than raw sexual violation, is perversion nonetheless.

James in the Preface expressed particular pleasure with two key and parallel scenes in the novel, the one where Beale takes Maisie to visit his Countess, and the other the encounter with Ida and the Captain when Maisie is walking in the Park with Sir Claude. It is James' point in the Preface that it is Maisie's "bewilderment" that makes the otherwise "small sterilities" of the various adulteries to be "*appreciable*". But within the novel there is still other implication in the scene in Kensington Gardens where Sir Claude and Maisie stroll hand in hand. They have entered the green world very much like lovers, with very particular reference. "It's the

Forest of Arden," says Sir Claude. Typically, he has rather offhand and vague knowledge of the text. "I'm the banished duke," he says, "and you're—what was the young woman called?—the artless country wench. And there... is the other girl—what's her name, Rosalind?—and (don't you know?) the fellow who was making up to her." But if his recollection of *As You Like It* is deficient in particulars, Sir Claude nonetheless is engaged in enlisting Maisie in love-game comedy. That artless country wench, Audrey presumably, one among the several "country copulatives", is to be Touchstone's bride.

When Sir Claude takes Maisie to Folkestone at the beginning of the lengthy final movement of the novel, it is given to Maisie, by James, to have "embraced the implication of a kind of natural divergence between lovers and little girls" by way of explaining Sir Claude's authority in taking her off to a seaside hotel, but that divergence is very soon, within a few pages, to be considerably narrowed. In the coffee-room at luncheon in the hotel, the two discuss Sir Claude's irregular connection with Mrs. Beale and the claims she is making; the sense plainly and entirely of Sir Claude's action is that he is running away with Maisie. The scene is interrupted by Ida's abrupt appearance, but that episode having concluded, Sir Claude gives Maisie his arm and escorts her to dinner where everything, "the bedizened banquet, the savour of dishes, the drama of figures," speaks to her of the joy of life, and after dinner the two smoke together on a porch—if not quite literally, nonetheless that is "exactly what," it is said, that Maisie felt that they were doing. After which, Sir Claude, stooping a little, draws Maisie to him, holds her a little, and kisses her good night. And the next day they will be in France.

The "simple, good, mild chap, bullied, hustled by his wife," having been submitted to James' imaginative probing and prodding, seduces a child. However, that proves not yet to be the end of the possibilities for the character. Mrs. Wix will say of Sir Claude that he is "just a poor sunk slave," a slave to his passions—and so indeed he is, but therein also is plausibly an ennobling principle of character. Far from having corrupted Maisie, from having killed her "moral sense" just when it was beginning to bud, as Mrs. Wix accuses him of doing, Sir Claude can now say, with convincing eloquence, that he has not killed anything, that "on the contrary I think I've produced life. I don't know what to call it—I haven't even known how decently to deal with it, to approach it; but, whatever it is, it's the most beautiful thing I've ever met—it's exquisite, it's sacred."

As for Mrs. Wix, to follow the Notebooks is to see that she began as a mere necessity, supererogatory to the main event. Having started the writing—the Notebook entry is for December 22nd, 1895—and having put Miss Overmore in Beale's house, James needed another governess for Maisie when she was at Ida's house. At this point Mrs. Wix is, repeatedly, "the plain governess," "the honest frump," "the frump," "a widow," "the tattling frump," "old frumpy," "Mrs. Something" who has lost her only little girl, although James does foresee that she might also serve by carrying Maisie off at the end, to save her and to bring her up. A few months later, when he was well into the writing, James was delighted to conceive a nice complication for that ending, that Mrs. Wix might offer herself to Sir Claude as a replacement for Mrs. Beale. "ADMIRABLE, this," he exclaims to himself. "They will be together—they will make a *trio*. The small touching oddity (with her secret passion for him) of her offering *herself* as a rescue from the temptation: the impropriety of Mrs. Beale."

The governess' offer of herself when it comes will in fact carry a charge considerably beyond being oddly touching, and when she gets into the novel the honest frump is in fact grotesque and is so from the very first. Much as he had done with his portrait of Rosy Muniment in *The Princess Cassimassima*, discovering the malice lurking within a Jenny Wren, so with Mrs. Wix, straight as she is out of Dickens, James pressed so as to expose the stunningly plausible nether side of lovable quaintness.

The critic Juliet Mitchell was certainly right in saying, flatly, that "Mrs. Wix is quite simply one of James' nastiest characterizations," although that is in a measure to overstate the kind of James' investment in the character.[11] Mrs. Wix is ignorant, morbid, vengeful, righteous, narrow-minded, quite corruptible, and secretly lustful, and it is an ultimate joke of the novel that she represents moral convention.

As is true of the novel in its entirety, in the characterization of Mrs. Wix sentimental expectation is abruptly submitted to dispassion. She is a poor widow who has lost an only daughter, which latter fact especially affects six-year-old Maisie, as well it might, but the very telling of the matter suggests opportunism, a rehearsed self-identity. It is said, and so Maisie is informed, that Mrs. Wix "had had a little girl quite of her own, and the little girl had been killed on the spot." The brief sentence which begins in pathos ends in the abrupt language of a police report, and the insinuating ironies continue: Mrs. Wix "had had absolutely nothing else in all the world, and her affliction had broken her heart. It was comfortably established between them that Mrs. Wix's heart was broken." It is established between them, moreover, by Mrs. Wix's imposition, that "the little dead Clara Matilda, who, on a crossing in the Harrow Road, had been knocked down and crushed by the cruellest of hansoms," is Maisie's "little dead sister," about whom Maisie is to know everything "that could be known, everything she had said or done in her little mutilated life." That hansom was of course cruel only in that a kind of infantile bathos makes it so. The "mutilated" in Clara Matilda's "little mutilated life" is James' own cruel, quick, undermining shorthand. Even the name, Clara Matilda, bespeaks the emotive triteness which is the mark of Mrs. Wix's imagination. As Maisie's bespoke tutor, Mrs. Wix avoids "subjects," but knows swarms of stories taken from the novels she has read, "all about love and beauty and countesses and wickedness." Her conversation is "an endless narrative, a great garden of romance, with sudden vistas into her own life and gushing fountains of homeliness." She lingers especially, in her telling, on accounts of persons who have wronged her. Maisie knows, once again, that in the eyes of the world Mrs. Wix is a figure mainly to laugh at, and for James, too, she is at once pathetic and an occasion for amusement, but she is also something much more malign. For Maisie, Mrs. Wix bespeaks safety, but she is, explicitly, just "as safe as Clara Matilda, who was in heaven and yet embarrassingly, also, in Kensal Green," which is quickly to portend that, whereas Sir Claude will plausibly claim that he has created life, in the figure of Mrs. Wix safety is death. It is also said that when she is first put into her hands, Maisie senses immediately that Mrs. Wix, like mortality itself, will never let her go.

All of this above is in the beginning, in Chapter Four, when Mrs. Wix first enters the novel. What then follows is determined extrapolation.

Poor widow that she is, and because she is a poor widow, the honest and principled frump is susceptible to bribery. She will be willing to be used by Ida. She will accept Sir Claude's generosity when he goes off to see Mrs. Beale, for all of her great disapproval of Sir Claude's susceptibility to Mrs. Beale. In Boulogne, while Sir Claude is back in London, she will have a carriage and hotel service, so it is promised, and it is then that, to Maisie's sense, Mrs. Wix emits her "faint fragrance of depraved concession." It has been given to Maisie to realize "the way her humble companion had sidled and ducked through life." Material comforts have been few. She has arrears of dinner to make up and moral passion is both the loser and is the likely loser. Her fantastic idea, moreover, early and late, that she and Maisie might go off to live together with Sir Claude, has all along had its ballast of practical calculation. Poor widow that she is, and lacking in job skills, she needs a place to stay.

Honest and principled frump that she also is, and old and ugly as she is, she is also a woman, a fact which is coerced into active play by this novel about sex. Except that she is old and ugly, she is indeed not different from Miss-Overmore-become-Mrs. Beale. Her position, her motives, and, finally, her desires, are the same, and as for her being older than Sir Claude, so of course is Ida older than Sir Claude, and so of course is Sir Claude older than Maisie, and so in fact the novel discovers that there is no reason other than literary expectation that she should in fact be exempt from the sexual dance. (The matter of age is thematized. Maisie is led to reflect that persons in her life "were not of the age they ought to be.") Having begun as a convenience, Mrs. Wix comes quickly to be perfectly at home in the novel, an actor in the main action—and then she is also something still more because, old and ugly as she is, by act of her amorous imaginings and efforts, she provides, by incongruity, abrupt comic perspective on the main action, like a Shakespearian fool. She sheds light, like indeed Maisie herself. If in her the amorous impulse is grotesque, then, plausibly, so is the thing itself—or to say, as James does, that her action comprises a "small touching oddity," is to see the thing in Olympian perspective, with humor beyond cruelty.

Her passion, if grotesque, is not at all a secret passion but is candid, overt, vehement, importunate, and quick. She wrestles Mrs. Beale for Sir Claude's photograph. In the nursery, talk about

Sir Claude substitutes for instruction, and to Maisie's impromptu question, "And you, my dear, are you in love with him too?" as are all the ladies, Mrs. Wix plumps out, "Over head and ears. I've *never*, since you ask me, been so far gone." Her initial proposition to Sir Claude for the constitution of a *trio* occurs approximately a third of the way into the novel, in Chapter Twelve; when Mrs. Wix has quarreled with Ida and fears that she will be cut off, she proposes to Sir Claude that he share (and pay for) their asylum whenever and wherever she and Maisie should seek refuge, an arrangement which, she says, will have the added benefit that Sir Claude will thereby be saved from some other woman, a real bad one. In Boulogne, the latter reason becomes primary and Mrs. Wix becomes flirtatious. Why, asks Sir Claude, is she so happy that he is free of Ida, and Mrs. Wix answers with an upward grimace and "a great giggling insinuating naughty slap." "'You wretch,'" she says, "'you *know* why!'" And she turns desperate, becoming the pleading lover: "'Take me, take me,'" she implores. "'Here I am, here I am.'"

It is no small irony in the novel, moreover, that if an innocent Maisie is to be contaminated, it is, explicitly, quaint Mrs. Wix who is the primary agent. By way of enabling herself to gush, to speak her own passions and fantasies, to make Maisie the confidante of her desires, and by way of convenient rationale, she assumes that the poor child is already and early so sufficiently corrupt, so knowing about passion (and jealousy and adultery), that after all nothing need be held back. Still in the early time in the nursery Mrs. Wix's talk of Sir Claude takes her far, as she herself admits, to the point where her conscience almost is engaged, but then is not. "There were hours," it is observed, "when Mrs. Wix sighingly testified to the scruples she surmounted, seemed to ask what other line one *could* take with a young person whose experience had been, as it were, so peculiar." "'It isn't as if you didn't already know everything, is it, love?,'" she says to Maisie who at this point is probably not more than nine years old,[12] and "'I can't make you any worse than you *are,* can I darling?'—these were the terms in which the good lady justified to herself and her pupil her pleasant conversational ease."

That "moral sense" which eventually she will decree, in Boulogne in the climactic scenes of the novel, will serve her nicely, by way of seducing and intimidating Sir Claude, as also by way of providing a weapon against her rival, Mrs. Beale, and it will as well have eventual use for her as blackmail to secure Maisie's compliance to her version of a trio. Mrs. Wix invokes the peculiar, and for Maisie baffling, idea, only and for the first time when, in Boulogne, she has assented to the carriage and the hotel service, when Sir Claude is free of Ida, when there will be only Mrs. Beale to contend with, and when the matter of Maisie's choice seems crucial. If Sir Claude and Mrs. Beale are to use Maisie by way of disguising the illicitness of their union, so equally might Maisie enable Mrs. Wix as Mrs. Wix substitutes for Mrs. Beale. Maisie has protested that really it is Mrs. Beale she wants to be with. "'I never, *never* hoped I wasn't going again to see Mrs. Beale!'" she says. "'I didn't, I didn't!'" and, again, "'She's beautiful and I love her! I love her and she's beautiful!'"—and it is following upon that profession that Mrs. Wix, who is not beautiful, puts forth moral compulsion. "'Haven't you really and truly *any* moral sense?'" she demands of Maisie. Maisie herself begins by scarcely knowing what the moral sense might be but proceeds then to a sort of striking up of an acquaintance with it, when Mrs. Wix elucidates wickedness for her.

Meanwhile, in a further and lovely ironical twist, Mrs. Wix will charge Maisie with corruption of her own besieged innocence. "'You want me to be as bad as yourself!'" she accuses when Maisie says that she loves Mrs. Beale. "'Have I lost all delicacy,'" she will demand, "'all decency, all measure of how far and how bad?'" "'I've done it for *you*, precious ... don't let me have been thrust for nothing into such horrors and such shames. I never knew anything about them and I never wanted to know! ... There are lines I've crossed with *you* where I should have fancied I had come to a pretty pass—!'"

III

As for Maisie herself, Mrs. Wix is not far from wrong in her assumption, however self-serving, that Maisie has already and early on come to know "everything". From the very beginning, and to the end, Maisie learns in fact very little that she does not already know, and nothing essential. Her supposed prior pure innocence is just that, a supposition, a construct, which occurs mostly prior to and outside of the novel, which the novel exploits by way of impertinent denial. She is a wise child who is subjected to a situation which will tease forth inner knowledge and bring it to the point of discernability and understanding. The important question is not, what did Maisie learn, but what did she know.[13]

The novel is in fact emphatic in asserting that in the usual sense Maisie does not learn anything. The matter of her "studies" is brought up again and again. Great plans are made and are inevitably frustrated. The idea is broached that Maisie be sent off to school, perhaps to one of the splendid schools at Brighton, but nothing comes of it. Miss Overmore says of Mrs. Wix that she cannot possibly teach Maisie anything because she is as ignorant as a fish, which is the case, but it is equally the case that, as Mrs. Wix says, with Mrs. Beale Maisie learns nothing whatever. To Maisie's winsome pleading Mrs. Beale responds, "You shall have such lessons as you've never had in all your life. You shall go to courses.... At institutions—on subjects.... All the most important ones. French literature—and sacred history. You'll take part in classes—with awfully smart children." But the issue of this promise is attendance with Mrs. Beale at some public lectures where "the fountain of knowledge, in the form usually of a high voice that she took at first to be angry, plashed in the stillness of rows of faces thrust out like empty jugs," and where in any event Mrs. Beale's hoped-for object is improvement of another sort, to meet Sir Claude. The matter is sounded even at the end, as Maisie and Sir Claude try to work out the details of an agreement to go off together. If Mrs. Wix is to be abandoned, then, asks Maisie, "who'll teach me?" and she must concur that Mrs. Wix really does not teach her very much. Sir Claude vaguely proposes home schooling with himself and Mrs. Beale as teachers, but that is not to be, either.

Maisie is almost entirely deprived of learning in the sense such as might be supposed to be the main occupation of a little girl with governesses. James insists on the fact, and thereby he eliminates a primary variable. By so much is Maisie disengaged from a greater world. She is isolated. There are also no playmates. Excepting, moreover, only the nursemaid Moddle and the general maid Susan Ash, Maisie's sole companions are those who comprise the variously sexualized quintet: her parents, her step-parents, and Mrs. Wix, none of whom properly proposes a sense of a family. One of the things Maisie does learn about is money, but what in particular she learns is that in her case money is short, that for lack of money she will not go to the school in Brighton, that it is the nature of plans in general to be too expensive, that Paris is beastly expensive, and so on, and more important, that money is a basic means of exchange which in her case she does not have. When money is tendered to her—by the Countess, by Ida—it is made quickly to disappear. Money, too, this is to say, figures as a subtraction for Maisie.

Aside from the content of the public lectures, such education as she might have is entirely of a kind that is forbidden, which is to say that it is another negative. What indeed Maisie may be said to *learn* is that information is something which is withheld, not to be had at all except by practices of slyness. She learns whatever she learns by hanging over the bannister, by picking up on innuendo, by silent observation, having previously learned to keep her mouth shut. She is not a participant in the world she inhabits, at least until the end, with the result, as James perceives, that there is disjunction between what Maisie learns and what essentially she knows, and this too is a point upon which James insists. She is covert. She practices cunning and concealment. She early on embraces apparent stupidity when, at age six, she experiences the feeling of danger and then greets a remedy, namely "the idea of an inner self or, in other words, of concealment." It is the practice of that idea that enables her to achieve, in James' striking phrase, "a hollowness beyond her years" together with an appearance of "harmless vacancy". She displays an odd air "of being present at her history in as separate a manner as if she could only get at experience by flattening her nose against a pane of glass."

This split in Maisie's consciousness precipitates the truly terrifying brief scene in which the little girl Maisie plays with her doll Lisette, as a little girl might do, taking the part of mother to child as little girls do. Lisette asks questions and Maisie is "convulsed" by Lisette's innocence. There were things she really couldn't tell even a French doll. Lisette would like to know where Maisie has been. Lisette on one occasion asks a particularly indiscreet question and Maisie, imitating her mother, says to her, "'Find out for yourself!'"

Forced back upon herself, what Maisie most surely knows is her uninstructed inner self, but that—her instincts, her innermost desires—is sufficient knowledge; by reference to what she already knows she can know what at least basically her various companions are up to and, finally, can take her place among them. This too is a point upon which James insists. Maisie really does not have to ask questions. She is from the beginning equipped with "a subtlety beyond her years". When her mother's beau Mr. Perriam begins to frequent the upstairs chambers, it is "extraordinary the number of things that, still without a question, Maisie knew." When Maisie begins to make out the nature of the relationship between Sir Claude and Mrs. Beale, she knows that nothing further is to be had by questions. "It was in the nature of things," James says, "to be none of a small child's business, even when a small child had from the first been *deluded into a fear that she might be only too much initiated*." [My italics.] For there is nothing to have been feared. Maisie's knowledge is of the nature of things, and, James adds, ""Things, then, were in Maisie's experience so true to their nature that questions were almost always improper."

Late in the novel, in Boulogne, within dialogue concerning Maisie's knowledge of Ida's affairs, James interrupts to say directly to the reader, "What [Maisie] knew, what she *could* know is by this time no secret to us," which he can say because the novel from the beginning and almost page by page has been a demonstration of what Maisie knows, knew, and has known. Chapter One has her in her father's house where male visitors pull her hither and thither and kiss her and pinch her and blow smoke in her face. Some of these men also make her strike matches and then light their cigarettes; others put her on their laps and pinch her calves "til she shrieked," it is said, and "her shriek was much admired," which—that shriek is crucially revealing—is to suggest exactly that she might be the maid in a French farce. No doubt that those pinches hurt, but no doubt either that the six-year-old acts a part in these sex games, voluntarily or not.

When Sir Claude's photograph is introduced, not only is the six-year-old Maisie immediately smitten but, in this early episode, she is aware of her advantage in competition with another woman, in this case Mrs. Wix. When soon thereafter the real Sir Claude manifests himself, she gapes at his shining presence, thinking to herself, "It was as if he had told her on the spot that he belonged to her" while at the same time she intuits a relationship between Sir Claude and Mrs. Beale. Playfully petulant Mrs. Beale says to Sir Claude that he belongs to a horrible sex. "'Isn't it a horrible sex, little love?'" she demands of Maisie, with her cheek upon her step-daughter's, and the six-year-old replies, "'Oh I like gentlemen best.'" In the nursery with Mrs. Wix all the talk is of Sir Claude. Are you in love with him, too? asks Mrs. Wix, and Maisie says of course, "'Why, *rather!*'" as if, so she thinks, the matter had not already been self-evident.

Sir Claude is the evident and ultimate singular target of Maisie's desire. She has some reason to love him given her circumstances and also his peculiarities. Other experiments in desire have, however, been made available to her. She has had her earlier experience with the gentlemen at her father's house. To come back to it again, James in the Preface calls special attention to two scenes in the novel, the one in Kensington Park when Sir Claude and Ida confront each other and Maisie is sent off for twenty minutes with the Captain, the other when Maisie is whisked away by Beale to the Countess' house. In the Preface, James' point is the transformative effect of Maisie's mere presence; it is Maisie's presence that makes these otherwise thin or merely deplorable scenes to be "appreciable". In fact, however, this presence of hers is not really merely passive, nor, despite James' later assertion in the Preface, is it her "freshness" either alone or primarily that casts portentousness.[14]

The Kensington Park scene begins with Chapter Fifteen, with Sir Claude's fumbling attempts to place himself and Maisie within the precincts of bucolic love-game comedy. Sir Claude is Maisie's play lover. They meet Ida in company with her most recent conquest, the Captain. Now an exchange of partners takes place; Sir Claude and Ida confront each other and Maisie is sent off for a twenty-minute interlude with the Captain, which will be the material of Chapter Sixteen. Maisie immediately likes the Captain very much, with his eyes like little pale flowers and his altogether "funny" face and his deep voice and smell of cigars and the big military hand he offers her, and his general air of By-Jove Englishness. Your mother, says the Captain, "has told me ever so much about you. I'm awfully glad to know you," and Maisie thinks to herself that she had never been so addressed as a young lady, not even by Sir Claude. "It struck her," says James," as the way that at balls, by delightful partners, young ladies must be spoken to in the intervals of dances." Even as she presses the Captain to declare, to her, his love for her mother, at the same time she notices her own lesser concern for Sir Claude. She assures the Captain that she can keep a secret. "Oh there are lots of things I've never told," she says. When the Captain suggests that she, Maisie, might come to live with himself and Ida and minus Sir Claude, Maisie wants to be assured that indeed the Captain will be there. And when at the termination of the interview Sir Claude demands information from her, she falls back upon that practiced show of imbecility by means of which she has been used to keeping information to herself—which at this point goes to mark a significant advance in the young girl's maturity.

There is much in this scene, this is to say, beyond additional proof of Ida's awfulness. The Captain's testimony in fact creates a possibility of pity for Ida, and even, for Maisie, the incredible possibility that her mother might be loved. But for the scene as a whole, what happens is that the fact of adultery, here made flagrant, is at length provided with its prelude, namely flirtation and courtship, in which all of the characters are involved and most notably Maisie herself. That is the action of the scene. Maisie is excited, she trembles, she weeps, she is thrilled. And there is even a kind of anticipation of the fact of adultery in her—quick, facile, secretive—transfer of affection from Sir Claude to the Captain.

Chapters Fifteen and Sixteen take place in the plausibly pastoral world of Kensington Gardens. The parallel episode, comprising Chapters Eighteen and Nineteen, takes place first among the sideshows of the "thingumbob" at Earl's Court, a street fair of some sort, where, by way of a perfect parody of Arden, Mrs. Beale and Maisie pause before the booth of "the Flowers of the Forest," "a large presentment of bright brown ladies—they were brown all over—in a medium suggestive of tropical luxuriance." Beale then emerges from the booth with his brown lady with the scarlet plume, pushes Maisie into a hansom, and drives her to the brown Countess' tropically-luxuriant love bower.

The intermediate scene, the ride in the hansom, is a matter of less than half of a paragraph which, while so brief, nonetheless brings almost to the point of full candor a fundamental possibility—a fundamental truth, as James' contemporary, Freud, had it—of father-daughter relationship. And also daughter-father. As Maisie is said later to have recollected the event—present tense would have encumbered agitation to the point of incoherence—Beale had put an arm about her and drawn her close so that she had been either charmed or scared into silence, she scarcely had known which. She had known that Beale was trembling "and this had the effect of making her, with an emotion which, though it had begun to throb in an instant, was by no means all dread, conform to his portentous hush." And so they drove and drove, as she recalls, and he had kept her close and she had held her breath, the while she had found herself to "vibrate with the sense that [Beale] had jumped up to do something and that she had as quickly become a part of it."

The Countess' drawing room is dazzling, with its curtains and cushions and mirrors and palm trees drooping over brocaded and gilded nooks, and Maisie's first thought is that in the matter of taste the Countess far outshines the two other women in her life, Ida and the new Mrs. Beale, leaving out Mrs. Wix. These two women practice allurement, it is their principle activity, and the ugly Countess relegates them to relative obscurity. Then it is Maisie's second observation that Beale is grandly at home in this dazzling scene. All idea of danger slips away from her. Beale, with his back to the fireplace, his light overcoat—"the very lightest in London"—wide open, smiles "at his young lady," "his wonderful lustrous beard completely concealing the expanse of shirt-front." He is a handsome man, so Maisie thinks. After a little, and after showing Maisie some of the Countess' fine and fetching little things—no doubt, Beale says, that the Countess will give Maisie something jolly—he offers the little girl some candy, from the pink satin box with six rows of chocolate bonbons, something better, so Maisie reflects, than any Sir Claude had ever come up with. Seated on a yellow silk sofa under one of the palms, Beale takes Maisie on his knee, "stroking her hair, playfully holding her off while he showed his shining fangs and let her, with a vague affectionate helpless pointless 'Dear old girl, dear little daughter,' inhale the fragrance of his cherished beard," and it is of significance as to what Maisie knows that she senses that in the interim of her separation from her father she had grown for him, that Beale now knows that she is a person in her own right, to be reckoned with.

With Maisie still on his knee, and following numerous sighs, Beale lights a cigarette and begins to smoke in her face, and there follows a moment of profound muteness. Beale is confused. Maisie's whole desire, it is said, is "to give something," to offer "an immense surrender"... of an undefined something, to which incidentally, as she reflects, her relationship to both Sir Claude and Mrs. Beale would be irrelevant. It is here that there occurs James' notoriously intense observation: "if [Beale] had an idea at the back of his head she had also one in a recess as deep, and for a time, while they sat together, there was an extraordinary mute passage between her vision of this vision of his, his vision of her vision, and her vision of his vision of her vision." If there can be little doubt that James was delighted by this sentence of his, nonetheless the description of the complex, likely interchange between the two could not have been put more plainly, nor could the intimacy of daughter and father have been rendered more adequately, more intensely. This is the climax of the interchange between the two, after which there is a sad falling-away. "What," James says, "there was no record of indeed was the small strange pathos on the child's part of an innocence so saturated with knowledge and so directed to diplomacy." Beale will make his offer to take Maisie to America. In a final attempt to extend the proffered intimacy Maisie says to Beale, "I'll do anything in the world you ask me, papa," but she knows that she is meant to turn down the trip to America.

Instead, and in the chapter immediately following, Maisie is taken by her step-father to a hotel in Folkestone.

That phrase at which James has finally arrived, "an innocence so saturated with knowledge," says, now, everything we are to know and might be taken to be the novel's final statement except that, at some length, demonstration is to follow, beginning with this elopement with Sir Claude. Or, rather, what more Maisie is to know is only a matter of expression, which, as James suggests, perhaps requires the enumeration of some series of mental steps, but James also, and several times, says that now he is himself at a loss for expression. Having brought Maisie and Sir Claude to the Folkestone hotel, James tells us,

> Maisie had known all along a great deal, but never so much as she was to know from this moment on and as she learned in particular during the couple of days that she was to hang in the air, as it were, over the sea which represented in breezy blueness and with a summer charm a crossing of more spaces than the Channel. It was granted to her at this time to arrive at divinations so ample that I shall have no room for the goal if I attempt to trace the stages....

And again, still at Folkestone, James to the reader: "Oh decidedly I shall never get you to believe the number of things she saw and the number of secrets she discovered." And again, now in Boulogne as Maisie begins to divine Mrs. Wix: "I so despair of courting her noiseless mental footsteps here that I must crudely give you my word for its being from this time forward a picture literally present to her." All of this—these quite un-Jamesian confessions of speechlessness, this throwing up of his hands—is to say with some eloquence that really there is nothing more to say, at least nothing basic, about the question of what Maisie knew. Here as elsewhere James borrows convention to make France to be a site and symbol of romance, and it is said, when Maisie first arrives in France, that "she recognized, she understood, she adored and took possession; feeling herself attuned to everything and laying her hand, right and left, on what had simply been waiting for her." Untutored though she is, when she hears the strum of a guitar and the drawl of a song about 'amour,' she knows what 'amour' means.

Various arrangements for her future are to be considered. She might make one of a trio, in France, with Sir Claude and Mrs.

Beale. She might make one of a trio with Mrs. Beale and Mrs. Wix, while Sir Claude would live nearby. She might make one of a foursome. But what clearly Maisie wants is Sir Claude, and with some cunning and then boldness, she goes after what she wants.

So early as the arrival at the hotel in Folkestone, when the question of the absence of Mrs. Beale is in the air and unspoken, Maisie has the sense, as never before, of her "giving [Sir Claude] a lead" and of his being grateful. Arrived in Boulogne, Maisie urges and will urge that Sir Claude take her to Paris because, as somehow she knows, Boulogne is only the threshold and Paris is the goal, where, as we know, all the true lovers go: "... she found herself inquiring of Sir Claude—and without a single scruple—if he were prepared as yet to name the moment at which they should start for Paris," and when Sir Claude hesitates, she presses, "Well, isn't that the *real* thing, the thing that when one does come abroad—?" A moment later she is speaking to Sir Claude about "our affairs", the matter of their comprising a household together. Having to deal with Mrs. Wix, Sir Claude turns in despair to Maisie and is met by her "more than filial gaze." Not, as James makes explicit, that Maisie is simply enraptured. She knows that Sir Claude tells lies. For that matter, she lies to him when she says that, during his absence in London, Mrs. Wix had not said anything about him.

In the terminal chapter Maisie and Sir Claude walk hand in hand through the streets of Boulogne, where the gilded Virgin is a local landmark. There at the station is the train to Paris, about to leave. In the fraught moment Maisie proposes that they just go. Sir Claude is momentarily tempted, but then of course his fear gets the better of him and the train leaves without them. And it is at that moment, still at the station, when Sir Claude is seated on a bench with his back to the wall and is still frightened, as Maisie perceives, that Maisie proposes that she give up Mrs. Wix, that he give up

Mrs. Beale, that there will be just the two of them.

At the end and necessarily Maisie will leave for England in the care of Mrs. Wix. The novel could not have been brought any further, and, as had occurred to James when early on he had projected a Mrs. Wix, Mrs. Wix serves nicely to provide a way out of the novel. But that is dying fall which in fact leaves the subject as open as ever.[15]

The end of the action proper is that Maisie frightens and appalls everyone who is left. Sir Claude has been tempted but backs away from the proffered invitation, although temporizing by making his pretty and plausible speech in behalf of passion. Mrs. Beale, having been asked directly by Maisie to give up Sir Claude, expostulates, "To *you*, you abominable little horror?," which is to put the matter reasonably. At the very end, in the boat and looking back at the hotel room balcony from which Sir Claude has disappeared in order to be with Mrs. Beale, Maisie says to Mrs. Wix that she knows so much as that, and Mrs. Wix, it is said, "still had room for wonder at what Maisie knew." But "wonder" is a term of many possible tonalities, and here it really cannot mean that Mrs. Wix really and simply is non-plussed because we have long ago come to know that Mrs. Wix has known what, in every essential, Maisie knows, nor has Maisie here signaled any great new insight. "Wonder" in this instance is a refusal definitively to know, but instead to continue to wonder. By so much as Mrs. Wix wonders or will continue to wonder, she will suppress knowledge of what Maisie knows—and so the novel ends where it began, by affronting those sentimental conventions which were inscribed in the literature of the golden age of the literature of childhood, amounting, as in the case of Mrs. Wix with her conventional morality, to frightened refusal to know what little girls know.

Chapter Five

The Awkward Age

I

The Awkward Age had been planned "in perfect good faith," James said, "for brevity, for levity, for simplicity, for jocosity, in fine, and for an accommodating irony," but as to the first of these, brevity, this novel too had got away from him. Like the other novels of the nineties. The seed had sprouted. "The truth is," James said by way of a kind of apology, writing in the Preface, "that what a happy thought has to give depends immensely on the general turn of the mind capable of it, and on the fact that its loyal entertainer, cultivating fondly its possible relations and extensions, the bright efflorescence latent in it, but having to take other things in their order too, is terribly at the mercy of his mind."

So he had cultivated "possible relations and extensions" of the original thought, which consisted, presumably, of what the Notebooks reveal to have been the original plan for the novel, but—in a way that seems to have confused generations of readers, beginning with the earliest of them—he had kept to the intended tone. Clearly James felt that the levity had been retained, along with the jocosity and the irony, and then, as well, the simplicity, at least in the sense of a clear casting of situation and plot.

In his single and brief Notebook entry for the novel (in contrast to the serial elaborations for *The Spoils of Poynton* and *What*

Maisie Knew) James had considered that the subject would be a young girl, "the little London girl," who, at the age of seventeen or eighteen, comes to "sit with the free-talking modern young mother" when her mother entertains what would be her talky social circle. Although the conversation within the circle would then be supposed to be expurgated for the girl, she "inevitably hears, overhears, guesses, follows, takes in, becomes acquainted with horrors," so James speculated. Therefore it will be suspected that this girl may know more—about sex and sexual relations, particularly and clearly—than a young marriageable girl should know, thus to make her ineligible for marriage. There would also be a young man who would like the girl and want to rescue her from knowledge, but finally would reject her just because of what she has already become acquainted with. Another mother might be introduced who would be "foreign or foreignized" and clever, who has married off her own daughter very virtuously, having rescued her from overhearing horrors, but has married her very badly, very unhappily. There might be a larger subject, James had here added, namely the general question of non-marrying girls and the desperation of mothers. When he wrote the novel that larger subject had not more than a shadow of a presence, but the central situation did remain much as had been planned, although extrapolated, extended, and provided with an ado.

Thus: The mother, Mrs. Brookenham ("Mrs. Brook," sometimes "Mrs. B"), will have her eighteen-year-old daughter Fernanda, called Nanda, transferred from the upstairs of her childhood to the downstairs of Mrs. Brook's witty group of free-talking friends. By a kind of legerdemain James will posit an "inner circle" whose function it will be to gossip wittily about others, whose own function it will be to circle about the inner circle, but by actual count the inner circle itself will come to consist of just three, perhaps four persons, including Mrs. Brookenham, the young man Vanderbank ("Van"), who is to be Nanda's might-be rescuer, another young man, Mr. Mitchett ("Mitchy"), who is to marry the other young girl, and maybe the "Duchess," who is the foreignized one, the widow of a Neapolitan nobleman and guardian to the nobleman's niece, in charge of marrying off the young girl virtuously. The single major change in the original plan would be the introduction of Mr. Longdon, a wealthy older man who for the past thirty years has been rusticating at his country estate at Beccles. It must have occurred to James that in the matter simply of plot he would have to have a way of disposing of Nanda after Van rejects her. Just as he had invented a Mrs. Wix to be the terminal rescuer of little Maisie in *What Maisie Knew*, he could have a Mr. Longdon for Nanda. Mr. Longdon might take her away, back to Beccles, and out of the novel, as does happen. And it must have occurred to James as well that a Mr. Longdon, long gone from London, would provide a useful and amusing perspective on modern London society as represented by Mrs. Brook and her circle.

All of this was a material for drawing-room comedy, which James resolved—so the Preface makes clear—to keep light and ironic. He did also say, again in the Preface, that he had witnessed many actual instances of the problem of what to do with the young girl who has come to marriageable age when, as here, there was the circumstance that her modern parents had created the kind of self-conscious and intimate social circle to found in this novel, the crucial and explicit principle of which was freedom of talk. "Half the attraction [of the subject]," he said, "was in the current actuality of the thing." He had observed the circumstance "repeatedly, right and left," he said. But if so, certainly this would not have constituted a widespread social phenomenon, and, whatever the amount of the actuality, fortunately for the kind of story that James said that he had had in mind, the proffered situation had the feel of artifice.[1] James most especially, moreover, would have found comedy in the fact that others might want to believe, or might want to pretend to believe, and maybe even truly would believe, that a girl of eighteen would know nothing about sex. Sexual knowledge on the part of young girls was after all something of a specialty of his and had been at least from the time of *Daisy Miller*, not to mention that just preceding *The Awkward Age* there had been the precociously knowledgeable six-year-old heroine of *What Maisie Knew*. In any event, coming back to the novel at the time of the writing of the Preface, James seems clearly to have found less interest in the endangered girl herself (the "merciless maiden," now) as in her effect on the others.

Clearly it was the drawing room that attracted him. "My idea was to be treated with light irony," said James once again—"it would be light and ironical or it would be nothing," and by way of conveying the tone, so he said, he had resolved to write a novel entirely in dialogue, specifically after the manner of the French novelist "Gyp", *but* without ever mentioning the name or otherwise giving away his source. The result of that fine discretion, however, so he complained in this oddest of all of the Prefaces, was that nobody had understood what he was up to nor what he had accomplished.

Here in the Preface he in fact advertised the ignorance and the rudeness with which his novel had been greeted. He recalled the letter he had received from his English publisher, on his return from a time abroad. "I'm sorry to say," wrote the publisher, "the book has done nothing to speak of. I've never in all my experience seen one treated with more general and complete disrespect." (The American publisher, Harper, would restrict its run to a thousand copies.) And the reviews which the English publisher would have had in mind were in truth not only almost entirely negative but were almost uniformly sarcastic, about James' style, or his subject, or his general abstruseness. So, for instance, the reviewer for *Pall Mall Gazette*: "the surest way to induce a novice to Mr. Henry James' work never to attempt another book of his would be to start the patient with 'The Awkward Age'.... Mr. James' verbal style is a revelation to the normal slipshod person; for his awkward adverbial inversions ... are due, not to carelessness, but to some perfectly unintelligible but consistent reason." And *Bookman*: "The honest reader in search of a story will stare dazedly through perhaps a third of Mr. James' new book, and then shut it with a snort." And *The Spectator*, haughtily: "All of the resources of Mr. James' subtle analysis and ingeniously elaborate style are lavished on the portrayal of a set of smart degenerates, whose very nicknames—e.g., 'Mitchy' and 'Tishy'—enhance their odiousness." Along with other reviews the same.[2]

Not, either, that even well-intentioned friends seemed to have got the point. William Dean Howells had been primarily responsible for arranging for the serialization of *The Awkward Age* in *Harper's Weekly*—and for getting James top dollar for it, three thousand dollars, a sum for which, it happened, James was the more grateful because it enabled him to buy the house in Rye which he coveted. Howells wrote about *The Awkward Age* in 1903, several years after publication of the novel, in a general essay about James' later work, saying that it was one of James' great novels, comparable to *The Wings of the Dove*. He praised "the intensity of its naturalness," comparable, he said, to that of Hardy, although then he added what might have been understood to be contrary implication by praising the "pathos which aches and pierces through [the] closing scenes" of the novel. "What beautiful and gentle souls the new-fashioned young girl [i.e., Nanda] and the old-fashioned man [i.e., Longdon] are," he said, "and how beautifully and gently they are revealed to us."[3]

So much, so James might have despaired, for the attempt to be light and ironical or nothing, but he responded to the general misunderstanding by asserting his pride in this novel, both publicly and privately, and insistently. Just following the American publication of the novel and before Howells' essay, he had written to Howells to say that "Nothing I've ever done is better." To his own perception, he said, nothing he had ever done was "firmer, fuller, more unbrokenly sustained; in every way more expert and mature." To his friend Henrietta Reubell, who had been puzzled, he wrote that his character Mrs. Brookenham was "the best thing I've ever done".[4] Later, in 1908 in the Preface, a decade after the novel had appeared in serial, he confessed that upon rereading it he found himself to be on unexpectedly good terms with the work; he lingered with pride, he said, and stood ready to justify his complacency—which, with some considerable belligerence, is what for the most part in the Preface he did.

In fact at the time of the publication of *The Awkward Age* he had despaired, privately, and would seem to have been deeply embarrassed by the fate of the novel. In that same letter in which he said to Howells that he felt that he had never done anything better, he also said that currently, following publication of the novel, the new silence of "Editor & Publisher" had convinced him that he had awakened their disgust, but for the reason, he supposed, that once again a novel had taken off on its own, far beyond the 70,000 words he had originally promised, with the result, he said, that "I've sat in darkness ever since, under the dreadful sense of having failed (as if I were 25 again) in the chance you had got for me."

Now, however, in this Preface, he was ready to excuse himself for the length of the novel, and attributed the incomprehension of his critics to their strange antagonism to dialogue. He said that actually he had anticipated that his decision to write a novel in dialogue, which would be to say lacking dependable authorial guidance, would be likely to encounter a "certain extraordinary benightedness on the part of the Anglo-Saxon reader." "One had noted this reader," he wrote, "as perverse and inconsequent in respect to the absorption of 'dialogue'", likely to regard the practice as "uncanny and abhorrent" especially when, as in the present case, dialogue was really constructive, organic and dramatic, speaking for itself, representing and embodying both substance and form. It was because of their peculiar aversion to dialogue, he submitted, that English playgoers rejected Dumas and Ibsen. James had taken Gyp for his model of lightness and irony in dialogue, but, he suggested, not even a pure English or an American Gyp would have fared any better with English or American readers.—No doubt that James did not know that Gyp herself had in fact been published regularly in English translation in the middle to the late nineties, with her dialogues sometimes set up in play form and sometimes in straight narrative form.[5]

Certainly James' insistence spoke to a sense of something both striven for and accomplished, not, however, that he was really helpful by way of explaining just what in the novel's actual complexity of dark and light, or of lightsome rigor, he felt that he had accomplished.

James to the contrary, it was not the form in itself that, on the one hand, seems really to have challenged his benighted Anglo-Saxon reader. None of those among the unenlightened did complain of just that, either in the moment or afterwards. But it was not the election of the form of the *roman dialogué*, that, either, explained the achievement. Gyp herself would say, in a letter to a friend, that she had adopted the dialogue form because it was "revoltingly easy, whereas narrative requires a semblance of effort," while she confessed to having "neither respect nor esteem for [her] readers since I see what they like." ("Gyp" was Sibylle Gabrielle de Mirabeau, described by her biographer as a "Bonapartist of Legitimist descent". She was also a prominent anti-Dreyfusard and anti-Semite, and not a lovely person.)[6]

Nor is the form of *The Awkward Age* really that of a Gyp-like dialogue beginning to end, but for James the form would have particularly beckoned. Since *The Other House*, three years before, he had been attempting to adapt stage drama to the uses of prose fiction, and in this novel now, at least after his rereading, he apparently felt that he had found the way, or in any event a new way—this perhaps by way of implied response to Edith Wharton, who had asked, smartly, whether there was any singular virtue in writing a novel as if it were a play.[7] The *roman dialoguè*, or in any event allusion to it, might now be seen to have provided the refreshment of another and a new technique by which he had done again, but anew and more strictly, perhaps therefore more profoundly, that which he had been doing. Characters would be seen to have been relentlessly revealed, to have revealed themselves, comically and ironically to have exposed themselves, according to the seemingness of a purely objective process. Dialogue would be discovered to have elicited more and more dialogue, whereby characters might become themselves beyond their knowing, all the way. Given characters whose function it would be to talk, they might be observed, or heard, as, compulsively, they proceeded to their limits. The procedure would meanwhile have been in no way obvious, but it would be fierce.

All of this ambition is to be taken subjunctively, however, because while in fact the novel is long on dialogue, especially in the later chapters, the objectivity and the distancing—the chill of it—which the novel does achieve, is accomplished quite as much by other means: by physical descriptions of characters, by play-like composition of scenes, by stage directions, by attention to gesture, by presentation of character backgrounds before the characters are allowed to proceed, and so forth. In a repeated trick James displaces himself as author by invoking a supposed outside observer, as he will do again in the next novel, *The Sacred Fount*. "An observer disposed to interpret the scene," he writes; and "the ingenious observer" might have detected; and, again, "the acute observer we are constantly taking for granted" would have detected.... It is not therefore to be said that James as author does not intrude, or that, as James himself was satisfied to express the matter, that there was no "going behind," but on the other hand and more emphatically what is markedly, positively, and essentially missing is not authorial direction but authorial sympathy for characters and their situation, a sympathy which is so conspicuously missing as to become a positive element in the telling.

The result is indeed a kind of a lightness and irony, but a lightness which certainly is not froth and an irony which goes very deep. As he composed his ado, James invented the other characters who were to circle about the inner circle, and they became important in their own right and not only as entertainment for the inner circle. If anything, they are the further distanced from sympathy because they are offered as objects for observation on the part of James' inner circle which itself has been composed as an object for objective, dispassionate observation. They will be revealed, they will be undressed, but in a way to reflect back on Mrs. Brookenham and Van and Mitchy and the Duchess, who themselves are being subjected to a process of revelation and undressing, and as also, neither beautifully nor gently, will be the new-fashioned young girl Nanda and the old-fashioned man Longdon.

James' ironies might even be seen to have gained another

complexity, incidentally and all inadvertently, by the milieu in which they were serialized. *Harper's Weekly,* with its immense distribution, could pay him well. The paper gave him money and James provided the paper with prestige. He had previously written a series of monthly letters for the editors, which, however, they had suspended after the tenth of them. There was irony first of all in the fact that this satire on what would at most have been a very special instance of Edwardian society in London would make its appearance in this most American and demotic of journals. *The Awkward Age* was not the sort of thing that *Harper's Weekly* did, but there it was, surrounded, by way of lightness and irony, with a profusion of illustrations and by advertisements for soap and watches and soup-by-mail and Buffalo Lithia Water and Oneida Elastic Ribbed Union Suits. Moreover, as happened, the novel was also overwhelmed by the news of the day. The serial ran from October of 1898 to January of 1899, when the pages of the paper were dominated by news of the Spanish-American War.

Nor has the novel ever really recovered, in the more than a century since its appearance. Where James prided himself on the novel's levity, simplicity, and jocosity, and on his judgment that he had never done anything better, Edmund Wilson, for one, offered the opinion that "One is dismayed in reading [James'] comments on *The Awkward Age,* which he seems to have considered highly successful, to realize that he is unaware of the elements in the book which, in spite of the technical virtuosity displayed in it, makes it unpleasant and irritating.... James could never have known how we should feel about the gibbering, disemboweled crew who hover about one another with sordid, shadowy designs." And so for other esteemed critics over the years. F.O. Matthiessen would refer to "the strained virtuosity" of the novel, along with that of *The Sacred Fount.* R.P. Blackmur, rejecting the idea that the failure of the book was due to its formal qualities, as had often been said—that is, by James' presumed (and claimed) restriction of presentation to scene and dialogue—took the novel to be a failure nonetheless. The true cause was, rather, in the fact of the lifelessness of the novel, "the inability of all the characters in the book, including its presumably fresh and plastic young heroine, to bring into the conventions to which they restrict themselves the actual emotions and stresses that the conventions are meant to control, but of which they never, in a living society, are meant to be equivalent." Ezra Pound was all but unique in recommending the novel to readers, in his role as universal cultural educator, and he wrote about it at length, but nonetheless discovered it to be "a study in punks, a cheese *soufflé* of the leprous crust of society."[8]

II

In this oddest of the Prefaces James said that he had drawn a figure on a sheet of paper in order to explain the form of the novel to his prospective editors at *Harper's Weekly*. The figure consisted of a circle which in itself contained "a number of small rounds disposed at equal distance about a central object." The central object, he said, was his "situation, my subject in itself, to which the thing would owe its title," with each of the other small rounds, or "lamps," functioning "to light with all due intensity one of [the subject's] aspects." Each of these "lamps", then, would be "the light of a single 'social occasion' in the history and intercourse of the characters concerned," and would "bring out to the full the latent colour of the scene in question and cause it to illustrate, to the last drop, its bearing on my theme." Also, this scheme allowed him to treat "the respective divisions of my form" as successive Acts of a Play.

The complicated sketch is not to be found in the Notebook entry for the novel nor anywhere else, so that it is possible that James' memory of having manufactured and submitted it was a late invention of memory, made to account for earlier struggles with the form of the novel as it had begun to get away from him. He had in fact been writing the novel on the fly, trying to keep up with the demands of weekly serialization.[9] And in any event the sketch as described in the Preface elides all of the most important points. What is the "subject in itself"? What is the "theme"? Are "situation" and "subject" the same thing? If the "situation," the "subject in itself," delivers the title of the novel, "the awkward age," whose age is it? Is "the awkward age" that of Edwardian modernity? Or does it refer to adolescence, namely Nanda's? The two quantities are related only verbally. Nanda is offered as a young girl like any other of her years. Society in this novel, on the other hand, is at once special and is to be seen as being decadent rather than being on the cusp of maturity.

James' account of his sketch may or may not be only later rationale, but whichever, *The Awkward Age* holds together by something other than formal tidiness. It is divided into ten "Books" of varying lengths, each of them named for a character in the novel, some of them major in terms of the plot (Mrs. Brook, Vanderbank, Nanda), and the others not, but then even the division into the ten books was a later imposition on the novel, for the American edition and after the fact. The English edition had been divided into the fourteen parts of the original serial. Book One is named for Lady Julia, who is the once beloved of Mr. Longdon and who has been dead for some time. It is only Book Ten that is named for Nanda. Moreover, the individual Books go their own ways and do not necessarily concentrate on the characters for whom they are named. The plot breeds the novel's personnel, and thereafter the real binding agent is the tone, which is to say the perspective, which also is to state what is the underlying idea of the novel, to be found in the levity, and the jocosity, and the lightness, and above all the irony, which is continuous and unforgiving and goes deep.

At the center of this novel which succeeded *What Maisie Knew* is the problem of what Nanda knows, but as in the case of Maisie there is unannounced presumption that fundamentally Nanda already knows everything, both sex and the ways of the world with it. In large part the novel is given to characters who will not really be edifying but who will be providers of comic extension to what she already knows.

In the outer circle there are, for beginners, Tishy Grendon and her sister Carrie Donner, both of whom are married and both of whom are, in the Jamesian vocabulary, on the pounce. Tishy is Nanda's friend, and one of the Books is named for her, although she will have no direct part in creating Nanda's fate. A climactic event occurs at a party in her apartments, but that is all. Tishy is married, unhappily, to Harry, who doesn't like her, while Harry James finds her to be an occasion for great fun. It is said of her that her "sign" is "a retarded facial glimmer." In conversations she is typically behind. Her apartment—to come to the sex of it—is all lemon and pink. The walls are covered with delicate French mouldings. The French chimney has a French fire. Her sister, on the other hand, has a different way with her similar desperation but provides James with similar opportunity. She has a husband somewhere. She makes a "startling appearance." "In the manner of certain shiny house doors and railings, she instantly creates a presumption of the lurking label 'Fresh Paint.'" She has "committed herself to a 'scheme of colour' that was practically an advertisement of courage." "Irregularly pretty and painfully shy," it is said, "she was retouched from brow to chin, like a suburban photograph—the moral of which was simply that she should either have left more to nature or taken more from art."

Carrie Donner has been jilted by Mr. Cashmore, who also has a Book named for him and who has nothing at all to do with Nanda's fate in any way directly. Mr. Cashmore is very rich; he has more cash. He is "somewhat massive without majesty." He "would have been very red-haired if he had not been very bald." With his monocle and a long upper lip, he is given to little petulant movements and intense ejaculations. He rather hankers after young Nanda, having jilted Carrie Donner, the while he is married to Lady Fanny Cashmore, who has little fancies of her own. And as for Lady Fanny, in turn, for James the name "Fanny" always has droll implications. This Fanny is "magnificent, simple, stupid," with an unsurpassably low forehead and "an air of sombre concentration just sufficiently corrected by something in her movements that failed to give it a point."

Lady Fanny is the sister of Lord Petherton, age thirty-five, a constant companion of the widowed Duchess and thereby companionate to the Duchess' young marriageable charge, by everyone called Little Aggie, who also has a Book named after her. Lord Petherton has "for his main facial sign a certain pleasant brutality, the effect partly of a bold, handsome parade of carnivorous teeth," partly of a broken nose. He would have been ugly, it is said, if he had not been happy. He smiles as he listens to the social chaff, "in a way that would have been a mistake, and indeed an impossibility, if he had really been witty." With his large teeth, he advertises "a kind of brutal geniality".

There is no wickedness in any of these, nor any moral intrusion at all on the part of the author. It is only a likelihood that Lord Petherton with his carnivorous teeth will find Little Aggie to be delicious, and furthermore—James relentlessly goes so far, by way of his own kind of brutal geniality—that Little Aggie herself will delightedly play her own part.

As little as anyone, indeed, is Little Aggie to be let off the hook. She is present in the novel in the first place in order to be Nanda's opposite, as according to James' initial Notebook notation. The Duchess has raised her and prepared her for marriage according to the Duchess' idea of the Old World order. Until marriage she was to be preserved in the cage of childish childhood innocence, and is so preserved. Like Pansy Osmond, she is a product of acquired Europeanism, except that James' irony will now take her to the point of what James terms her "emphasized virginity". She is exactly Nanda's age and, until marriage, is nevertheless a very little girl to whom one is tempted to speak baby talk. Her formal education has consisted of readings in Modern Light Literature and *Stories from English History*, with the horrors left out. Her speech continues to be marked by "the prettiest, faintest foreignness". "Since," it is observed, "to create a particular little rounded and tinted innocence had been aimed at, the fruit had been grown to the perfection of a peach on a sheltered wall." She has been "prepared for consumption"—and it is one of the more candid jokes in the novel that no sooner is she married, to Mitchy, than the little peach bounds into what is euphemistically called "knowledge", with principle opportunity provided by her aunt's lover, Lord Petherton. At the party at Tishy Grendon's, she and Lord Petherton play a game in the other room, with the door locked. She has hidden a book, a naughty French novel, which Lord Petherton is to find, but he won't because she is sitting on it, unless he pulls her off, in order, as it is said, to "compass his desperate end".

The presence of Little Aggie in the novel does serve in its way to augment that "question of non-marrying girls and the desperation of mothers" which James had foreseen in the Notebook entry, but not in a way to make it weighty. To the contrary, and apparently contrary to James' initial thoughts, with Little Aggie, as James came to make her, the question in itself becomes subject for comedy. According to the Duchess, Little Aggie will prove the advantage of the Continental, versus modern English, theory for preparation of young girls for marriage, but proves in fact that the theory has prepared her for adultery, and so Little Aggie becomes another amusement for Mrs. Brook's talky inner circle.

III

The outer circle exists for the amused comment of the inner circle, which should be to say that authority goes to the latter, that the reader's judgment is to be based upon the witty observations of the witty Mrs. Brook and her chosen few. But in fact no one is spared.

The inner circle, this "collection of natural affinities," in Mitchy's phrase, meets principally in Mrs. Brook's drawing room. This drawing room is said to be a "temple of analysis," but it is a temple which by way of immediate subtraction of the sacred has a street address. The Brookenhams live in an apartment in Buckingham Crescent. The apartment looks out not on the streets of London but, rather, commands a prospect rearward, consisting of "a medley," as James nicely puts it, of smoky brick and spotty stucco, of roofs and chimney-pots and stables, all "unnaturally near". Within, the place has an air of "confessed out-of-season vacancy", due to the fact that the Brookenhams have remained in the city out of season because they are doing poorly in the way of household income—a fact which in its turn may be seen either to depress this drawing-room comedy or to add to it still another comic effect.

Mrs. Brook's social fluency is undermined not only by the presence of Nanda but also by the relative seediness of her circumstances. By so much she is not the less witty but is tainted by pretension.

And Mrs. Brook has a family. She has a husband, and his name is Edward. There is "something in him," it is said, "that had long since pacified impatience and drugged curiosity." He has a pale, cold face marked by a hardness of line "in which, oddly, there was no significance, no accent," suggesting "a stippled drawing by an inferior master." Edward has a government job and has had it for about a year. It had been secured for him by Mrs. B, somehow. His job has something to do with Rivers and Lakes. He makes twelve hundred a year, which is not enough. As always, James is precise about figures.

The Brookenhams also have a son, and his name is Harold. He is small and has a slight stoop, which gives him "a character somewhat of the insidious sort, carried out in the acuteness... of his smooth fair face, whose lines were all curves and its expression all needles." He has the voice of a man of forty. He is a leech. He begins life in the novel by stealing five pounds from his mother. His characterizing activity throughout the novel consists of touching one or another of the friends for five pounds. He makes unannounced and uninvited visits to the country houses of wealthy distant acquaintances, at his mother's urgent direction.[10]

But Mrs. Brookenham herself—that best thing, so James said, that he had ever done—is submitted to very far-reaching imagination of her possibilities. For all of her attested authority, she is neither imperious nor devastatingly witty nor even handsome, although she is pretty in her way. In this *roman dialogué,* she is a conversational tactician, making strengths from her weaknesses. Her special sign, says James, is "an innocence dimly tragic". She suggests "the luxury, the novelty, of woe, the excitement of strange sorrows and the cultivation of fine indifferences," which complex of intimations provides "immense effect to her other resources"—her relative youth, mainly. She has "lovely, silly eyes," "absurdly pathetic eyes," and a quavering tone of voice. Her face at any moment will show itself to be "charged with the woe of the world". The characteristic mark of her conversation is a "muffled exaltation". James refers to her "whimsical woe".

That woe, in turn, is at once genuine and is a pretense. It is an ironic exaggeration of the domestic problems which do constantly intrude upon her drawing-room life—Nanda, Edward, Harold, money. (There is suggestion as well that she feels guilty about the way she has raised her daughter.) Rather than suppressing these after-all commonplaces of domestic life, she uses them in order to secure an intimation of wisdom: the woe of the world regarded whimsically.

And there is more, namely an underlying genuineness which has awful consequences. Considering that she is a mother (of four), she is young. She is forty-one years old. The fact of her youth is underscored. She has about her "the pure light of youth". She is "still charmingly pretty," somehow as a result of rather than despite her expression of woe. She is light and flexible—all of which goes to say that that interest of the inner circle in liaisons and adulteries is of interest to her. She is younger than she should be—to what extent of desperation will be seen when she provokes the peculiar climax of the novel. Particularly, she is in love with the young man whom her daughter also loves, the thirty-four-year-old Vanderbank. She will once admit to being a vulgar person, and she is that. She sends Harold off to impose on wealthy people and just in the same way, by exercise of the same possibilities of character, she both encourages and manipulates a connection between her daughter and the elderly and wealthy Mr. Longdon. If he will take her off to Beccles, as indeed he will do, Mrs. B will have at once mitigated her financial worries and rid herself of her rival.

The odd climax of the novel occurs on the occasion of Tishy Grendon's dinner party, where Little Aggie sits on the French novel. The novel itself figures. It is French and naughty. Aggie, who is now married and therefore fully adulterous, is licensed to play with it. The unmarried Nanda should not have read it, but she has. It had been given by Vanderbank to Mrs. B, taken from her by Nanda, and brought by her to Tishy. (We know that both Vanderbank and Mitchy have regularly plied Mrs. B with French novels of the same character, which is to indicate something more of the nature and the affinities of the collection of natural affinities.) At the climactic moment everyone has gathered—James, in a scenic *tour de force*, has eight people in the room, all of them talking—and Mrs. B forces Nanda to confess to everyone that, although she slightly tergiversates, she has read the book and also had written Van's name in it. Nanda is by so much now to be known to be less than adequately virginal. Her marriage prospects, such as they might have been, have been canceled. And Mrs. B at the same time makes it known that it was to her that Vanderbank had made the insinuative gift, thus publicly to establish her claim in the contest between herself and her daughter. But Mrs. B has gone too far. Her five minutes of tactical candor will have the consequence that the inner circle will be destroyed. As Mrs. B herself will soon admit, the members will never grow together again. —All of this only for the reading of a *risqué* novel, except that in the case of Nanda it implies the young girl's sexual experience, and except that the gathering tensions have led up to it.

The swains, meanwhile, are Mitchy and Vanderbank, and they too submit to James' probing ironies.

Mitchy is Nanda's would-be suitor. He is the son of a shoemaker, and is not good-looking, but he is very rich and therefore is of the inner circle. (He has forty thousand pounds, to be compared with the Brookenham's twelve hundred-plus-something from a rental property.) He is shrewd. He agrees to recognize a class difference between himself and the others. He is plain-spoken and generous, and he is the one who does not get the girl. He is in love with Nanda, and marries Aggie at Nanda's request. Vanderbank is the favored young man, with "a handsome face of good humor" and an effect of "long, cool fairness". Women want him. He is a source of what Mitchy calls "the sacred terror," a phrase and an adjective which clearly came to resonate with James. The phrase is here repeated several times. James' next novel would be *The Sacred Fount*. In the next novel after that, *The Ambassadors*, Waymarsh exhibits an instance of his long-suppressed "sacred rage". In each instance, as here, "sacred" means the something within which civilization and propriety and duty suppress: desire, passion, and, plainly, sex, although perhaps the more suppressed in the case of Waymarsh. While here the adjective is coupled with terror.

It is reasonable to suppose that Mitchy had started out in James' thinking as a blunt and honest fellow, a sturdy plebeian, until then the novel took hold. Mitchy has prominent colorless eyes and a retreating chin. The Duchess says of him that he is "supremely hideous," and if she hyperbolizes, Mitchy himself seems nevertheless to agree. But, then, in the same way that Mrs. B capitalizes on her deficiencies, so does Mitchy. He ironizes himself. His dress is deliberately outlandish. There was comedy, says James, "in the form of his pot-hat and the colour of his spotted shirt, in the systematic disagreement, above all, of his coat, waistcoat and trousers." "It was written all over him," says James, "that he had judged once for all his personal case and that as his character, superficially disposed to gaiety, deprived him of the resource of shyness and shade, the effect of comedy might not escape him if secured by a real plunge." Conscious as he is of his commoner status within this circle, with its assumptions, and conscious as he is of his looks, he converts what he knows to be an expectation of humility on his part, to brazenness. And by measure of the same, he is a brutal man. He has agreed to marry Aggie at Nanda's request, but he expects to be paid, by Nanda, who unlike Aggie is not emphatically virginal, and at the end of the novel he comes to collect. He says to Nanda that he supposes that he makes her flesh creep, but nonetheless there is obligation. In the final scene of the novel, in which Nanda entertains her three beaux successively, Vanderbank, Mitchy, and Longdon, Mitchy takes up the lengthiest part. Nanda toys and evades, and Mitchy, having none of it, frightens her.

Vanderbank, the elegant young man, is a civil servant who has a very decent berth, at least by his own reckoning, which is to say that, decent or not, he too is vaguely anomalous in Mrs. B's circle according to its own vaguely aristocratic presumptions. He is Deputy Chairman of the General Audit. Money is his profession and is also a problem for him. Because of his need he may be presumed to be susceptible when Mr. Longdon offers to bribe him. Mr. Longdon will pay him an unspecified large sum to marry Nanda. He will finally refuse, but it remains unclear as to whether pride is his primary reason, or the fact that Mrs. B has made the offer public, or that, as Nanda suspects, he cannot abide the inadequacy of her virginity, or because he will not love any woman. He evades Mrs. B's direct offers, and has done so for ten years, while, faithfully every Sunday for ten years, doing his part in verbal intercourse. "How can any one love you," asks Mrs. B of Vanderbank, "without wanting to show it in some way? You know all the ways, dear Van ... in which *I* want to show it," but he changes the subject. Early on, discussing, with Mitchy, Nanda's love for Vanderbank, Mrs. B predicts that

Vanderbank will "never, never... he'll never come to the scratch," as she can know given her own experience with Vanderbank and as James can know because Vanderbank is one of those charming young men like Tony Bream in *The Other House* and Sir Claude in *What Maisie Knew* who are victims of their own charm. The sacred terror, like the fact of being very handsome, is cause for flight. Vanderbank is deeply, fundamentally unengaged. He is a source of passion—naturally so, with his great good looks, one of "the great cases of privilege," says Mitchy. And at the same time he is elusive, equivocating, self-protective, with the result altogether that, not quite a mountebank, there is something sadly dishonest about Vanderbank. In his final interview with Nanda, requested by her for the reason that she has wished to see him for the one last time, his response is kindness of that kind which is designed to repel intimacy. "Vanderbank had not been in the room ten seconds," writes James, "before he showed that he had arrived to be kind." He emits "a kindness that almost immediately filled the place, to the exclusion of everything else." He projects "a familiar, friendly voice, a brightness of good looks and good intentions, a constant though perhaps misapplied laugh, a super-abundance almost of interest, inattention and movement." He admires Nanda's flowers. He says that she ought to have a bird or two.

IV

It is those "beautiful and gentle souls," as William Dean Howells put it, "the new-fashioned young girl and the old-fashioned man," who drive the plot. Nanda is the primary problem and Mr. Longdon is the anticipated solution. They also—the character Mr. Longdon in particular—considerably complicate, not at all the plot of the novel, but the texture and tone of it, and therefore the meaning of the novel. The two characters are precisely *not* "beautiful and gentle souls". Nanda is not merely her mother's victim, if she is that at all. Longdon is only superficially, if also self-righteously, a chastening shade, with his old-fashioned manners, come as from the grave (as he himself puts it) to be a visitation upon modern London society. He also has his own purposes.

Nanda, by way of a preliminary complication, is a girl with too much forehead. "There's a great question," says Vanderbank, "whether Nanda is pretty at all." She lacks her mother's grace, according to the Duchess. Vanderbank and Mitchy agree that she has no sense of humor while at the same time she is not, either, becomingly shy. She is "as bleak as a chimney-top when the fire's out," according to her mother. Also, her experience, of the kind with which the novel is concerned, extends, so it is hinted, considerably beyond the reading of French novels.[11] Tishy is her best friend. She spends nights at Tishy's house. Things happen at Tishy's house, as everyone seems to know. Mitchy is often there with the seamy Lord Petherton. "What," provocatively asks Nanda, "is it you so like in Lord Petherton?" Mr. Cashmore, who has been dallying with Tishy's sister while his wife has been philandering elsewhere, fancies Nanda, and we are to know that Nanda has met with Mr. Cashmore secretly. Nanda smokes—always, in James, an erotic signal. When Van takes a cigarette from his case, she reaches for the case and rubs her cheek on the polished silver. She wants one just like it, that will hold twenty cigarettes.

She will have been rejected by the man she loves for the sole reason, so she mistakenly supposes, that the supposition of her sexual knowledge, whatever that might have amounted to, has been made public. She is love-lorn. At the end, in the act of accepting Mr. Longdon, she weeps. But not only is she not merely the victim of a young girl's inevitable knowledge—"there was never a time when I didn't know *something* or other," so at the end she says to Mitchy—she is also devious in manipulating that knowledge, and shockingly so, like little Maisie before her. She has persuaded Mitchy to marry Little Aggie in order, as Mitchy knows, that Vanderbank might be encouraged to be more forward. She creates the disaster of a marriage in order to clear the field. And she does so with clear implication that Mitchy will have the reward he seeks. "I think there's no adventure I'm not ready to undertake for you," says Mitchy, "yet my passion... is still enough of this world not wholly to have renounced the fancy of some small reward," by which he means, specifically and as he says, an arrangement by which he and Nanda will be drawn more together. Nanda knows, because Mitchy has already told her so, that her more-or-less candid sexuality positively attracts him. He says now that he would "like so terrifically to have a secret" with Nanda, to which she replies that he can easily be gratified. "I'm full of secrets," she says; "I think I'm really most secretive." And when at the end Nanda evades what had been her clearly implied promise, as also Mitchy's insistence, it is with the facile advice that Little Aggie has turned out as she has merely because she is trying to find out what sort of a person she is, and that the best thing that the cuckolded husband Mitchy might do is to be helpful.

The final moments of her final interview with Vanderbank are given by Nanda to, in effect, procuring for her mother. Vanderbank has absented himself since the episode of Tishy's dinner party. Nanda now says to him that perhaps he hasn't known how awfully much her mother likes him, that she's in love with him. "Not, for that matter, that father would mind," she adds, so that Vanderbank might know that there is literalism nestled within what she says. "She's so fearfully young," Nanda says. She has heard that her mother had once confided to a friend that Vanderbank had done more for her than anyone else, "because it was you who had really brought her out," and when a person has brought a person out… and Vanderbank understands, yes, he says, a person should take the consequences and see a person through.

"You're indeed," says Vanderbank, "the modern daughter!" Nanda has just said that she is natural, "as natural as a cold in your head." It is not to be supposed that Nanda is also a grateful daughter, nor, in the present circumstances, a generous daughter. Rather, given the present subject matter, which is to say hypocritical sexuality, she is facing both her mother and her lost lover, and rubbing their noses in it.

But no other character in James' fiction heretofore had been so slyly made as to be so perverse as this present instance of a Jamesian poor sensitive gentleman, Mr. Longdon.

Except for a few short visits, Mr. Longdon has stayed away from London for thirty years, having retired to rural Beccles in order to nurture his memory of his lost love, Lady Julia. "Lady Julia," he says, "had everything." Coming to the promiscuous Brookenham circle, supposedly therefore he represents not only the old-fashioned virtues generally, but loyalty and true love in particular.

In the lengthy first scene of the novel he has just been paying an evening visit to Mrs. B and her friends and, because it is raining, he has accepted a ride from Vanderbank, which ends at the latter's apartment. What is to be known about Mr. Longdon immediately, aside from his age, is that he is a dandy.[12] Vanderbank remarks on the perfection of his evening dress and the smartness of his sleeveless overcoat. Longdon has in effect thrust himself on Vanderbank, and in this scene it is to be noted secondly that an immediate warmth is established between the two. They discuss Longdon's ancient courtships, the difference between generations—"Oh, you young men, you young men!" murmurs Longdon—and the situation of the Brookenhams. Soon it is near midnight and Longdon moves to leave, but Vanderbank objects. "There are satisfactions you must give," he says to Longdon, and presses another cigarette upon him. Although he doesn't usually smoke, Longdon's resistance rings hollow. He sat there, it is said, "like a shy singer invited to strike up." He does eventually leave, but later, talking to Nanda, he will say of Vanderbank that "he dazzles me," and "I think one has a natural nervousness at being carried off one's feet."

This hinted homoeroticism, not more than that, is subsidized by the facts as they come out, that as a young lover of Lady Julia, and of another woman just before her, Mr. Longdon had not been a success. He will come to reflect that even in his prime he must have passed for old-fashioned. Lady Julia, who had everything, apparently had also had her own other tastes. Reflecting on his failure, to Vanderbank, Mr. Longdon suggests that "the better a woman—it has often struck me—the more she enjoys, in a quiet way, some fellow's having been rather bad, rather dark and desperate about her—for her." Before Julia he had courted Vanderbank's mother, who had introduced him to Lady Julia. When Lady Julia had turned him down, he had turned back to Vanderbank's mother, who by now had four children. He had come to her for episodes of comfort. "She was," says Mr. Longdon, "the one person with whom I could always talk and who always understood."

There is something creepy about Mr. Longdon.

The plot turns on the fact that Lady Julia was Mrs. B's mother and therefore Nanda's grandmother, whom, however, Nanda had never known, because Lady Julia had died. It is established at the very beginning that Mr. Longdon does not like Mrs. B, whom he has just been visiting. It is established within a following few paragraphs that he does like Nanda, and likes her even before he has met her. Vanderbank has a photograph. Nanda is not a pretty girl, as everyone agrees, but Mr. Longdon exclaims immediately that "Lady Julia was exquisite, and this child's exactly like her." "She has Lady Julia's expression," he insists. "She absolutely *has* it." It is said that he is "delightfully positive" when he adds, "She's much more like the dead than like the living." And as a matter of plot, everything flows from this necrophiliac excitement of his. Having missed out on Lady Julia, Mr. Longdon will in some manner be a friend to the granddaughter.

Nanda needs a husband and is in love with Vanderbank. Vanderbank needs money. Mr. Longdon attempts to have Vanderbank marry Nanda by providing funds, in an amount which promises to be significant. For his own reasons, Vanderbank refuses, but meanwhile Longdon has attempted to marry off the child who might have been his own granddaughter, whom he has as well identified with his own might-have-been dead lover, with Vanderbank, who might have been his son, and for whom his feelings are warm beyond being filial, who will take his, Longdon's, place, as the lover of Lady Julia now risen from the dead, for Longdon knows that Lady Julia would have preferred a man like Vanderbank, equipped as he, Vanderbank, is, with resources of the sacred terror, which is to say that he is someone who is rather "bad," as Longdon himself had not been, although now he will try to prove himself. Longdon is one who is risen from the dead, having raised himself in order once more to have a shot at Lady Julia. That is why he is in London, and when he returns to Beccles, it will be to his proper place. Meanwhile, prior to that end, he attempts incest by surrogates, by making a payment, or in any event by making an offer to pay, thus to participate in such a way as he might.

In the last scene of the novel, Nanda is in her upstairs childhood room where, serially, she entertains the three men in her life:

first, Vanderbank, who refuses her; then Mitchy, who frightens her; and then Longdon. Mrs. B has pressed the girl. "We must all help, in our way, to pull the coach," she had advised Nana, "with money, money, money, at every turn, running away like water," nor does Mrs. B care whether the "little fussy, ancient man," as she thinks of Mr. Longdon, will marry her daughter or adopt her. Nanda has in fact sometimes seemed to flirt with Mr. Longdon, while there is no doubt that it is Vanderbank she wants. "We've become, you and I… one of the couples who are invited together," she has said to Mr. Longdon, on an occasion. But the kind of Longdon's interest in Nanda has been clear from the beginning. Thus, seated on a bench at the summer estate that Mitchy had rented, Longdon had invited Nanda to come to *his* place, and to come alone. "Have you arranged it with mamma," asks Nanda, and he says that he has arranged everything. In the last scene, now that Vanderbank is definitely gone, along with Mitchy, and now that Nanda is without other choices, the old man comes forth candidly as a suitor. And he will have the girl. There can be no doubt of this. Mr. Longdon tells Nanda that he had left early for his appointment with her, so as to be sure to be on time "for our trysting place". For the past ten minutes he had been roaming in front of her apartment. She might do anything with him; "so you may dance, if you like," he says to Nanda, "on the absolutely passive thing you've made of me." But this nervous lover soon, almost instantly, becomes a demanding lover. It would be good for him, Longdon, he says to Nanda, if she didn't continue to love Vanderbank. Whereupon Nanda says that she doesn't, and collapses in tears. If she will come with him, as she will, then, says Longdon, "You understand clearly, I take it, that this time it's never again to leave me—or to *be* left," although of course it had been Lady Julia by whom he had been left. Nanda now makes it clear to Longdon that she is the kind of girl whom a Vanderbank would reject, which is to say a sexual girl, and Longdon kisses her—albeit on her forehead, her somewhat excessive forehead. And off to Beccles the girl will go.

V

James' Notebook entry for the novel, dated March, 1895, is peculiarly brief considering the kind of planning and ruminating that had gone into the other novels which he had begun to contemplate at the same time and which were immediately to precede *The Awkward Age*. Main elements of the plot are there, but Longdon in particular is not, while what might be thought to be the serious part of the ambition for the novel—"the question of the non-marrying girls, the desperation of mothers, the whole alteration of manners"—has no more than a trace of a presence as the novel came to be. As little as *What Maisie Knew* is a manual for proper parenting, is *The Awkward Age* an instruction on how not to prepare a young girl for marriage. Nor is the novel a sociological study of Edwardian manners. It is a comedy with a Restoration feel and texture. Characters are assembled and exposed, and that is the cold fun of it. No loveliness is allowed to intrude. If the novel is not really a *roman dialogué* after the manner of Gyp, nonetheless James took care to see the actors in the novel distantly, thereby to deprive them of authorial fellow-feeling, and he did so with so fine a relentlessness and so intense a clarity of focus that, looking back when he was writing the Preface, he might very well have been so exceptionally proud as he was of this novel that he had written.

Chapter Six

The Sacred Fount

The Theory, The Theorist, and The Lady

I

The single notable thing James said about *The Sacred Fount* (other than that he "mortally loathe[d] it"—he did not include it in the New York Edition) was that it was a joke. A joke, he said, was all that it could be, but, he said, it was "a *consistent* joke"; although "doubtless very disgraceful," it had "its own little law of composition" which had been "applied quite rigorously and constructively".[1] He might also have said that never before had he applied and constructed any more rigorously than in *The Sacred Fount,* within any more constraining a law of composition, nor ever before had application been more severe, and subtle, and deliberate and detached and deadpan—with the disheartening result, as clearly he had not anticipated, that absolutely no one seemed to have caught on, so that in one way the joke was on him. And therefore, perhaps, and reasonably, his mortal loathing of the thing.

Nor, for that matter, would he be better served in time to come. *The Sacred Fount* has lived on to be the primary case for late-James obscurity, no doubt first of all just because of the fact of that very *consistency* upon which James prided himself, which is to say the almost total disallowance of any "going behind," but then also because if joke it is recognized to be, as usually it is not, it requires an adjusted kind of perception to see the humor of it. The novel hovers over matters which are funny only from the most austere and detached point of view, now and then dipping down to alight upon horrors.

It is told entirely in first person by an unnamed narrator who, in the way of late James, is unreliable, but who, now, is singularly persuasive, to the point of intimidation; he intimidates the reader, by force, sheerly, of his intelligence, while, as eventually becomes clear, he is not merely unreliable but almost entirely untrustworthy because almost totally self-deluding. (The "almost" of it adds to the confusion.) He is an inventor and a wielder of "theory" (the word is constantly at his lips) and is himself, like his author (but he is not the author), at once terrifically rigorous and marvelously subtle in both his constructions and his applications, and is mostly mistaken as to the facts—which would be to make him comical by way of being a fool and an object of satire, adrift in his elegant constructions, but then, as also eventually becomes clear, accumulatively and retrospectively, by way of both further complication and enrichment, the narrator is also at once a tormented person and a nasty person whose character is at once displaced into and is serviced by his theorizing. Beyond his own knowing, of course, but as the reader is to come to know. For the dawning joke of the matter.

Particularly, the narrator constructs a theory about love and lovers, which, as the novel plays out, requires serial intricate adjustments and ever-renewed strenuous intellectual concentration, as new materials intervene or as the truth of things comes too close. By applying his theory—it is his main activity—he believes that he will discover who among his fellow weekend guests at the country estate Newmarch is engaged in dalliance with whom—and in the disproportion between the tremendous effort and the small object occurs the broader part of the joke of the novel. According to the theory, one party to a love affair will wax, in beauty or wit or vitality, and the other will wane. The giver gives of himself or herself as from a sacred fount. "One of the pair," says the narrator, "has to pay for the other." Investigation will be a matter of discovering who has done which, who has given and who has received, although primarily, as the novel works out, the search is for the losers in the transaction, and one especially.

The narrator is himself odd man out among these weekenders. In his way, and therefore, he is more intensely occupied with romantic liaison than anyone else in the brief novel, while for the same reason, for lack of authorizing experience, his conclusions are at once elegant and incredible, beyond credence. Again, as in *The Turn of the Screw* three years earlier, the novel is at once enclosed within the report of its narrator, and, although one tends to forget, is in fact presented as a recollection of events, and so there is the more reason to doubt the telling as well as to question the motives of the telling; the narrator's tale has been composed, seemingly some long time after the events, and is—candidly—self-serving. And like his predecessor the governess, once again, the narrator interrupts the flow of his perceptions intermittently in order to congratulate himself on his perceptiveness, thereby to forestall questions about the accuracy of his perceptions. What actually had happened that weekend at Newmarch, what there is of evidence, is only to be deduced, and only from interstitial or dropped or otherwise seeped revelations. At the end of the novel, however, the narrator will recall plainly that Mrs. Brissenden, a fellow guest and probable adulteress, or anyway a would-be adulteress, had told him, point blank, that he was crazy. Which is the case.[2]

"Alas," said James in behalf of his novel, "for a joke it appears to have been, round about me, ...to have been taken rather seriously," although in fact the general note of the contemporary reviews was one of exasperation. So Harry Thurston Peck, in *Bookman*:

Henry James, he said, seemed really "to be sinking into a chronic state of periphrastic perversity". Said the reviewer for *Athenaeum* (England), "the whole book is an example of hypochondriacal subtlety run mad." "Mr. James has out-Jamesed himself," said the reviewer for *Current Literature*. James had written "a book which must stagger some of his most unflinching admirers, and of which the effect upon the reader first making the acquaintance of his work could be only a conviction of its absolute lack of sense." Told entirely in first-person, in the late Jamesian manner, at the length of a novel, by a narrator who is crazy, no doubt the novel made really unreasonable demands upon hard-working reviewers with their obligations to both deadlines and knowingness—which left little room for fun, while the intended joke, which reviewers did not get, was intricate with the fact of the difficulty.

But the case was not different among James' friends and well-wishers. "Harry James has upset me," said Henry Adams in a letter to Mrs. Elizabeth Cameron. "[*The Sacred Fount*] is insanity, and I think Harry must soon take a vacation... in a cheery asylum." He reported that John Hay, too, had found the novel "close on extravagance". Later, writing to his daughter and having just read *The Wings of the Dove*, which he liked, Hay himself would say that James had written *The Sacred Fount* "just to scare us". James' one single notable discussion of the novel occurs in a letter to Mrs. Humphrey Ward, and was occasioned by the fact that she had failed to understand it. James had to tell her that the novel was meant to be a joke, that it was "the merest of *jeux d'esprit*". Meanwhile, Edith Wharton mourned. "I could cry over the ruins of such a talent," she said. William Dean Howells certainly was the most loyal of James' readers and perhaps even the most understanding. He would say, in a late general essay on James, that he had mastered "the secret" of *The Sacred Fount*, but, he added, "for the present I am not going to divulge it." Nor did he ever.[3]

For that matter, even James himself would seem, later, to have had second thoughts about his application and construction, although not really to the point of what were the actual difficulties of the novel. *The Sacred Fount* is unique in James in being the single instance of a novel-length use of first-person narrative. In his Preface to *The Ambassadors*, by way of explaining why he did *not* in this later novel use first-person, James would write that "The first person, in the long piece, is a form foredoomed to looseness". But the problem for *The Sacred Fount* was entirely the opposite, in being all a matter of compression and intensity. Not only is it confined within the narrator's crazed head, but the novel even approaches a condition of unities in the classical sense, of time and place. Except for some matters in the first chapter, it has its single setting, the country house called Newmarch, and an action going from beginning to end in thirty-six hours.

In a word, *The Sacred Fount* is concentrated, intricate, and tricky, beyond anything else James had ever written or was to write (to speak to the matter of the law of its composition, only). And the fact that nobody seemed to have caught on to what he had been doing would have been reason enough for his promise, as James put it in his letter to Mrs. Ward, that this would be the last joke of the sort that he would ever make. (But in fact the novels that follow would also have their comedy, their furtiveness.)

II

Rebecca West was accurate and witty, if humorless, when she said of *The Sacred Fount* that it was a record of how "a week-end visitor spends more intellectual force than Kant can have used on

The Critique of Pure Reason in an unsuccessful attempt to discover whether there exists between certain of his fellow-guests a relationship not more interesting among these vacuous people than it is among sparrows."[4] But it is to be seen that the very momentum of her sentence carried West to nice insight. For all of the negatives, she was right to see that while the narrator provides the force, the vacuity of the fellow-guests is also material. For James they too are a part of the joke and are not opportunity, merely, for the narrator's folly. In and for themselves they participate in the chill Jamesian regard, defined by their merely commonplace kinds of deceits, philandering, desperations, and jealousies, only magnified by the fact that the narrator so intently gazes upon them.

The weekend party at Newmarch is said to be a very large one. At one point the narrator says that there are forty people there. But the characters of importance in the novel are just seven, three women, three men, with the narrator coming in seventh. Grace and Guy Brissenden are married. The others are not. Grace Brissenden dallies—the term is Lady John's—with Gilbert Long, who in turn, and to Grace Brissenden's dismay, dallies sometimes with Lady John, sometimes with May Server. Guy Brissenden also makes overtures to Lady John and sometimes to May Server. May Server makes overtures to both Guy Brissendon and Gilbert Long, sequentially, and also to the painter Ford Obert, who also interests Lady John, while, meanwhile, everyone is engaged in deceiving everyone else. The narrator observes each of these others as they sequester with each other, serially, in niches and pathways and rooms of Newmarch.

These other characters have their different kinds of compulsions, and they have their names and other tics of individuality, but it is important that they have something less than personalities; it confirms the humdrum and mere typicality of their affairs that

James, furthermore, mostly deprives them of backgrounds. Ford Obert, the painter, has sometime in the past painted May Server's portrait, but otherwise these others seem to know each other only by virtue of being regular guests at weekends at Newmarch. May Server is provided with two sentences of background. She goes from man to man. She is "on the pounce," so it is said, and there might be a cause for that. Guy Brissenden tells the narrator that May Server's circumstances "are nothing wonderful. She has none too much money; she has had three children and lost them; and nobody that belongs to her appears ever to have been particularly nice to her." But that, significantly, is the entirety of that. The narrator pays no attention to what he has just been told. Rather, he now asks Brissenden how *he* gets on with her, certainly thereby to confirm the narrator's obsessed obliviousness, but it is also informative that these seemingly salient circumstances do not at all become significant datum in the novel—which could perhaps indicate simple forgetfulness on James' part, but probably does not, and which of a certainty signifies that in this case exploration was to rest in typicality. No other reference to May's circumstances finds its way into the novel, earlier or later. Like the others, May Server has the reality of her typicality, merely. She is only the kind of frantic flirt whom one might well encounter at a party. And so for all of these characters: their tawdry ordinariness—their *vulgarity,* in the two senses of the word—is what is to be said about them.

The same, however, is not to be said for the narrator except for the authorial distance, which is the same. The narrator too has been detached from informing background and circumstance. He has neither name nor address nor physical presence (we know that he is older than young Guy Brissenden, but not more than that), nor occupation, nor past other than his engagement with Newmarch and its guests. All of the complicated gnarled inwardness of the character is to be revealed in performance alone, without comment or gloss or explanation, which latter might otherwise secure, or even just allow, sympathy. The narrator is radically on his own. The governess was a governess, the daughter of a poor parson, etc. We have no idea who this narrator is aside from his being one of those who are invited to Newmarch, but then his lack of defining circumstance makes for the situation in which he becomes the story, to be studied and explained and unraveled. Ambition for dramatic neutrality has now taken James this far; more than the governess or any of the other of James' characters of the nineties, the narrator enacts himself and is allowed to betray himself, in the senses both of self-revelation and subversion. And if the novel is difficult, that is the result primarily, finally, of the reader's—one might say the audience's—having to be aware of the continuous irony of the character's self-betrayal. That is where the density and the twistings of the prose come in. Plot, setting, and characterization are suppressed, and the narrator ever more ingeniously goes on and on, until the final diagnosis, that he is crazy. Although he doesn't altogether stop there, either. At the very end, like the theorist he is, he is still congratulating himself on the superiority of his "method".[5]

He might be another of James' poor sensitive gentlemen. As he enacts himself we can know that he is alone, lonely, and yearning, and is sensitive at the expense of sense, but he is also thin-skinned, petty, jealous, sneaky, meddling, vain, smug, impertinent, vicious, a voyeur and, by so much, a sexual parasite, fearful of passion. Clearly he is related to Mr. Longdon of the previous novel, *The Awkward Age*, and to Lambert Strether of *The Ambassadors*, soon forthcoming, as also to John Marcher, forthcoming in a little while, in "The Beast in the Jungle". And for that matter not only is he a poor sensitive gentleman, but for all of his abstractness, he explicates the type: subterranean implications in those other characters in James' fiction (vanity, voyeurism, parasitism, and so on) are here released into action. And this too is a part of the joke. The characterization—the self-characterization—is brutal, if complicated, and is relentlessly so, and comic in that way, indeed outrageous. We are made witness to what amounts to pratfalls of characterization, where what seem to be reflections indicating honor or sensitivity or fineness of sensibility, are repeatedly brought to earth.

What must be the initial presumption of a straightforwardness on the part of the speaker, which inevitably goes along with a first-person narration, is in fact sabotaged in the first sentence of *The Sacred Fount*. The novel begins in London at Paddington Station where the narrator is about to take the train to Newmarch. Here at the station he will meet Gilbert Long and Grace Brissenden, also on their way to Newmarch and traveling together. "It was an occasion, I felt—the prospect of a large party—to look out at the station for others," he says, "possible friends and even possible enemies, who might be going"—and it is that "enemies," dropped into the sentence as a seeming afterthought, that strips the statement of what was to be expected, namely an expository directness. The statement's authority resides now in its unintended irony. Why "enemies" and why, also, "possible"?—which is not to say that this narrator is saying that he actually has enemies (or friends either, for that matter) but that wariness, as a quick second consideration, is policy for him, no matter how perfectly mundane the occasion. And now the narrator goes on, looking forward, but apprehensively, to what we will learn is to be nothing more than a one-hour train ride: "Such premonitions, it was true, bred fears when they failed to breed hopes, though it was to be added that there were sometimes, in the case, rather happy ambiguities"—which last, as he puts it, is quickly *not* to say something like "happy eventualities". Persons in the train compartment who glowered at one, he says, sometimes after breakfast the next morning proved to be charming, but on the other hand it would happen that "one was spoken to first by people whose sociability was subsequently to show as bleak; and"—worse still—"one built with confidence on others who were never to reappear at all, who were only going to Birmingham."

And if some go to Birmingham, only, now we are to know (by his none-too-forthright account), as the first chapter proceeds, that others have slighted him more deliberately, Gilbert Long in particular. The narrator had met him at Newmarch and in the interval since, Long had "failed to know [him]," which snub, as he takes it to be, he attributes to Long's being "stupid unless I held him as impertinent". But Long "was stupid in fact," he says, and he suspects that Long had been invited to Newmarch in the first place only because of his striking good looks, his six feet and more of stature and his low-growing, tight-curling hair—which it is to be supposed the narrator has not. But on this occasion this "fine piece of human furniture," "the heavy Adonis, who had so often 'cut' me," approaches him like an old friend, speaks of common acquaintances, says that he is glad that the narrator will be going to Newmarch—and much of the plot of the novel springs from the bewildering event. The narrator observes that Long's manners "had distinctly gained in ease". Now it appears that Grace Brissenden has arrived with Long. She is a woman of a certain age—in her early forties (but the narrator quickly speaks of her previously having flaunted her "fifty years"). She too shows a difference. The narrator says that he had mainly remembered her as having been "rather ugly," whereas now she "was rather handsome," and seeming to be much younger than she had been. She has married a man, Guy Brissenden, who is in his late twenties, with whom she is not now traveling, for he will be taking a later train, with Lady John. (Mrs. Froome and Lord Lutley will also be traveling together, "in the wondrous new fashion," as

Mrs. Brissenden says.)

The two, Long and Grace Brissenden, speak of each other to the narrator, separately, and seem, to the narrator, to confirm and elaborate his judgments. Gilbert Long says of Grace Brissenden that she has charms which her young but dull husband can't appreciate, that while she has not got younger, her clock has simply stopped, that she has grown no older since her marriage. Grace Brissenden says of Gilbert Long that she had never seen a man so improved, that suddenly he has a mind and a tongue, and that this transformation must be the result of the influence of a very clever woman.

There is information in all of this, of a casual and a passingly sordid sort, which for the narrator, baffled, distraught, and teased as he is, is the beginning of theory and the termination of knowledge.

The reader will know that Long and Grace Brissenden are at play with each other, contemplating a weekend, and think themselves to have been caught by this prying narrator, who is outside of the wondrous new fashion. (Long asks the narrator why he is staring at him so hard.) As is to be suspected from the beginning and as will be clear at the end, there have in fact been no transformations, while that the narrator should so entirely misinterpret, and think, or at least begin to think, that these two have undergone basic change, in mind and body, confirms and compounds what already, from the first paragraph on, is to be known of the narrator's lonely estrangement—from what in James' view is an amusing ordinariness of civilized sexual arrangements outside of marriage. Gilbert Long and Grace Brissenden also talk to each other. The reader but not the narrator will surmise that Gilbert Long has had a relationship with Lady John, which perhaps continues, that Grace Brissenden knows it, that it was for that reason that she had arranged for her husband to travel with Lady John.

Arrived at Newmarch, the narrator will find Ford Obert, May Server, Lady John, and Guy Brissenden, who together complete what he calls his "little gallery". Now, scrutinizing, he sees, or thinks that he sees, that Guy Brissenden has suddenly aged. Brissenden seems to be about sixty years old, while his wife seems to be about twenty. Gilbert Long, meanwhile, so the narrator says, has become predominant among the guests and commands everyone's attention as he could not possibly have done two or three years before without making a fool of himself. And that, at the end of Chapter Two, is sufficient for explicit formulation of the theory of the sacred fount.

For all of the rest, and as for plot, the narrator addresses himself primarily to discovering which woman it is who has been responsible for the transformation of Gilbert Long (who had snubbed him and now does not), with the evidence, according to the theory, having to consist of the woman's mental deterioration, in the narrator's words, her "cerebral lesion". The only candidate among those present is May Server, but there are intervening, intertwining complications: first that at first impression, before he catches himself, the narrator thinks May Server to be extraordinarily pretty, markedly responsive, and conspicuously charming, and secondly that he is, or thinks that he is, or wants to be in love with her. But of course the theory of the sacred fount will be the more importunately sacred, more so than love.

Not, so James has it, that the narrator is without some moments of self-reflection. While he had felt from the first, so the narrator says, that he was on the track of something ultimate, a law that would fit his observations, he does acknowledge that, at least at first, he had thought that he might be exaggerating them, "grouping them into a larger mystery (and thereby a larger 'law') than the facts, as observed, yet warranted"—but, he quickly goes on to say, "that is the common fault of minds for which the vision of life is an obsession. The obsession pays, if one will; but to pay it one has to borrow." He cautions himself "not to yield further to my idle habit of reading into mere human things an interest so much deeper than mere human things were in general prepared to supply," but after all, having neither irony nor humility, nor fellow-feeling for those "mere human things," on, nevertheless, he goes.

On the other hand, his larger law is not really implausible, thus to make the narrator seem to be the less so himself. The theory in itself is even basically commonsensical—that there is likely to be some kind of inequality between lovers, that one of a pair is likely to be more sacrificing than the other—but of course the common wisdom stops short of vampirism, as the narrator does not. This lonely theorizer makes of it something at once absurd, theatrical, and vicious. Theory for this crazy person is a weapon, as well as being subsidy to vanity. He has insistent exchanges with each of the other persons in his little gallery, but by way of visiting his obsession upon them. He probes, he queries, eliciting responses ranging from casual interest to annoyance to fear (many of his observations are of backs turned to him, in flight), and converts everything he is told into endorsement of his intelligence. Grace Brissenden has her own reasons for wanting to have the narrator think that the woman in the case of Gilbert Long is not herself, and joins him, therefore, in the search for a case of female cerebral lesion, pending her final judgement, that the narrator is crazy. (The weekend is over and so also is the affair. Long, she says, is the prize fool he always was, "every appearance to the contrary notwithstanding," and "his stupidity is unimpaired.") Ford Obert offers an interest in the theory, which ultimately, however, he withdraws. (He has been having his own fluctuating relationship with May Server.) These are dubious encouragements, which, for the narrator, are nevertheless sufficient. Fortified, he is ready to misinterpret anything in behalf of his brilliance, or, as he puts it, explicitly, "his joy of the intellectual mastery of things unamenable, that joy of determining, almost of creating results."

He is a fantasist. He is immured in a frenzy. He is driven by a single idea. But if by so much he is a traditional kind of comic figure, James has also singularly embellished him. He is crazy, *and* by the sheer energy of his intellect he all but commands plausibility. With his fine distinctions and acute precisions, he sounds like Henry James. Just as "The Turn of the Screw" was an *amusette,* as James was to say, and, for the fun of it, meant to catch those not easily caught, so with the characterization of this narrator.

Moreover—and this too is part of the fun of it, within the perspective which the novel invents—that same intellectual energy almost but not quite conceals the sheer nastiness of the character. He is vain, smug, impertinent, and is a snoop, a meddler, a boor. His "extraordinary interest in my fellow creatures," as he puts it, is both outrageous and malicious. His theory of the sacred fount creates victims, and clearly it is victimization that delights him. Theory is sadism for him, with the erotic charge in it provided by the fact that the field of his inquiry is, explicitly, sexual dalliance. Hence his metaphors. May Server becomes his "prey". There is broad hint in the novel that the narrator is also if passingly interested in Guy Brissenden who, he says, was "intellectually speaking, plastic wax in my hand." Observing May Server, he recognizes, as he says, "the last, the expiring struggle of her native lucidity," as she moves "groping and panting, in the gathering dusk of her fate." The theory demands that May Server and Guy Brissenden must be fellow victims, related in "a fellowship of doom," she by forfeit of her mind, he by sacrifice of his youth—proceeding in both cases, perhaps, so he contemplates, to a grand climax and *coup de théâtre*, where May will have attained "the point of final simplification" and Guy "the limit of age recorded of man." And as for his enjoyment: "I could look at neither of these persons," he says, "without a sharper sense of the contrast between the tragedy of their predicament and the comedy of the situation that did everything for them but suspect it. They had truly been arrayed and anointed, they had truly been isolated, for their sacrifice." Their ignorance is his knowledge, a condition which provides him, he says, with an ultimate "intensity of amusement".

In a lovely turnabout, he asks himself if he had not "fallen so much in love with Mrs. Server that the care for her reputation had become with me an obsession," which, if so, will demand that he cancel the obsession and thereby enable cancellation of his care. The one way he might square his loving with his theory would be to transmute his love into pity, which he does. Like a sighing lover, with only the one critical term, love, transposed, he says, exactly, "I knew how far I was gone in pity for her". He had in fact been stirred in the first place by a presumption of her vulnerability. Ford Obert early on had advised him of two things, first that Mrs. Server had designs on him (but Obert had had his own reasons for saying so), and that she was beastly unhappy, to which the narrator had responded in terms only not quite leering, "But isn't that just one's advantage?" Most of a chapter will be given to the narrator's attempt at a seduction, which he recalls as sheer pastoral. It happens in the garden, on the primrose path to dalliance: "There was a general shade in all the lower reaches—a fine clear dusk in garden and grove, a thin suffusion of twilight out of which the greater things, the high tree-tops and pinnacles, the long crests of motionless wood and chimnied roof, rose into golden air. The last calls of birds sounded extraordinarily loud," and so on, he almost sings, with, in any event, an eloquence unlike anything else in the extended monologue of the novel. But these are borrowed terms, as the narrator himself recognizes: "She came slowly and a little wearily down the vista," he says, "and her sad, shy advance, with the massed wood on either side of her, was like the reminiscence of a picture or the refrain of a ballad." Seated together, he puts his hand on hers. Debonairly, he tells her that he has been in love for one whole day, thereby to approximate the attitudes and morals of the other weekenders. But he fails, of course. May is distracted. The reader will know that really she is thinking about Gilbert Long. The narrator removes his hand, which she allows him to do "with as little sign as on her first feeling its touch".

It is another piece of James' cruel joke that the narrator, ever the odd man out at this weekend frolic, is entirely impotent in the ways of Newmarch. Sex, like everything else, is in his head. Supposing May Server's interest in him (confirmed, so he conceives, by the fact that she has *not* flirted with him while she has flirted with all of the other men at Newmarch, thereby, so he infers, to hide her feelings for him) he considers what he might or might not tell the others who might suspect May's interest in him. "It would have been almost as embarrassing to have to tell them how little experience I had had in fact," he thinks to himself, for he is nothing if not candid about himself if also mistaken, "as to have had to tell them how much I had had in fancy." Pitying May, he blames passion. "I saw," he says, "what consuming passion can make of the marked mortal on whom, with fixed beak and claws, it has settled as on a prey. She reminded me of a sponge wrung dry and with fine pores agape. Voided and scraped of everything, her shell was merely crushable." And therein is a general lesson, which in this narrator's case is redundant. "Who of us all," he asks, "could say that his fall might not be as deep?" For himself, he has managed to obliterate passion in behalf of theory, which, critic that this narrator is, becomes its alternate. In an ultimate extravagance of misunderstanding he offers Mrs. Brissenden his conclusion that it was not his person that gave charm to his theory, but rather, he says, "I think it was much more my theory that gave its charm to my person." Which is to say that theory is his allure, is safe sex, while being at the same time a kind of continuous pleasant indulgence of his very own sacred fount.

III

On the other hand, if the narrator's idea about passion, that it consumes and rends, is here a component of the ongoing joke, at the expense of the narrator, that does not mean that he might not really have something to fear. Whether or not James was right in complaining that readers seemed to be taking the novel seriously, the narrator's idea has its inevitable double nature. Passion, for James, is opportunity for comedy. (In "The Given Case," a light tale contemporaneous with *The Sacred Fount,* the lawyer Barton Reeve feels himself "in the grip of his passion, shaken as a rat by a terrier.") And, as often, passion is dreadful, and, almost always, as here in *The Sacred Fount,* it is both at the same time—as it was from *Watch and Ward* forward, and especially in the novels of the nineties, with their special attention to sex. In the novel just prior to *The Sacred Fount,* in *The Awkward Age,* the name for passion was "the sacred terror". The joke part of it in *The Sacred Fount* is in the fact that the narrator wildly exaggerates the ravages (if any there actually are here to be observed) of what in the milieu of Newmarch is less than love. He theorizes about what he does not know (his awkward dabbling with May going to prove that he knows nothing) but that, in a way further to perplex the reader, does not mean that he does not, essentially, know what he is talking about.

It is in any event a universal stuff of literature as well as a common wisdom, that passion is both funny and awful, but the more particularly Jamesian idea for exploitation, here and elsewhere, is that if passion has its ravages, so does fear of passion, with its ravages, but then the fear, too, is both terrible and funny, as this strangely ambiguous, this strangely grave fool of a narrator goes to show.

The insanity of the narrator is explicated by his immediate successors, who similarly will devote their lives to avoidance of passion. In *The Ambassadors,* which James had begun to write within a month after finishing *The Sacred Fount,* Lambert Strether, middle-aged and in Paris, has for his major function the discovery that passion—with sex explicitly at the core of it, in the illicit arrangement between Chad and Mme. De Vionnet—is a metaphor for life itself, and it follows that his previous life, the life of Woollett, had been a death. "Live all you can; it's a mistake not to," he cries out to Little Bilham, bursting forth from a lifetime of restraint and repression. Notwithstanding his final retreat into sacrifice and rectitude, when he rejects the proffer of romance with Maria Gostrey, the whole of the novel has in fact been given over to enlightening him as to the joy, as may be said, of sex, and particularly the payment exacted by fear of the joy. Lambert Strether, this is to see, casts clarification backwards, even as the narrator of *The Sacred Fount* anticipates Strether—quite exactly, to the point of certain atrocious implications of temperament. For all that Strether is a sympathetic character, like the narrator he is a voyeur and, by so much, a sexual parasite. But then also, to look backwards, Strether on his side implies the suffering, struggling, agonistic side of the narrator.[6]

And so for "The Beast in the Jungle," which James wrote in 1902, just a year after the publication of *The Sacred Fount.* There is echo of *The Sacred Fount* even in the names of the characters: John Marcher somewhat recalls Newmarch, and May Bartram recalls May Server. It is also the case that from a certain and available point of view "The Beast in the Jungle" is a jokey kind of a tale. John Marcher's reluctance to recognize what May Bartram offers him is peculiar in itself and is based on an obsessive notion, which in turn is based on hardly anything, that an extraordinary but otherwise unspecified fate awaits him, which so long as it doesn't arrive has the function of subsidizing his vanity. Unlike Strether, who had the Puritanism of Woollett, Massachusetts with which to contend, and whose final renunciation will be based on a moral discrimination, John Marcher has only his dim foreboding which, relentlessly, he converts into metaphor—the beast which is waiting to spring—which, like theory and however vivid, is a poor substitute for a life. He is a fool. He frustrates nature. Marcher fails to get into May. But of course the tale is in fact painful and eloquent, made so by a concordance of elements: May Bartram's constancy in her love for Marcher, for one thing, and the advance of the years for the two of them, and May's death, and, finally, the fullness of Marcher's realization of his fate. "The escape would have been to love her; then, *then* he would have lived," he now knows. "*She* had lived—who could say now with what passion?... whereas he had never thought of her (ah, how it hugely glared at him!) but in the chill of his egotism." And these are words which exactly, with only a slight shift in authorial perspective, and by way of reconversion, might have been uttered by the narrator in *The Sacred Fount.*

And so for the governing conceit of *The Sacred Fount*, simply that between lovers one gives and the other receives, that the giver is consequently depleted while the other is enriched. As invented and elaborated by this narrator, the theory of the sacred fount is absurd. But the idea had a history in James' imagination going back almost to the beginning, similarly enhanced, and expressed in similarly ultimate terms, and not always to be regarded as the stuff of a joke.

In the initial episode of *The Sacred Fount,* at Paddington Station, when the narrator takes Grace Brissenden to be younger than she had been, and Gilbert Long to be more sociable, he says to Mrs. Briss with reference to Long, that "'it's a most extraordinary case—such as one really has never met,'" and she says "'Oh, but it happens'".

There is in fact a borrowing here, both verbal and substantive, going back to 1868, when James was twenty-five years old. He had written a story called "A Most Extraordinary Case". In it a young soldier, back from the War, is sick of a mysterious disease. He falls in love. The young woman thrives. In the crucial scene of the story, he has struggled from his sick bed in order to attend a party. He is near collapse while the young woman along with some others make much of him. The moral is uttered by a friend, Mrs Mason: "'Was there ever anything like the avidity of these dreadful girls?'" she asks. "'They like a man to look as if he were going to die,—it's interesting.'" The soldier does die; the young woman marries his doctor.

Again, another story of James' twenty-fifth year, "De Grey: A Romance," is almost a template for *The Sacred Fount,* except that the accents are gothic. There is a curse upon the male De Greys, as recorded in an old bible which is in the possession of a wise priest. The first women whom the De Grey men love, always die. Paul De Grey loves Margaret. In defiance of the curse, they plan to wed. Margaret falls ill. In order to stymie the curse, and because he loves the girl, Paul kills himself, by willing himself to die. The priest speaks prophecy and doom. To Margaret, prior to the climactic event, he says, "'My dear child, Paul is very ill. God grant that, if you manage not to die, it may not be at his expense!'" She resists, but the curse is seemingly absolute, and, says the author in her behalf, "she blindly, senselessly, remorselessly drained the life from [Paul's] being. As she bloomed and prospered, he drooped and languished. While she was living for him, he was dying of her. Execrable, infernal comedy!" It is noteworthy, moreover, that James did not quite end the story on that exorbitant note, but retreated towards psychological credibility. Old Mrs. De Grey, Paul's mother, clings to belief that Paul had died by falling from his horse. The old priest had loved the boy and says to his mother, Suppose that Margaret had died, would to heaven that she had. (Margaret has merely gone crazy.) Mrs. De Grey says, "'Ah, suppose! Do you make that wish for the sake of your theory?'" At which terminal point it becomes a question as to whether in the first place there had really been a curse upon the male heirs of the De Greys, and if not, then what is left is the secular fact that as Margaret, the bride-to-be, had bloomed and prospered, her lover, mistakenly convinced of the curse, had drooped and languished of his own conviction, so that while she was living for him, he was dying of her.

"Men have died from time to time, and worms have eaten them, but not for love," says wise Rosalind. The narrator of *The Sacred Fount*, with his theory, urges the contrary. Not only will it be the case that one of a pair of lovers will be more loving than the other, but one of the pair has to pay for the other, and the payment will proceed to the end, to the maximum of depletion. Young Guy Brissenden will die long before his older wife. May will be an empty sponge.[7] The narrator congratulates himself that he is "on the scent of something ultimate." To comic effect, he imposes his great law upon the passingly sordid, largely commonplace intrigues of Newmarch. As well, the great law serves the narrator personally. Paradoxically, it saves him from passion while it renders the woman, May, vulnerable to what must be his passion. But at the same time there is a jolt to it; it forces a different way of thinking about Newmarch. For all that the narrator is both mistaken and underhanded, he does also speak truth. (And if he is rejected, that is the usual fate of seers.) The love game, while it is a game, also is not. Perhaps some do die of heartbreak. In any event, the narrator's theory goes all the way, to urge the realization that these weekenders are at play with fundamental matters, with, exactly, something ultimate. Oddly enough, the narrator has dignified the place and the persons. With all of their trysts and their fumbling liaisons, Life and Death are informative metaphors for what the weekenders are doing. And by so much, and in this way as well, the novel again undermines its own comedy.

Early on, in Chapter Four, the characters assemble in order to view a painting, and here for the moment the comedy gives way entirely, to the sinister. The narrator has invited May to visit one of the galleries at Newmarch. As they proceed, he reflects on May's beauty. Her beauty reflects that of the gallery itself, he says: She might herself have been "all Greuze tints, all pale pinks and blues and pearly whites and candid eyes—an old dead pastel under glass." Come to the painting, they discover that Gilbert Long and Ford Obert have arrived before them. The painting is of a young man in black, "a quaint, tight black dress, fashioned in years long past," and he has "a pale, lean, livid face and a stare, from eyes without eyebrows, like that of some whitened old-world clown." In his hand he is holding "an object that strikes the spectator at first simply as some obscure, some ambiguous work of art, but that on second view becomes a representation of a human face, modelled and coloured, in wax, in enamelled metal, in some substance not human." The object appears to be "a complete mask, such as might have been fantastically fitted and worn." We are told by the narrator that Long has commented on it brilliantly, impressing the painter Obert, but we don't know what he has said. Asked what the painting means, May Server says that it might be called the Mask of Death. The narrator objects. "Isn't it much rather the Mask of Life?" he asks. "It's the man's own face that's Death. The other one, blooming and beautiful ... is Life, and he's going to put it on; unless indeed he has just taken it off." May says that the mask wears a horrible grimace. The narrator says that he doesn't see it. May says that she sees nothing else. Obert and the narrator agree that mask and face resemble someone. It could be May (the mask; she has already been identified as a dead pastel), or Long, or Brissenden (the face) or someone else among the guests, and the matter is left at that.

There is nothing of a joke in this scene, in this novel which James said was a consistent joke, nor does the scene in any obvious way advance what there is of a narrative. Rather, it provides a grotesque deepening to the affairs of Newmarch. The painting, located in a gallery which, it is said, has the aspect of a shrine, is plainly frightening. The young man in his quaint tight black suit is a Newmarch forebear, who augurs. He proposes a riddle—to these playful weekenders—having to do with Life and Death. Nor does the painting propose a hectoring, moralizing kind of statement, such as to tell observers how to behave. It is its own sacred fount; the young man has begot the beautiful artifact, has given his own face to it. The statement it makes is bleak and metaphysical. And the answer to the riddle is that May and the narrator are both right, on the side of Death. The livid face without eyebrows, staring, is as much without life as is the wax or enamel artifact—May does not in fact contradict the narrator when he says that the face is Death.[8] The depleted face is Death and so is its alternative. The narrator's decision that the mask is Life, meanwhile, is akin to his converting May, the beloved, into a dead pastel, an artifact of life, and is akin to converting Love, for that matter, into Theory.

Edmund Wilson was probably right when he said, long ago, that if anyone ever really got to the bottom of *The Sacred Fount,* he would throw a good deal of light on Henry James.[9] Leaving aside biographical matters, certainly the novel does bring together strategies and concerns and attitudes of much of James' fiction, and particularly of the time following the playwriting years, and brings everything to an extreme, to the point of tour-de-force. The novel illuminates what has gone immediately before: the ambition for an absolute of objectivity, the interest in desire, in sex, the tenacity of imagination and the pitilessness of it. The novel has clear relation to *The Turn of the Screw,* and as well to *The Other House,* with its distraught heroine who murders a little girl, for love, and to the investigations of desire in *The Spoils of Poynton* and *In the Cage* and the others. It is appropriate climax to James in the nineties. But *The Sacred Fount,* of 1901, is also all but contemporaneous with the large novels which quickly followed: *The Wings of the Dove* (1902), *The Ambassadors* (1903—but it was written before *The Wings of the Dove*), and *The Golden Bowl* (1904). While in these later novels James obviously was letting loose—he had given up on the struggle for compression—the intelligence after all was the same. And to realize so much is to consider that *The Sacred Fount* was also the tour-de-force version of what was immediately to follow, in what are usually thought to be James' great novels. *The Sacred Fount* is demanding, sly, and tricky in its approach to great matters, and is entirely ironic, and being so, casts a light both backwards and forwards.

Chapter Seven

The Major Phase

In *The Wings of the Dove,* Kate Croy, having left Lancaster Gate, has gone to stay with her sister, Marian Condrip. She says to Densher, who has found her there, that she has come in order to help with her father, Lionel Croy, who has shown up "in a state which made it impossible not to take him in." "Do you mean in such want—?" Densher asks. But it's not that. "No," says Kate, "not of food, of necessary things—not even, so far as his appearance went, of money." "He looked as wonderful as ever," she says, "But he was—well, in terror." "In terror of what?" Densher asks, and Kate says, "I don't know. Of somebody—of something. He wants, he says, to be quiet. But his quietness is awful," and she adds, after a moment of self-questioning hesitation, "He cries." Densher asks, "What *has* he done?", but Kate stops him. "If you love me—now—don't ask me about father," she says, and Densher does love her, so he says, and he doesn't ask, and that is all of it.

The brief episode near the end of the novel makes for a moment of suspense. Densher delays his offer of the letter from Milly Theale in which presumably she has left him her fortune. He will not open it. He has been holding it behind his back. It is in the next line of text that he extends it to Kate. And the interchange functions also by recalling and emphasizing for the reader, this several hundred pages later, what had been established in the very beginning of the "long-drawn fiction," as James called it, of the sordid circumstances of Kate's origins, to which she will be likely be returned, as contrasted with the promises and plans and locales which have now been the conditions of most of the novel. Or, rather, what at the beginning had been a state of dismalness and meanness is now the more so for the passage of time. Poor widowed Marian, who will never shimmer like her radiant sister Kate, always in want, with her four bouncing children, is the more in need and therefore the more obligating. Lionel Croy, who with his Dickensian name had been almost comically a grasping schemer and manipulator of the filial pieties, has become frightening. He is demented, out of his mind.

The episode has these uses as plot device, but nonetheless in a novel which is almost always read as a drama of subtle apprehensions leading to an exquisite sacrifice on the part of an ideal heroine—a dove—and ending in moral realizations, it comes as a surprise leading, then, to other realization, of the far reach of possibilities of imagination in the novel which have been there all along only mostly obscured—by the subtle playing of calculations on the part of all of the characters, and the elaborations of consciousness, and the play of moral rationalizations and equivocations, and not least by the densities of James' late style. Here is confirmation that underneath everything, as we should have suspected, there has been something much indeed like a madness which has compelled this plot.

To go back and strip the plot to its essentials is to see first of all that the scheme which has been hatched by Kate and Densher is at least morbid, depending as it does on the seduction of a dying girl, whom by the way the schemers scarcely know, in order to get hold of her money. It is hardly too much to say that Kate as con artist is sociopathic, no matter how plausible her motives and reasons and needs, and no matter that ultimately she fails. She deceives the reader, as well. As for Densher, he starts out comically vague. "You would have got fairly near him by making out in his eyes the potential recognition of ideas; but you would have quite fallen away again on the question of the ideas themselves," James writes. Midway, Densher seems to have a conscience. At the end, however, he is a sexual blackmailer looking to be twice lucky; his price for seducing Milly is to have Kate sleep with him. Even mild and benign Susan Stringham, a writer, while of course she does Milly no intentional harm, is a busybody whose life is a composition and maybe a fiction based upon the supposition of Milly's forthcoming death. For all of the seeming drama of consciousness in the novel, moreover, every one of the characters who constitute Milly's "others"—James' term in the Preface—one way and another is self-seeking, self-rapt, and, as regards Milly in herself, indifferent. Including the doctors whom Milly consults.

But Milly in herself also proposes some nice questions for consideration.

She is of course at the center of the novel. "The idea, reduced to its essence, is that of a young person," James writes in the Preface, "conscious of a great capacity for life, but early stricken and doomed, condemned to die under short respite, while also enamoured of the world; aware moreover of the condemnation and passionately desiring to 'put in' before extinction as many of the finer vibrations as possible"—which is to say that everything in the plotting of the novel depends on the fact that Milly is sick, that her death is imminent, and that she knows it; this knowledge it will be that will propel her interest in meanwhile "having lived"—James again, in the Preface—which in turn will mean having a love affair whether or not physically consummated. (James had raised that latter issue for himself in his first Notebook jottings for the novel, reflecting that an episode of actual "physical possession" of the sick girl would be "vulgar" and "second-rate.") And die of course Milly does, when she finds out that Densher has been spoken for—we don't know that she knows anything more than that—and she does so by turning her face to the wall, as is several times said.

If this, then, is the essence of the matter, then Milly's consciousness is the plot within the plot. Not only does the supposition of her early death provide Kate and Densher with their opportunity, which will be spun out in an ado, but the same creates Milly's own story, only just not quite independent of what others think and do. Her own story, moreover, there underneath and simmering almost throughout, and occasionally coming to a boil, is more curious than the others know.

James carefully skirts specifying just what is Milly's ailment. Obviously, clinical diagnosis would have been a distraction at best. Nonetheless, the nature and cause and progress of Milly's illness is the one constant mystery in the novel, and it is the case, as has been demonstrated notably by John Landau (pursuing his argument regarding the constant of the instability of representation in all of the late novels), that nowhere in the text is there distinct evidence that in blunt physical terms Milly is sick at all. Milly's illness, as Landau says, is "the black hole, the tantalizing absence" at the "ostensible but illegible center of the action."[1]

It is Susan Stringham, who is a provincial New England writer of short stories and is a reader of Pater and Maeterlink, who in the first instance creates the supposition of Milly's doom, which supposition in itself is a creative extension of her fancy that Milly is a princess and that she, Susan, is her confidante. She is a figure not unlike Catherine Sloper's Aunt Penniman, in *Washington Square*, who makes her charge into a heroine of a romance. Early in the novel, seeing Milly seated on an Alpine rock with a view of a valley below, Susan immediately suspects the possibility of a "latent intention... of some betrayed accordance of Milly's caprice with a horrible obsession," but then in the next moment thinks that, after all, Milly will not jump, "for she now saw that the great thing she had brought away was precisely a conviction that the future was not to exist for her princess in the form of any sharp or simple release from the human predicament." In the next moment after that the two women are at supper, it having been agreed between them "that lighted candles at wayside inns, in strange countries, amid mountain scenery, gave the evening meal a peculiar poetry." Milly—casually but more pertinently than might first have been guessed—has said to Susan that yes, she, Susan, bullies her. The whole of the Alpine trip, planned and conducted by Susan, has already been likened by James to a Wagnerian overture. And it is at this point that Milly for the first time in effect elects to participate in the romantic cliché, or perhaps it is the case that in a manner she has been bullied into it. She asks Susan, abruptly, "What was it, that, in New York, on the ninth, when you saw him alone, Dr. Finch said to you?" In fact, as Professor Landau points out, Milly has merely guessed that Susan had seen Dr. Finch, but not without reason, as we might surmise given the kind of companion Susan has turned out to be. And in fact Dr. Finch in New York had not said anything that mattered, only that Milly had had a slight illness, causing only a few hours of anxiety.

What follows is ambiguous both substantively and tonally. Milly might well be teasing the overly-solicitous, overly-imaginative, and overbearing Susan Stringham, or she might have now become co-author, as it were, of her fate, but in any event the actual state of Milly's health is in no way resolved.

It is an important moment. Susan asks Milly, are you feeling unwell? And Milly says, "I don't know—haven't really the least idea. But it might be well to find out." "Are you in trouble—in pain?" Susan asks, and Milly says, "Not the least little bit." "But," she adds ominously and also incongruously, "I sometimes wonder—!" Wonder what?, Susan asks. And the series of Milly's responses is in the same way truncated or evasive and roundabout. Milly says that she wonders "if I shall have much of it," leaving the "it" to be deciphered. What then is the "it"? "Everything," says Milly, "everything I have." What is the matter?, asks Susan. "That's the matter," says Milly, "that I can scarcely bear it," the "it" now being "The power to resist the bliss of what I *have*"—which, whatever is meant (that she feels herself to be excessively happy? and for the sake of a story, her story, wishes to be less so?) is something other than the name of a disease.

By the time—not much later—that Milly in company with Lord Mark stands before the Bronzino portrait of the woman who resembles her, she seems to be confirmed in her attitude composed of bravado and mystery and high melancholy. Here in the misplaced middle of the novel, as James thought it, Milly confronts her likeness with tears in her eyes, and interprets: the face of the woman in the portrait is handsome in sadness, she is a very great personage "only unaccompanied by joy," and "she was dead, dead, dead," whereupon Milly says "I shall never be better than this." The "this" is, again, ambiguous. The scene has the kind of uncertainty that is in the similar portrait episode in *The Sacred Fount*, published the year before *The Wings of the Dove*. Milly's reference might be either to the woman in the portrait, dead and memorialized in an act of great art, or the reference might be to Milly's own situation in this moment, accompanied as she is by a solicitous and obviously interested Lord Mark, at a house party with caring lovely British people, but probably both references come to bear, and in either event the princess has assumed a role which almost demands a pavane.

All of this occurs in the earlier parts of the novel, but in the much that follows there is no other actual confirmation that Milly is really a sick girl. In London she visits the great physician Sir Luke Strett, twice. Her first visit is an affair of ten minutes, for the great physician is in a hurry. What did he say?, asks Kate, and Milly says, gaily, "That I'm not to worry about anything in the world, and that if I'll be a good girl and do exactly what he tells me, he'll take care of me for ever and ever." The doctor had in fact scarcely asked her anything, so Milly herself reports, but, she says, he didn't need "to do anything so stupid"—and it is difficult to escape the conclusion that for James, nearing age sixty when he was writing these lines, the twenty-two-year-old Milly Theale was after all a very young girl, anxious to be a princess, while her estimation of the wisdom of doctors, especially of society doctors of the type of Sir Luke, was not one necessarily shared by James. "But I hope," says Milly of Sir Luke, "he didn't like me too much." And when next she consults Sir Luke, fearing that he would perhaps take advantage "of her being a little romantic to treat her as romantic altogether," he tells her in effect to get a life—the phrase here has a precision. Shall I suffer, Milly asks the doctor, and he says, "Not a bit." "And yet then live?" asks Milly, and he says, "My dear young lady... isn't to 'live' exactly what I'm trying to persuade you to take the trouble to do." If there is diagnosis here at all, it occurs in the couple of lines previous when Milly asks, "So you don't think I'm out of my mind?" and Sir Luke answers, "Perhaps that *is*... all that's the matter."

The pertinent further actions in the novel are not many and are of the same order.

Susan Stringham on her own and of her own volition visits Sir Luke. When Mrs. Lowder asks Susan if the doctor is interested in

Milly's case, she must say that the doctor had said that Milly didn't have a "case," that his only advice was that Milly was to be happy. When near the end Sir Luke appears in Venice, he is on vacation and recommends that Milly be watched by the resident Italian doctor, Tacchini, who spends his time gossiping with Susan because Milly will not see him. Milly by this time has taken to her bed. Sir Luke takes one last look at her, and his final words are, "she's better."

There can be little doubt, finally, that at the very least we are to suspect that Milly wills not only her own death—that much is explicit—but that she has also willed her sense of doom. For whatever complex of motives. For all that Milly is the "dove," and for all that her portrait might be James' tribute, as is often said, to his cousin Minnie Temple, who had died young and with whom he might have been infatuated, the novel considerably exceeds, or, better, undermines the manners of elegy. Nor does it moralize. Milly, the dove, is the victim of a plot, but she is also sly; her final act of charity, leaving the money to Densher, is also an effective act of revenge.

Thus it is that the novel can at the end, rather peripherally in terms of plot but nonetheless illuminatingly, permit a glimpse of overt madness, in the case of Lionel Croy, as a reasonable potentiality within human fate and motives, just as it has made capital of a series of grotesque (no matter if infinitely calculating) brutalities, just as it leads to the suicide of a young girl, the latter being climax to a seductive delusion. The novel proceeds to a level quite beyond merely moral realization.

To see so much now, after the fictions of the nineties, just preceding, is to know that James, in this time of what is usually said to be his greatest achievements, is—still and again—very slippery, and sly, and by so much and certainly not without humor, and that the vision is at once disengaged, dry, bleak, and amused.

As for the other novels of The Major Phase:

In *The Ambassadors,* to look at the nub of the matter, the poor sensitive gentleman Lambert Strether wakens from puritanical proprieties to hanker after the naughty French lady who is the paramour of the boy who is promised to be his stepson. In *The Golden Bowl* the premise of the action is a scarcely disguised settled routine of father-daughter incest. (He will be "peculiarly paternal," she will be "passionately filial," according to the first of James' Notebook entries.) It is the complacency of the relationship between Maggie and Adam, her father, that provokes the action to follow—leading again to another guise of incest when Maggie provides her father with Charlotte as a surrogate for herself, by way of repaying him for providing her with his own surrogate, Prince Amerigo.

James himself is not appalled. A quick clue to his attitude is to be discovered in his apparent fondness for funny names for his characters: in *The Wings of the Dove* Susan Stringham, in *The Ambassadors* the Pococks, Mamie and Jim, and Miss Barrace whose name secures its proper pronunciation by reference to the many "fanny" jokes throughout later James. There are: "Fanny Knocker" in "The Wheel of Time" in 1892–93, "Fanny Hurter" in "The Death of the Lion," and in *The Golden Bowl,* Fanny Assingham, (The rake "Captain Everard" in *In the Cage* will also come to mind.) In *The Golden Bowl* in particular there would not seem to be room for either sly nudges, random anality,[2] or romping good humor, but the crude joke is nonetheless in there and doing work, something like that of the clown in *Othello.*

"Fanny Assingham" is in fact particularly an illumination—just the name, not necessarily the matter of the character—because in all seeming it is an abrupt discrepancy in the tale of incest and betrayals and manipulation. The joke is broad and in fact vulgar, and in its insistent crudeness—buttocks tripled—it becomes a sarcasm which distances the whole of the action, thereby to create space for skeptical scrutiny of the action, that rather than fear or pity or anything else like. And, to stay with *The Golden Bowl,* there is more of the same if not to the same degree of obviousness, with other of the lesser characters who get into the novel: the Lutches (Dotty and Kitty), Mr. Blint, Mr. Gutermann-Seuss. There is a callousness here which is evidenced and created by the fact that in all proper seeming this is no proper place to make fun, wherefore that callousness, amounting to brutality, itself serves to adjust one's idea of the main event, namely the adventures of Maggie and Adam and Charlotte and the Prince. The author who creates the world of this novel is so very knowing that he can be unsympathetic, making broad jokes at the expense of Maggie and Adam and the others, with their trials and desires, and so the novel comes to be at once cruel and comic.

It is matter to the same point, it may be added, that especially in the later fictions James' metaphors tend to an extreme, taking the reader to an awareness of, exactly, the presence of the excessive in the world of the fictions and thus to the probability of compulsions and disruptive energies beyond or beneath the manifest consciousness of the characters in the fictions. James' theatrical experience continues its dividends, with characters allowed their own performances and beyond the author's direct involvement. Characters reveal themselves and specifically the violence within themselves more than they know, and are therefore the victims of themselves. Metaphor might at any moment be a pratfall. Or it is to be said that James betrays his characters in the same moment that they are being portrayed. The Prince says to Maggie (by way of flirtation), "I'm like a chicken, at best, chopped up and smothered in sauce; cooked down as a *crême de volaille,* with half the parts left out." Charlotte says to the Prince, "We hang, essentially, together," and the Prince repeats, "Yes, I see. We hang, essentially, together"—the "essentially" creates the pause which changes the commonplace expression so that the verb is very nearly literalized. These two are *hanging*, as on a gibbet. "A fascination with concealed meanings lurking in well-worn phrases, with dramatic plots which suddenly emerge from cliché metaphors, runs ... through all late Jamesian prose," as Ruth Yeazell has said.[3] Maggie, again, looks upon Charlotte's face "as that of a prisoner looking through bars," and Charlotte a moment later is seen to be an animal at large.

The procedure reaches its utmost irony in "The Beast in the Jungle" in 1903, in which his own literalizing obsession with an extravagant metaphor ruins John Marcher's life. The idea that some kind of special fate awaits him is in itself not more than unreasonable. Anyone might entertain the same. Perhaps most people do, to some degree of self-sustenance. But John Marcher is fascinated by his figuration of the idea. He lives a secret. His life is lived in a jungle and he is in constant terror.

John Marcher, to stay with the same example, is in no way admonitory. It is not the case that the reader out there is advised against, perhaps, egotism. Nor does Marcher stand forth, by way of negative example, as an encouragement to good relationship skills. The tale is not driven by moral consideration, one way or the other. It is not helpful. Nor is the etiology of John Marcher's peculiar condition at issue. We are not led to ask why it is that he cannot or will not, whichever it is, recognize love and life. He is not a subject for diagnosis. James' tale, rather, is at once eloquent, moving, and frightening and risible. We observe Marcher's anfractuosities, of which, the more ironically, he himself is unaware, while he enmeshes himself in his actually quite tawdry metaphor. Meanwhile, the story is tenacious in making him reveal himself, but—by way of one more turn of the screw—not *to* himself except *maybe* at the very end.

T.S. Eliot was right. "James' critical genius," he said, "comes out most tellingly in his mastery over, his baffling escape from Ideas; a mastery and an escape which are perhaps the last test of a superior intelligence. He had a mind so fine that no idea could violate it."[4] To one who would be a novelist James himself had said: "Try to be one of the people on whom nothing is lost!" This was in his essay "The Art of the Novel" in the 1880s, written in response to the critic Walter Besant who had demanded that the novelist reveal "a conscious moral purpose". James would have none of that, and more than that, no "purpose" of any sort is to be discovered in these later works.[5] Rather, James gazed, relentlessly, until people in the world about him—nice people, the usual fry—gave themselves up.

Notes

Preface

i. For extended discussion of James' guilt in the matter of Fenimore's suicide, see Lyndall Gordon, *A Private Life of Henry James: Two Women and His Art* (NY: W.W. Norton, 1999). For response see Michiko Kakutani, "Casting Henry James as an Artistic Cad," *NYTimes* (Apr. 23, 1999); Marcus Klein, "A Portrait of Two Women," *The New Leader* (Jun. 14–28, 1999) 32–33.

ii. For Edel and almost everyone who has followed, this incident is to be seen to be horrific, deeply affecting an already burdened and guilty James. It comes therefore as tonic revision of one's idea of James, in this period and perhaps altogether, to have evidence that he might well have thought the incident to be comic. Sheldon Novick reprints a recollection of James' Venetian friend the Countess Pisani:

> "[James] made a frightfully funny story, I thought, of it, because he said he took all these things out into the laguna and there were a lot of clothes, a lot of her black dresses, so he threw them in the water and they came up like balloons, all around him, and the more he tried to throw them down ... the more they came [up] again, and he was surrounded by them." Sheldon Novick, *Henry James: The Mature Master* (NY: Random House, 2007) 207.

iii. Elizabeth Robins, *Theatre and Friendship: Some Henry James Letters, with a Commentary by Elizabeth Robins* (NY: G.P. Putnam's Sons, 1932) 15–16, 172ff. Leon Edel didn't like Elizabeth Robins. In his account her talent was narrow—she was good at Ibsen but that was the extent of her range—and she was manipulative. She had, said Edel, "a way of disarming those who talked with her—and she talked mainly to the great. She was all attention; she turned on them her lustrous blue eyes; she created an effect of hearing and understanding everything. By means of her quiet intensity she had managed with extraordinary skill, within a week after landing in London, to involve a dozen leading stage figures, among them Beerbohm Tree and Oscar Wilde, in her personal affairs and ambitions. Only Bernard Shaw cut through her pose." She played the part of Claire de Cintré in the London production of *The American* (at James' own request), a part for which, by this account (and also according to reviews) she was all wrong. Leon Edel, *Henry James: The Treacherous Years, 1895–1901* (Philadelphia: J.B. Lippincott, 1969) 34. Robins, on the other hand, had been gratuitously gracious towards Edel, acknowledging the value of Edel's Sorbonne dissertation, published in 1931. "Those interested in Mr. Henry James whether as novelist or dramatist," she wrote, "will, I think, be glad to know of the two volumes of scholarly research and faithful documentation published by M. Léon Edel [as she would have known him], *Henry James: Les Années Dramatiques and The Prefaces of Henry James*"—which volumes, she said, had come to her too late to be the help they might otherwise have been, which is probably the case given the relevant dates.

iv. In Fred Kaplan, *Henry James: The Imagination of Genius* (NY: William Morrow, 1992) 377–78.

v. In Edel, *Treacherous Years*, 84.

vi. F.O. Matthiessen, *Henry James: The Major Phase* (NY: Oxford UP, 1944) 1.

vii. Novick quotes later reflection by Edmund Gosse. On the morning following the hooting at the *Guy Domville* opening, said Gosse, "I was astonished to find [James] perfectly calm; he had slept well and was breakfasting with appetite... and he returned, even in that earliest conversation, to the discussion of the work he had so long neglected." Novick adds in a footnote that, contra Edel, other sources confirm James' immediate and continued cheerfulness. Novick, 220, 555.

viii. Henry James, "To Arthur Christopher Benson," Mar. 11, 1898, *Henry James: A Life in Letters*, ed. Philip Horne (NY: Viking, 1999) 298.

ix. "Gustave Flaubert", *Henry James: Literary Criticism*, vol. II, ed. Leon Edel (Library of America, n.d.) 311.

x. F.W. Dupee, *Henry James* (Garden City: Doubleday, 1951, 1956) 168–69.

xi. *Henry James Letters*, vol. III 1883–1895, ed. Leon Edel (Cambridge: Harvard UP, 1980). "Massive": To Grace Norton, Jun. 30, 1890. p. 296; "Interminable": To William James, Jul. 23, 1890, p. 300; To Robert Louis Stevenson, Jul. 31, 1888, p. 240; To William Dean Howells, Jan. 22, 1895, p. 513.

xii. Cynthia Ozick, "What Henry James Knew," in Ozick, *Fame and Folly* (NY: Knopf, 1996) 103. Henry James, "Ivan Turgeneff (1818–1883)," *Henry James: Literary Criticism*, vol. II, ed. Leon Edel (Library of America, n.d.) 1030, 1032.

xiii. For valuable elaboration see Marcia Jacobson, *Henry James and the Mass Market* (Univ. of Alabama Press, 1983).

xiv. *Henry James Letters*, vol. III, "To Mr. and Mrs. William James," May 28, 1894, p. 482.

xv. Henry James, Letter to A.C. Benson, Jun. 29, 1896, *Letters to A.C. Benson and Auguste Monod* (London: Elkin Mathews & Marrot, 1930) 35.

xvi. *Henry James: Literary Criticism*, vol. II (Library of America, n.d.): "Gustave Flaubert," 1893, p. 301; "George Sand," 1899, p. 768.

xvii. Henry James, "Niagara," 1871, *Portraits of Places* (London: Duckworth, 2001) 317. Henry James, *A Small Boy and Others*, 1913. In *Henry James Autobiography* ed. F.W. Dupee (NY: Criterion Books, 1956) 36.

xviii. Frank Moore Colby, "The Queerness of Henry James," *The Bookman* (Jul. 1902) 396–97. "Matilde Serao," *Henry James: Literary Criticism*, vol. II, 953–67.

xix. *Henry James: Literary Criticism*, vol. I (Library of America, n.d.) "The Art of the Novel," pp. 62–63; "The Future of the Novel," p. 103.

xx. This is to speak to processes of composition, not, here, to the ways in which James' characters come to discover each other, or don't, as the tales (and the plays) move forward. Dialogue in James "bristles," especially in the later fictions, and proceeds by feints and implication, and lies, often enough, but is always intricate with characterization which it progressively illuminates, as will be seen below. But, to the contrary, see: Tzvetan Todorov, "The Verbal Age," *Critical Inquiry* (Winter 1977) 351–71, tr. Patricia Martin Gibby; Sharon Cameron, *Thinking in Henry James* (Univ. of Chicago Press, 1989).

Chapter One

1. Theodora Bosanquet, *Henry James at Work* (London: Hogarth, 1924) 275.

2. Donadio cites a diary kept by one of James' neighbors in Rye. The neighbor

records a casual conversation, in 1907, in which James recalled an incident having to do with the prolonged wailing of a cat on his lawn, which had driven him beyond the limits of endurance, and "under the extreme provocation of its obscene caterwauling," he had killed the animal, the act followed by nausea and collapse. Donadio goes on to say that the startling anecdote reveals a range of emotions and responses not usually associated with James. Stephen Donadio, *Nietzsche, Henry James, and the Artistic Will* (NY: Oxford UP, 1978) 1, 4. Bosanquet, 244. When in 1905 James lectured in the United States, audiences were surprised by the size of the man. The reporter for the *New York Sun,* having met him at the boat, found James to be "immensely robust" and "anything but the man one is inclined to fancy from reading his delicate tales." Others, in his audiences, noted his "tremendous power," his "powerful" head, his "piercing" eyes. Marie P. Harris, "Henry James, Lecturer," *American Literature* 3 (1951) 304.

3. Henry James, To A.C. Benson, Jun. 29, 1896, *Letters to A.C. Benson and Auguste Monod* (London: Elkin Mathews & Marrot, 1930) 35.

4. Edmund Wilson, "The Ambiguity of Henry James," 1934–1938, in Wilson, *The Triple Thinkers* (NY: Oxford UP, 1948) 109.

5. Alice James, To William James, Oct. 13, 1867, *The Death and Letters of Alice James,* ed. Ruth Bernard Yeazell (Berkeley & Los Angeles: Univ. of California Press, 1981) 52.

6. Frank Moore Colby, "The Queerness of Henry James," *The Bookman* (Jul. 1902) 396–97. Henry James,"To Robert Louis Stevenson," Feb. 17, 1893, *Henry James Letters,* vol. 3, 1883–1895, ed. Leon Edel (Cambridge: Harvard UP, 1980) 406.

7. Henry James, "To William Dean Howells," Feb. 21, 1884, *Letters,* vol. 3, p. 28.

8. *Ibid.*

9. Henry James, "To William James," Jan. 9, 1895; "To Morton Fullerton," Jan. 9, 1895, *Letters,* vol. 3, pp. 509–10.

10. Preface to vol. XII, in *The Art of the Novel: Critical Prefaces by Henry James,* ed. R.P. Blackmur (NY: Charles Scribner's Sons, 1934) 228.

11. In *The Question of Henry James,* ed. F.W. Dupee (London: Allan Wingate, n.d.): Stuart Sherman, "The Aesthetic Idealism of Henry James," 1917, p. 91; Joseph Warren Beach, "The Figure in the Carpet," 1918, p. 116; Ford Madox Ford, "The Old Man," 1932, pp. 66, 70; R.P. Blackmur, "In the Country of the Blue," 1943, pp. 213–14.

12. Maxwell Geismar, *Henry James and the Jacobites* (Boston: Houghton Mifflin, 1963) 137–39.

13. James Thurber, "A Final Note on Chanda Bell," *The New Yorker* Oct. 15, 1949; repr. *James Thurber: Writings and Drawings,* ed. Garrison Keillor (NY: Library of America, 1996) 782–83.

14. Bosanquet, 271–72.

15. André Gide, letter to Charles Du Bos, in *The Question of Henry James,* 258.

Chapter Two

1. Henry James, to Mrs. Hugh Bell, Dec. 14, 1893; to Elizabeth Robins, Dec. 7, 1893. *Theatre and Friendship: Some Henry James Letters,* ed. and commentary

Elizabeth Robins (New York: G.P. Putnam's Sons, 1932) 142, 143.

2. In *Henry James: The Contemporary Reviews*, ed. Kevin J. Hayes (Cambridge: Cambridge UP, 1996), see *New York Tribune*, Sept. 27, 1896, p. 245; *Athenaeum*, Oct. 31, 1896, p. 248; *Saturday Review*, Oct. 31, 1896, p. 249; *Bookman*, Dec. 4, 1896, p. 256. For discussion of form in the novels of the late nineties as affected by the lessons of the drama see especially, among many, Michael Egan, *Henry James: The Ibsen Years* (London: Vision Press, 1972); Walter Isle, *Experiments in Form: Henry James' Novels, 1896–1901* (Cambridge: Harvard UP, 1968); Sheldon Novick, "Henry James on Stage," *Henry James on Stage and Screen*, ed. John Bradley (NY: Palgrave, 2000) 18–19. In 1908 James converted *The Other House* back into a play.

3. "John Gabriel Borkman," *Henry James: The Scenic Art: Notes on Acting & the Drama*, ed. Allan Wade (New Brunswick: Rutgers UP, 1948) 293.

4. Levy: "Except for *The Reprobate* and *Guy Domville*, the plays are inescapably trivial." Leo B. Levy, *Versions of Melodrama: A Study of the Fiction and Drama of Henry James, 1865–1897* (Berkeley: Univ. of California Press, 1957) 70. Carlson: "The best of James' plays remain minor works by a major author." Susan Carlson, *Women of Grace: James' Plays and the Comedy of Manners* (Ann Arbor: UMI Research Press, 1985) xiii. Edel: "His plays became the prisoners of his theories"; "he had sought largely to be entertaining on a superficial level." Leon Edel, "Henry James: The Dramatic Years," *The Complete Plays of Henry James*, ed. Leon Edel (New York: Oxford UP, 1990) 36, 67.

5. Jacques Barzun, "Henry James, Melodramatist," *The Question of Henry James*, ed. F.W. Dupee (London: Allan Wingate, 1947) 268.

6. George Bernard Shaw, "Two New Plays," *Dramatic Opinions and Essays with an Apology by Bernard Shaw* vol. I (Brentano, 1907) 7–14.

7. See *Henry James: The Scenic Art: Notes on Acting & Drama, 1872–1901*, ed. Allan Wade (New Brunswick: Rutgers UP, 1948) 256.

8. Robins, 76.

9. "On the Occasion of Hedda Gabler," *Scenic Art*, 247.

10. Leon Edel, *Henry James: The Treacherous Years, 1895–1900* (Philadelphia: J.B. Lippincott, 1969) 167; Jean Frantz Blackall, "The Experimental Period," *A Companion to Henry James Studies*, ed. Daniel Mark Fogel (Westport: Greenwood Press, 1993) 171–72.

11. Kevin J. Hayes, "Introduction," *Henry James: The Contemporary Reviews* (Cambridge: Cambridge UP, 1996), xvi. Henry James, "to Clement K. Shorter," Feb. 24, 1896, Feb. 26, 1896, *Henry James Letters* , vol. 4, 1895–1916, ed. Leon Edel (Cambridge: Harvard UP, 1984) 30–31.

12. See *Complete Plays of Henry James*, ed. Edel, p. 720; *Theatre and Friendship*, ed. Robins, p. 98.

13. Henry James, "To John St. Loe Strachey," May 6, 1896, *Henry James: A Life in Letters*, ed. Philip Horne (New York: Viking, 1999) 291.

14. One of the few extensive, if implied, explorations of *The Other House* is in *Celine et Julie vont en bateau (Celine and Julie Go Boating)*, a 1974 film directed by Jacques Rivette, which conflates the novel with another mostly overlooked tale, James' "The Romance of Certain Old Clothes." For Rivette, James' continuous ironies become license for equal, alternate, and conflicting ideas of the truth of things. In the

film the two young women share a dream, or fantasy, in which they repeatedly visit a house where they find a young widower who has vowed never to marry, his small daughter, two women who pursue him, and a nurse. We never learn which of the women he fancies. In successive visits, the child is several times murdered, sometimes, seemingly, by the character who stands in for Rose, sometimes by the character who stands in for Jean, and often by the nurse, who has a drinking problem, with added implication that the character who stands in for Tony is complicit. The film is, if not quite a comedy, at least good-humored. For analysis see David Van Leer, "Frank and Jim Go Boating: Henry James and the French New Wave," *Henry James on Stage and Screen*, ed. John R. Bradley (New York: Palgrave, 2000) 84–102.

15. Nina Baym, "Fleda Vetch and the Plot of *The Spoils of Poynton*," *PMLA* lxxxiv (Jan. 1969) 102–11.

16. Additionally, in an essay of March 1888 James had been discussing the somewhat similar transaction in inheritance in Maupassant's *L'Héritage*. A young man and his wife, after the (supposed) death of the young man's mother, attempt to remove her furniture before the arrival of other claimants. "The story is a model of narration," said James, "but it leaves our poor average humanity dangling like a beaten rag." Henry James, "Guy de Maupassant," *Fortnightly Review* Mar. 1888; repr. *Henry James: Literary Criticism*, vol. 2, ed. Leon Edel (New York: The Library of America, 1984) 541–42.

17. Charlotte Perkins Gilmans story "The Yellow Wallpaper" had been published in 1892 in *The New England Magazine*, was widely known, and would later be anthologized by William Dean Howells. It would not be unlikely that James would have read that terrifying story and, if he did, that he would have read it with deliberate obliqueness, as a story about the effect of interior decoration on a sensitive soul.

18. Henry James, To Horace Elisha Scudder, Mar. 3, 1896. *Henry James: A Life in Letters*, ed. Philip Horne (New York: Viking, 1999) 289.

19. Fred G. See, "Henry James and the Art of Possession," *American Realism: New Essays*, ed. Eric J. Sundquist (Baltimore: Johns Hopkins UP, 1982) 119–37.

20. Anne Coon, "Widows, Spinsters and Lovers: The Controlling Female Figure in the Fiction of Henry James," diss., SUNY/Buffalo, 1986.

Chapter Three

1. Henry James, "Preface" to vol. XI of the New York Edition, in R.P. Blackmur, *The Art of the Novel* (NY: Charles Scribner's, 1934) 154ff.

2. For discussion of the social position of the telegraph girl in late-nineteenth-century London and for contemporary comment suggesting that telegraph girls were likely to be prostitutes, see Jill Galvan, "Class Ghosting 'In the Cage,'" *The Henry James Review* 22.3 (2001) 297–98.

3. See Andrew J. Moody, "'The Harmless Pleasure of Knowing' Privacy in the Telegraph Office and Henry James' 'In the Cage,'" *The Henry James Review* 16.1 (1995) 53–65; Eric Savoy, "In the Cage and the Queer Effects of Gay History," *Novel* 28.3 (Spring 1995) 284–307. Both discuss the extent to which upper-class customers in the late nineteenth century were aware of a threat of being blackmailed by telegraph workers.

4. Leon Edel, *Henry James: The Treacherous Years, 1895–1900* (Philadelphia: J.B. Lippincott, 1969) 249.

5. For elaborated speculation regarding the homoerotic elements of the novel see John Carlos Rowe, "Working at Gender: *In the Cage*," *Questioning the Master: Gender and Sexuality in Henry James' Writings*, ed. Peggy McCormack (Newark: Univ. of Delaware Press, 2000) 86–103. See also, Savoy.

6. Henry James, "To Paul Bourget," Aug. 19, 1898, *Henry James: A Life in Letters*, ed. Philip Horne (New York: Viking, 1999) 306.

7. Henry James, "Guy de Maupassant," in *Henry James: Literary Criticism*, vol. II, ed. Leon Edel (The Library of America, 1984) 536.

8. Edna Kenton directed attention to the passage in James' "The Lesson of Balzac" in which (quoting Taine) James remarked of Balzac's treatment of a character that, unlike Thackeray with his Becky Sharp, Balzac had left his character free, providing her with "the long rope, for her acting herself out, that her creator's participation in her reality assures her." Edna Kenton, "Henry James to the Ruminant Reader: The Turn of the Screw," *The Arts* VI (Nov. 1924), repr. *A Casebook on Henry James' "The Turn of the Screw"*, ed. Gereald Willen (NY: Thomas Crowell, 1960) 102–14.

9. In 1995, writing what had been intended to be a critical survey, the late Wayne Booth said that he had counted more than five hundred titles of books and articles about *The Turn of the Screw*, in English alone, before he had got too bored to go on. In *Henry James: The Turn of the Screw: Case Studies in Contemporary Criticism*, ed. Peter G. Beidler (Boston: St. Martin's Press, 1995) 163. Beidler presents convenient summary of the critical history. Virtually every book and article among the hundreds of them dealing with the little novel, he writes, deals at least indirectly with the question of whether or not the ghosts are real or are the governess' hallucinatory projections, with, in recent years, the emergence of criticism which in one way or another maintains the possibility of maintaining both conjectures at once. According to seemingly general consent, the principal document in support of this latter conjecture is Shoshana Felman. Where Felman' essay is not devoted to Lacanian revision of Freud, it addresses itself to revision of the supposedly strict "Freudian" reading of the novel, chiefly that of Edmund Wilson (in 1934, subsequently revised), maintaining that "the mystification" in the novel is "a game, a joke" in which the reader is in the same position as the governess, becoming an interpreter of signs. "Entering into the game," says Felman, "we ourselves become fair game for the very 'joke' of meaning. The joke is that, by meaning, everyone is fooled. Shoshana Felman, "Turning the Screw of Interpretation," ed. Felman, *Literature and Psychoanalysis: The Question of Reading Otherwise* (Baltimore: Johns Hopkins Press, 1982) 94–207.

10. The touchstone essay for the moral reading is Robert Heilman, "The Turn of the Screw as Poem," *The University of Kansas City Review* XIV (Summer 1948) 277–89, repr. *A Casebook on Henry James' "The Turn of the Screw"*, ed. Gerald Willen (NY: Thomas Crowell, 1960) 174–88. Heilman goes beyond moral interpretation to discover specifically Christian associations in the tale. The governess is a savior figure, using words like "atonement" and speaking of herself as an "expiatory victim".

11. Henry James, "Preface" to vol. XII of the New York Edition, *The Art of the Novel*, 169ff.

12. Henry James, "To Dr. Waldstein," Oct. 21, 1898; "To H.G. Wells," Dec. 9, 1898; "To Frederic William Henry Myers," Dec. 19, 1898, *Henry James Letters*, vol. 4, 1895–1916, ed. Leon Edel (Cambridge: Harvard UP, 1984) 84, 85–87, 87–88. Frederic Myers was a founding member of the Society for Psychical Research. See Peter G. Beidler, letter, *PMLA* 100 (1985) 96–97.

13. Millicent Bell, "Class, Sex, and the Victorian Governess: James' *The Turn of*

the Screw," *New Essays on Daisy Miller and The Turn of the Screw,* ed. Vivian R. Pollak (Cambridge: Cambridge UP, 1993) 91–119.

14. Steven Marcus, *The Other Victorians: A Study of Sexuality and Pornography in Mid-Nineteenth-Century England* (NY: Basic Books, 1966) 268.

15. Virginia Woolf, "Henry James' Ghost Stories," *TLS* (Dec. 22, 1921). *Collected Essays by Virginia Woof,* vol. I (London: Hogarth Press, 1966) 292.

16. But see Joyce Carol Oates, "Accursed Inhabitants of the House of Bly," *Haunted: Tales of the Grotesque* (NY: Dutton, 1994) 254–83. In Oates' lovely amusette Quint is a randy but good-willed fellow, understanding but embarrassed by Miles' affection, while Jessel, who in life had been a sweetly modest girl and impeccably groomed, is embarrassed by her current state.

17. See J.R. deS. Honey, *Tom Brown's Universe: The Development of the English Public School in the Nineteenth Century* (NY: Quadrangel/NYTimes, 1977). Honey writes: "...in the course of the nineteenth century the terms vice, immorality, wickedness, corruption, evil and sin with which public-school headmasters [said] that their schools would infect their pupils, together changed their connotation. In the first half of the century the emphasis was on 'rebelliousness'. Only by around 1860 did a mainly sexual connotation become common, and this reflected in the first instance fears about masturbation rather than homosexuality, which were not to intrude until after about 1880, and whose dominance by the end of the century involved a complete reversal of the early Victorian attitude to schoolboy friendships." p. 194. See also James R. Kincaid, *Child-Loving: The Erotic Child and Victorian Culture* (NY: Routledge, 1992).

18. "To H.G. Wells," op. cit.

Chapter Four

1. *Manchester Guardian* Sept. 1897; *Spectator* Oct. 30, 1897. Both in Kevin J. Hayes, ed. *Henry James: The Contemporary Reviews* (Cambridge: Cambridge UP, 1996). F.R. Leavis read the novel as social comedy, Marius Bewley as Jacobean comedy. Both in Marius Bewley, *The Complex Fate: Hawthorne, Henry James and Some Other American Writers* (London: Chatto and Windus, 1952) 96–144. Martha Banta agrees with Bewley. Martha Banta, "The Quality of Experience in *What Maisie Knew,*" *The New England Quarterly* Dec. 1969: 483–510. For forefronting of the character of the brown "Countess" in the novel, see Toni Morrison, *Playing in the Dark: Whiteness and the Literary Imagination* (NY: Random House, 1992) and response by Walter Benn Michaels, "Jim Crow Henry James?", *The Henry James Review* 16.3 (1995) 286–91. For readings of the novel as an account of child-rearing, see Muriel G. Shine, *The Fictional Children of Henry James* (Chapel Hill: Univ. of North Carolina, 1968) 109–26; Merla Wolk, "Narration and Nurture in *What Maisie Knew,*" *The Henry James Review* 4 (1982–1983) 196–206; Nicola Nixon, "Texts and the Single Girl: James' Novels of the Late 1890s," diss., Univ. of Toronto, 1993, 76–122 (although the emphasis here is a feminist one). For account of Burnett's gift, see Ann Thwaite, *Waiting for the Party: The Life of Frances Hodgson Burnett, 1849–1924* (NY: Scribner's, 1974) 229. For the corrupt Maisie, see Harris W. Wilson, "What Did Maisie Know?" *College English* 17 (1955–1956) 279–82, and especially Sally Sears, *The Negative Imagination: Form and Perspective in the Novels of Henry James* (Ithaca: Cornell UP, 1968) 18–34.

2. Bewley, p. 138.

3. Following a dinner with the Jameses, Louisa May wrote in her diary: "Henry Jr... was very friendly. Being a literary youth he gave me advice, as if he had been eighty, and I a girl.... My curly crop made me look young, though thirty-one." In Leon Edel, *Henry James: The Untried Years: 1843–1870* (Philadelphia: Lippincott, 1953) 213.

4. Henry James rev. Adeline Dutton Whitney, *The Gayworthys: A Story of Threads and Thrums, North American Review* (Oct. 1865); rev. Elizabeth Rundle Charles, *Hearthstone Series, The Nation* (Sept. 14, 1865); rev. Elizabeth Rundle Charles, *Winifred Bertram, The Nation* (Feb. 1, 1866), all repr. *Henry James: Literary Criticism*, vol. 1, ed. Leon Edel (The Library of America, 1984) 637, 826, 831–2. For anecdotes regarding James' personal awkwardness with children, see Simon Nowell-Smith, *The Legend of the Master* (NY: Scribner's, 1948) 90–91. Mrs. Joseph Conrad, for instance: "Our small boy... hated to be nursed by strangers. Mr. Henry James at once took him on his knee and forgot his existence, now and then giving him an absent-minded squeeze while talking to Conrad."

5. James wrote "The Future of the Novel" in autumn 1899. The previous August while he had been engaged in trying to finance the purchase of Lamb House, in a letter to William and Alice James he had confessed to his feeling "the bitterness of humiliation" as he regarded the market-place success of such writers as F. Marian Crawford and Hodgson Burnett. In 1833 he had reviewed one of Burnett's plays, *Esmeralda*, produced in London as *Young Folks' Ways*, suggesting that it signaled the depth to which London theater had sunk. James' letters to Burnett, whom he had known in London and then later as his neighbor, tend to an elegance elevated into irony—as this one, to thank Burnett for the gift of a basket of fruit:

> "Noblest of Neighbours and Most Heavenly of Women!—"
>
> "Your gorgeous, glorious gift shook Lamb House to its foundations an hour or two ago—but that agitated structure, with the light of purpose rapidly kindling its eye, recuperates even as I write, with a sense of futility, under the circumstances of a mere economical swoon.... It's too magnificent—we don't deserve the quarter (another peach, please—yes it is the 7th—and one more fig—it is I can't deny it—the 19th!) Well, I envy you the power to make a poor, decent body so happy—and still more, so proud." Etc.
> In Thwaite, 78–9, 184–5.

6. See Marcia Jacobson, "What Maisie Knew," in Jacobson, *Henry James and the Mass Market* (Univ. of Alabama: Univ. of Alabama Press, 1983) 100–20.

7. Quentin Anderson, *The Imperial Self* (NY: Vintage, 1971) 209–13.

8. Entry for Dec. 22, 1895. *The Complete Notebooks of Henry James,* ed. Leon Edel and Lyall H. Powers (NY: Oxford UP, 1987) 147–48.

9. Ruth Bernard Yeazell, *Language and Knowledge in the Late Novels of Henry James* (Chicago: Univ. of Chicago Press, 1976) 31.

10. F.W. Dupee, *Henry James* (Garden City: Doubleday Anchor Books, 1956) 168. On the "language of violence" in *Maisie* see also Dan McCall, "What Maisie Saw," *The Henry James Review* 16.1 (1995) 48–52.

11. Juliet Mitchell, "*What Maisie Knew*: Portrait of the Artist as a Young Girl," in John Goode, ed., *The Air of Reality: New Essays on Henry James* (London: Methuen, 1972) 184–87.

12. James does not specify, but in his extensive Notebook entry for Dec. 22,

1895, where he writes a detailed outline for the proposed ten-thousand-word story, he says that it will be in his Chapter Five that "the second wife" will have her second meeting with the character who will become Sir Claude, at which time Maisie will be ten, and this meeting will occur after Maisie has been installed in the nursery at Ida's house for a year.

13. Much of the critical literature is devoted to the manner and end of Maisie's learning. See for example Walter Isle: Maisie's "real education, her development as an individual, is marked by her growing ability to distinguish between real and unreal, between true and false.... She moves from an age of mere sensation, of simple, unrelated perceptions and feelings to one of complexity of implication and interrelationship of meaning." Walter Isle, *Experiments in Form: Henry James' Novels, 1896–1901* (Cambridge: Harvard UP, 1968) 154–55. Randall Craig: Maisie's practical education "must take place in spite of her teachers and consists primarily of learning 'to read' the text of her life." Randall Craig, "Reading the Unspoken into the Spoken: Interpreting *What Maisie Knew*," *The Henry James Review* 2 (1980–1981) 204. Dennis Foster: "Lacan's paradigm for the relation of subject to the other provides an approach to the book that suggests why Maisie is supposed to know and to be what she seems to be for the adults.... Maisie need not know dark truths... so long as she appears to satisfy the formal conditions of knowing, so long as she speaks the language of knowing." Dennis Foster, "Maisie Supposed to Know: Amo(u)ral Analysis," *The Henry James Review* 5 (Spring 1984) 207. Juliet Mitchell: "For the mature Maisie, and in this precisely does her maturity consist, seeing *is* knowing, vision and knowledge are one." Mitchell, p. 168. Marius Bewley: "... the novel is the most magnificent portrayal in the language of the unfolding discretionary powers of a human being." Bewley, p. 111. And finally Sasha Brookes: the novel can be considered and interpreted in terms of W. Bion's theory of thinking, and especially his concepts of K and –K and the container/contained relationship. Sasha Brookes, "It seemed to have to do with something else...: Henry James' *What Maisie Knew* and Bion's theory of thinking," *International Journal of Psychoanalysis* 83.2 (Apr. 2002) 419–31.

14. James' concerns in the Prefaces are by no means necessarily those that went into the composing of his fictions. (For discussion see Nina Baym, "Fleda Vetch and the Plot of *The Spoils of Poynton*," *PMLA* lxxxiv (Jan. 1969) 102–11. There is at least one indication that James was less than fully attentive in his rereading of *Maisie.* Calling special attention, in the Preface, to the scene where Maisie meets Beale, James says—not directly but clearly enough—that the "unattractive lady" with Beale is "Mrs. Cuddon". In the text the identity of the lady is matter for brief discussion. Maisie says that she is sure that she will like Beale's companion, whom she has glimpsed. "I thought she was Mrs. Cuddon," she says, and Beale says "You mean my wife did? My dear child, my wife's a damned fool!"—which does leave open the possibility that really she is Mrs. Cuddon, but lacking anything further, Beale's lie, if it is that, would be pointless.

15. A correspondent, Mrs. John Bancroft, had asked James what had become of Maisie. James said that he did not know: "... the case seems to me to illustrate the marked difference between that which is in old-fashioned parlance a 'story' and that which has the distinctive characteristics of what I call a Subject." A story, he said, doesn't end with the book, but a Subject does. Henry James, "To Mrs. John Chandler Bancroft," Mar. 21, 1898, *Henry James: A Life in Letters*, ed Philip Horne (New York: Viking, 1999) 299–300.

Chapter Five

1. Contemporary with James' conception and writing of *The Awkward Age*,

newspapers and journals were discussing the phenomenon of the modern daughter who sought emancipation from Victorian codes of innocence. James' friend Blanche Crackanthorpe was the author of one series of articles on the subject. See particularly Hamlin L. Hill, Jr., "'The Revolt of the Daughters' A Suggested Source for *The Awkward Age*," *Notes and Queries* (Sept. 1961) 347–49. See also Nicola Nixon, "Texts and the Single Girl: James' Novels of the Late 1890s," diss., Univ. of Toronto, 1993, 82–90. For James, however, the theme of the independent-minded young woman, considered according to various perspectives, sometimes comic, sometimes dire, had been virtually stock-in-trade since the beginning.

2. Other examples include: *The Indianapolis News*: "We do not want to scare anyone away from what might prove an entertaining study, but it is only fair to say that that inextricable confusion in which Mr. Henry James' redundancy of language and ideas has wrapped his later works of fiction has never been worse confounded than in [*The Awkward Age*]." *The Literary World*, with some astuteness lurking within the exasperation, said: "Oh, Mr. Henry James, why do you write like that? You...drain all the blood and warmth and goodness out of people.... Is this really the way you see life?" *The Nation*: "[Mr. James has] now arrived at a point of intellectual remoteness from the flesh where he regards men and women with almost as slight reference to their bodies as if he were a philosopher contending that nothing is real except what cannot be perceived by the senses." *The Manchester Guardian* scratched its head: "To us it seems enigma, the very quintessence of riddle; and yet one has the sense that there is an answer...that behind and beneath all this there is a very definite meaning, and a purpose that is quite clear to the author's understanding.... It is amazing in its way, a triumphant exercise in the art of hinting, but it breeds in the mind of the reader a wild desire to take a chapter or two of 'Rob Roy' afterwards with a view to correcting the subtlety." *Chcago Tribune*: "The volume is made up entirely of the talk of a certain London society set of which the author had made a study, and there is not enough action in the whole to move a butterfly's wing." *Bookman, Indianapolis News, Manchester Guardian, Pall Mall Gazette* in Kevin J. Hayes, ed. *Henry James: The Contemporary Reviews* (Cambridge: Cambridge UP, 1996); *Literary World, Nation, Spectator* in Roger Gard, ed. Henry James: *The Critical Heritage* (London: Routledge & Kegan Paul, 1968).

3. W.D. Howells, "Mr. Henry James' Later Work," 1903, *The Question of Henry James A Collection of Critical Essays*, ed. F.W. Dupee (London: Allan Wingate, n.d.) 26–39.

4. Henry James, "To William Dean Howells," Sep. 25, 1899; "To Henrietta Reubell," Nov. 12, 1899, *Henry James: A Life in Letters*, ed. Philip Horne (NY: Viking, 1999) 324–27, 329–30.

5. *A Gallic Girl (Le marriage de Chiffon)* was published in the United States in 1895; *Those Good Normans* appeared in 1896, as did *Bijou's Courtships: A Study in Pink; Miquette's First Dinner Party* appeared in 1898. Dialogue novels, moreover, as Marcia Jacobson has pointed out, were extensively present during the 1890s, sometimes set up as playbooks, sometimes like conventional novels. Jacobson speculates that indeed *Harper's Weekly* might have been influenced to take *The Awkward Age* just because of an established idea that witty dialogue was appropriate to popular journalism. Marcia Jacobson, *Henry James and the Mass Market* (Univ. of Alabama Press, 1983) 122ff. James certainly knew and had read the immensely popular dialogue novel *Dodo: A Detail of the Day*, published in 1893 by E.F. Benson. James had read the novel in manuscript. Benson was one of the sons of his friend the Archbishop of Canterbury, Edward White Benson. Benson's mother had sent the hand-written manuscript to James for advice. James replied that the novel fell short of his ideal of literary ferocity. See Geoffrey Palmer & Noel Lloyd, *E.F. Benson As He Was*

(Luton Beds: Lennard Publishing, 1988). The two novels, *Dodo* and *The Awkward Age*, are in some ways similar. Both confine themselves to a social circle notable for its talk, and much of the talk, moreover, is about boredom, which is to be dreaded. Dodo, the heroine of her novel, while younger than Mrs. Brookenham, is presented as being as independent, dramatic, unscrupulous, and as fascinating to her immediate audience as is James' character.

6. Willa Z. Silverman, *The Notorious Life of Gyp: Right-Wing Anarchist in Fin-de-Siècle France* (NY: Oxford UP, 1995) 61–62. Testifying at a trial in 1900, asked her profession, Gyp replied, "Anti-Semite". Silverman, 158.

7. In Maxwell Geismar, *Henry James and the Jacobites* (Boston: Houghton Mifflin, 1963) 169.

8. Edmund Wilson, "The Ambiguity of Henry James," 1934–1938, Wilson, *The Triple Thinkers* (NY: Oxford UP, 1948) 110. F.O. Matthiessen, "The Ambassadors," in *The Question of Henry James: A Collection of Critical Essays*, ed. F.W. Dupee (London: Allan Wingate, n.d.) 227; R.P. Blackmur, *Studies in Henry James* (NY: New Directions, 1983), 112; Ezra Pound, "Henry James," *Literary Essays of Ezra Pound*, ed. T.S. Eliot (1935; NY: New Directions, 1968) 323.

In recent years the novel has been variously revalued. See especially F.W. Dupee, who in 1951 was agreeing with James that the portrayal of Mrs. Brookenham was the best thing he had ever done, and who finds that Mrs. Brookenham's salon is "the human medium, the source of amiability, proportion, beauty, wit." Jean Frantz Blackall, in 1981, is of much the same mind, writing in response to a critic who had maintained that the novel was without significance and the characters without motivation. F.W. Dupee, *Henry James* (1951; Garden City: Doubleday, 1956) 170–75; Jean Frantz Blackall, "The Case for Mrs. Brookenham," *Henry James Review* (Spring 1981) 155–61. Cynthia Ozick thinks the novel to be Kafka-esque, that it "vibrates with cognitions that are ultimately not submissive to their creator," that the novel "knows far more than its author knew, and holds more secrets of panic, shame, helplessness, and chaos than James could candidly face." Cynthia Ozick, "What Henry James Knew," in Cynthia Ozick, *Fame and Folly* (NY: Knopf, 1996) 101–28. Tzvetan Todorov semantically says of *The Awkward Age* that it "is one of the most important novels of our time." His basis for saying so is that the characters seem usually not to know what each of them is saying to each other; "obliquity has reached such a degree that it is no longer obliquity; the connecting lines between words and things are not merely loose or tangled—they have been cut," and therefore the novel is to be seen as exploring "a path opened by language but unknown to literature." The subject of the novel "is about what it is to talk." (To which it may be objected, in wonder, that the characters in the novel do after all seem to be very much attuned to what they are saying each to each, and to very subtle nuance within.) Tzvetan Todorov, "The Verbal Age, A *Critical Inquiry* (Winter 1977) 351–71, tr. Patricia Martin Gibby.

9. The serial ran for fourteen issues, Oct. 1, 1898 to Jan. 7, 1899. On Dec. 9, 1898, James was writing to H.G. Wells that he had been "so ridden ... by the black care of an unfinished and *running* (galloping, leaping and bounding) serial that parting with a day has been like parting with a pound of flesh." On the 19th he was writing to Frederic William Henry Myers saying that he had just now finished the novel, that he has been "intensely & anxiously busy, finishing, under pressure, a long job that had from almost the first—I mean long before I had reached the end—begun to be (loathsome name & fact!) 'serialized'—so that the printers were at my heels ...." To H.G. Wells, Dec. 9, 1898, in Edel, *Letters*, vol. IV, p. 86; To Frederic William Henry Myers, Dec. 19, 1898, in Horne, *Letters*, pp. 313–14.

10. Mrs. Brookenham is said also to have two younger children. James

mentions the fact once, and then seems to have forgotten.

11. In the single Notebook entry for the novel, dated 1895, while his main concern was with the effect of the non-marrying girl upon the mother's society, at the end James speculated on the character of the girl herself. She would be conscious and aware. "I am modern," she would say, "I'm not a *jeune fille*." That, as it turned out, seems to have been an idea that he had to recover. When Nanda makes her first appearance in the novel, in Book III, about a third of the way through, she is oddly a little girl. Mitchy asks her to make tea. "I can make tea beautifully," she says. "Mother showed me how this morning." She usually has her tea upstairs, in a cup, with a piece of bread-and-butter, "because I'm so young." Mitchy takes three lumps of sugar, and she takes five. On the other hand, and more interestingly, James might have wanted from the beginning to present a Nanda who acts the little girl with mocking intent beyond the understanding of Mitchy and the others. In any event, a moment later, in response to something addressed to her, she says knowingly that "Yes, I've heard.... It' supposed to be awful, my knowing Tishy—quite too awful."

12. There is no idea of a Mr. Longdon in James' Notebook entry. He is fresh invention and as was pointed out by Seamus Cooney many years ago, in the crucial matter of Longdon's age, James was initially uncertain. Longdon must have been in his twenties when he proposed to Lady Julia. She had rejected him and married someone else, and had a daughter—it would not have been less than a year later. The daughter is now forty-one years old. Longdon cannot therefore be less than sixty-two years old, and likely about sixty-five. But the matter is elided in the very first pages of the novel, where James says that Longdon will not see fifty-five again, meaning by clear implication that he is fifty-six. By making Longdon the few years younger, James makes what happens later to be more likely. Cooney points out that there is a similar problem with Vanderbank's age. Seamus Cooney, "Awkward Ages in *The Awkward Age*," *Modern Language Notes* 75 (Mar. 1960) 208–09.

Chapter Six

1. Henry James, "To Mrs. Humphrey Ward," Mar. 15, 1901, *Henry James Letters*, vol. 4, 1895–1916, ed. Leon Edel (Cambridge: Harvard UP, 1984) 186.

2. Since even more stringently than in *The Awkward Age* James has here allowed himself no "going behind," and since in its entirety the novel is a monologue, it is possible to think that the novel is doubly fictional, that it is *entirely* a fiction—an untruthful narrative of untruths—which is the creation of the narrator. But James clearly intended otherwise. The narrator records both event and dialogue with others, which sometime stimulate him, sometime provoke him, and sometime, according to his own testimony, contradict his own presented perceptions. That first of all. Secondly, the other characters in the novel pursue actions and have fates which for the most part have nothing to do with the narrator, and which he typically misunderstands. That is a piece of the joke. And finally, in the letter to Mrs. Ward which contains his one discussion of the novel, James would say: "As I give but the phantasmagoric, I have, for clearness, to make it *evidential*," and he proceeds to explain how certain of the characters, excluding the narrator, bear on other characters. Henry James, "To Mrs. Humphrey Ward". Jean Frantz Blackall is certainly right in saying that "James' joke was meant to depend on the reader's gradually being able to see through the narrator.... [I]t seems unlikely that he meant to overwhelm the reader with insurmountable ambiguities because the joke depends upon the reader's attaining a dual perspective on the scene he witnesses." Jean Frantz Blackall, *Jamesian Ambiguity and The Sacred Fount* (Ithaca: Cornell UP, 1965) 10–12.

3. Harry Thurston Peck in *Henry James: The Critical Heritage,* ed. Roger Gard (London: Routledge & Kegan Paul, 1968) 308. *Athenaeum and Current Literature* in *Henry James: The Contemporary Reviews,* ed. Kevin J. Hayes (Cambridge: Cambridge UP, 1996) 346, 353. Adams and Hay in Leon Edel, *Henry James: The Treacherous Years: 1895–1901* (Philadelphia: J.B. Lippincott, 1960) 339. Hay to his daughter in George Monteiro, *Henry James and John Hay: The Record of a Friendship* (Providence: Brown UP, 1965) 37. Wharton quoted in Philip Horne, *Henry James: A Life in Letters* (New York: Viking, 1999) 350. William Dean Howells, "Mr. Henry James' Later Work (1903) in *The Question of Henry James,* ed. F.W. Dupee (London: Allan Wingate, n.d.) 37.

4. In Leon Edel, "An Introductory Essay," *The Sacred Fount* (NY: Grove Press, 1953) vi–vii.

5. This novel too, like *Maisie* and *The Awkward Age,* outgrew itself, apparently as James found it to be yielding more and more possibilities. In a letter to Jonathan Sturges James said that he had planned a short story of 7000 words, and that it had grown to 70,000. Henry James, "To Jonathan Sturges," Jul. 10, 1900," *Henry James Letters,* 153. In the letter to Mrs. Ward, supra, James wrote, "The subject was a small fantasticality which (as I have to write 'short stories' when I can) I had intended to treat in the compass of a single magazine instalment—a matter of eight or ten thousand words. But it gave more, before I knew it; before I knew it had grown to 25,000 and was still but a third developed." *Henry James Letters,* 186. He said the same in letters to his agent James Pinker and to William Dean Howells. *Henry James Letters* 154, 251.

6. Bernard Richards, from slightly differing point of view, lengthily extends the comparison: Both Strether and the narrator "have a characteristic in common: that of making wilful assumptions about life, and trusting too much in the truth of these assumptions before they have really had time to test them;" "Strether is a man who is timid, self-centred, ungenerous, over-diplomatic, untrustworthy and on many occasions untrusting. These qualities he shares with the Narrator of *The Sacred Fount* and with several other heroes of James' later novels." Bernard Richards, "*The Ambassadors* and *The Sacred Fount*: the artist *manqué,*" in *The Air of Reality: New Essays on Henry James,* ed. John Goode (London: Methuen, 1972) 219–43.

7. Chun-san Wang explores analogues to the narrator's theory in terms of nineteenth-century medical studies of sex, dealing specifically with unlimited "expenditure of seminal fluid," as one writer, William Acton, phrases the matter, in agreement with John Laws Milton and Herbert Spencer. Chun-san Wang, *Desire in the Later Novels of Henry James.* diss., SUNY/Buffalo, 1996.

8. "It's the picture, of all pictures, that most needs an interpreter," says the narrator. Many have volunteered. For instance: Walter Isle writes that "the sort of reality that is hidden behind the narrator's theory of the sacred fount is death-in-life... and this is the effect of the pale, livid man in black." Oscar Cargill: The painting refers to the narrator who has "thrust off the mask of life [and] carries the menace of death." Laurence Holland: The painting along with the speculations it arouses images forth the novel itself, "the hazard of smothering life's face with the death-like grimace of artifice; the chance of removing a death-like mask to reveal the features at once pale and livid, of life itself; the prospect of covering the face of death with a mask of life and beauty; the hope of so composing the grimace and the beauties of masking artifice, and so presenting the drama of using it, as to protect life while revealing its intimate presence and constructing imagined possibilities for it." Dorothea Krook: The painting "ensures... that the metaphysical problem itself—which is reality, which appearance?—shall remain unresolved, while at the same time allowing a bias

in favour of the narrator's view of the superior reality of the phantasmagoric over the evidential." Donna Przbylowicz: By means of the painting "James introduces a multiplicity of ambiguities and implications, emphasizing the impossibility of discovering a definitive and privileged interpretation."

Adeline R. Tintner says that James invented the painting but incorporated contemporary symbolist vocabulary, and notes that the mask, representing both disguise of the self and discovery of the self, was an obsession of the Belgian James Ensor, whose work was being shown in England about the time of James' writing of *The Sacred Fount.*

Walter Isle, *Experiments in Form: Henry James' Novels, 1896–1901* (Cambridge, MA: Harvard UP, 1968) 227; Oscar Cargill, *The Novels of Henry James* (NY: Macmillan, 1961) 292–293; Laurence Holland, *The Expense of Vision: Essays on the Craft of Henry James* (Princeton: Princeton UP, 1964) 198; Dorothea Krook, *The Ordeal of Consciousness in Henry James* (Cambridge: Cambridge UP, 1962) 177; Donna Przybylowicz, *Desire and Repression: The Dialectic of Self and Other in the Late Works of Henry James* (Univ. of Alabama Press, 1996) 72. Adeline R. Tintner, *The Museum World of Henry James* (Ann Arbor: UMI Research Press, 1986) 138.

9. Edmund Wilson, "The Ambiguity of Henry James," 1934–1938, in Wilson, *The Triple Thinkers* (NY: Oxford UP, 1948 ed.) 97.

Chapter Seven

1. John Landau, *"A Thing Divided": Representation in the Late Novels of Henry James* (Madison: Fairleigh Dickinson UP, 1996) 82.

2. See John Carlos Rowe, *The Other Henry James* (Durham: Duke UP, 1998). Rowe's subject is the homoerotic James. In Rowe's thinking, the succession of Fanny jokes "expresses James' obsessive anal humor."

3. Ruth Bernard Yeazell, *Language and Knowledge in the Late Novels of Henry James* (Chicago: Univ. of Chicago Press, 1976) 20.

4. T.S. Eliot, "On Henry James: In Memory," in *The Question of Henry James,* ed. F.W. Dupee (London: Allan Wingate, n.d.) 125.

5. But this is not true of James' last completed novel, *The Outcry,* published in 1911, which does seem to be driven by prior political and cultural ideas.

Works Cited

Anderson, Quentin. *The Imperial Self*. NY: Vintage, 1971.

Banta, Martha. "The Quality of Experience in *What Maisie Knew*." The *New England Quarterly* (Dec. 1969) 483–510.

Barzun, Jacques. "Henry James, Melodramatist." *The Question of Henry James*. ed. F.W. Dupee. London: Allan Wingate, n.d. 1943. 261–73.

Baym, Nina. "Fleda Vetch and the Plot of The Spoils of Poynton." *PMLA* 84(1969) 102–11.

Beach, Joseph Warren. "The Figure in the Carpet." *The Question of Henry James*. ed. F.W. Dupee. London: Allan Wingate, n.d. 1918. 107–19.

Beidler, Peter G. ed. *Henry James: The Turn of the Screw: Case Studies in Contemporary Criticism*. Boston: St. Martin's Press, 1995.

Bell, Millicent. "Class, Sex, and the Victorian Governess: James' *The Turn of the Screw*." *New Essays on Daisy Miller and The Turn of the Screw*. ed. Vivian R. Pollak. Cambridge: Cambridge UP, 1993. 91–119.

Benson, E.F. *Dodo: An Omnibus*. 1893. London: Hogarth Press, 1986.

Bewley, Marius. *The Complex Fate: Hawthorne, Henry James and Some Other American Writers*. London: Chatto & Windus, 1952.

Blackall, Jean Frantz. "The Case for Mrs. Brookenham." *Henry James Review* (Spring 1981) 155–61.

_______. "The Experimental Period." *A Companion to Henry James Studies*. ed. Daniel Mark Fogel. Westport: Greenwood Press, 1993. 147–78.

_______. *Jamesian Ambiguity and The Sacred Fount*. Ithaca: Cornell UP, 1965.

Blackmur, R.P. "In the Country of the Blue." 1943. *The Question of Henry James*. ed. F.W. Dupee. London: Allan Wingate, n.d. 202–21.

_______. "Introduction." *The Art of the Novel: Critical Prefaces by Henry James*. NY: Chas. Scribner's Sons, 1934. vii–xxxix.

_______. *Studies in Henry James*. NY: New Directions, 1983.

Booth, Wayne. "A Reader-Response Perspective." *Henry James: The Turn of the Screw: Case Studies in Contemporary Criticism*. ed. Peter G. Beidler. Boston: St. Martin's Press, 1995. 163–78.

Bosanquet, Theodora. *Henry James at Work*. London: Hogarth Press, 1924.

_______. *Paul Valery*. London: Hogarth Press, 1933.

Bradley, John R. ed. *Henry James on Stage and Screen* NY: Palgrave, 2000.

Brookes, Sasha. "Henry James' *What Maisie Knew* and Bion's Theory of Thinking." *International Journal of Psychoanalysis* 83.2 (2002) 419–31.

Cameron, Sharon. *Thinking in Henry James*. Chicago: Univ. of Chicago Press, 1989.

Cargill, Oscar. *The Novels of Henry James*. NY: Macmillan, 1961.

Carlson, Susan. *Women of Grace: James' Plays and the Comedy of Manners.* Ann Arbor: UMI Research Press, 1985.

Celine et Julie vont en bateau (Celine and Julie Go Boating). Dir. Jacques Rivette, 1974.

Colby, Frank Moore. "The Queerness of Henry James." *The Bookman* (Jul. 1902).

Coon, Anne. "Widows, Spinsters and Lovers: The Controlling Female Figure in the Fiction of Henry James." diss., SUNY/Buffalo, 1986.

Cooney, Seamus. "Awkward Ages in *The Awkward Age*." *Modern Language Notes* 75 (1960) 208–11.

Craig, Randall. "Reading the Unspoken into the Spoken: Interpreting *What Maisie Knew*." *Henry James Review* 2 (1980–1981) 204–12.

Donadio, Stephen. *Nietzsche, Henry James, and the Artistic Will*. NY: Oxford UP, 1978.

Dostoevsky, Fyodor. "The Friend of the Family." tr. Constance Garnett. NY: Holt, Rinehart, Winston, 1963.

DuMaurier, George. *Trilby*. NY: Harper & Bros., 1894.

Dupee, F.W. *Henry James*. Garden City: Doubleday, 1956.

_______. ed. *The Question of Henry James*. London: Allan Wingate, n.d.

Edel, Leon. *Henry James*. (5 vols.) Philadelphia: Lippincott, 1953–1972.

_______. "An Introductory Essay." Henry James, *The Sacred Fount*. NY: Grove Press (1953) v–xxxii.

_______. "Introduction." Henry James, *Watch and Ward*. London: Rupert Hart-Davis (1960) 5–18.

Egan, Michael. *Henry James: The Ibsen Years*. London: Vision Press, 1972.

Eliot, T.S. "On Henry James: In Memory." 1918. *The Question of Henry James*. ed. F.W. Dupee. London: Allan Wingate, n.d. 123–33.

Felman, Shoshana. "Turning the Screw of Interpretation," *Literature and*

Psychoanalysis: The Question of Reading Otherwise. ed. Shoshana Felman. Baltimore: Johns Hopkins Press (1982) 94–207.

Ford, Ford Madox. "The Old Man." 1932. *The Question of Henry James.* ed. F.W. Dupee. London: Allan Wingate, n.d. 64–70.

Foster, Dennis. "Maisie Supposed to Know: Amo(u)ral Analysis." *Henry James Review* 5 (1984) 207–16.

Galvan, Jill. "Class Ghosting 'In the Cage'." *Henry James Review.* 22.3 (2001) 297–306.

Gard, Roger. ed. *Henry James: The Critical Heritage.* London: Routledge & Kegan Paul, 1968.

Geismar, Maxwell. *Henry James and the Jacobites.* Boston: Houghton Mifflin, 1963.

Gide, André. "Henry James." 1930. *The Question of Henry James.* ed. F.W. Dupee. London: Allan Wingate, n.d. 258–60.

Gordon, Lyndall. *A Private Life of Henry James: Two Women and His Art.* NY: W.W. Norton, 1999.

Harris, Marie P. "Henry James, Lecturer." *American Literature* 3 (1951) 304–14.

Hayes, Kevin J. ed. *Henry James: The Contemporary Reviews.* Cambridge: Cambridge UP, 1996.

Heilman, Robert. "*The Turn of the Screw* as Poem." 1948. *A Casebook on Henry James' "The Turn of the Screw".* ed. Gerald Willen. NY: Thomas Crowell, 1960. 174–88.

Hill, Hamlin L. Jr. "'The Revolt of the Daughters' A Suggested Source for *The Awkward Age.*" *Notes and Queries* (Sept. 1961) 347–49.

Holland, Laurence. *The Expense of Vision: Essays on the Craft of Henry James.* Princeton: Princeton UP, 1964.

Honey, J.R. deS. *Tom Brown's Universe: The Development of the English Public School in the Nineteenth Century.* NY: Quadrangle/NYTimes, 1977.

Horne, Philip. *Henry James: A Life in Letters.* NY: Viking, 1999.

Howells, William Dean. "Mr. Henry James' Later Work." 1903. *The Question of Henry James.* ed. F.W. Dupee. London: Allan Wingate, n.d. 26–39.

Isle, Walter. *Experiments in Form: Henry James' Novels, 1896–1901.*

Cambridge: Harvard UP, 1968.

Jacobson, Marcia. *Henry James and the Mass Market.* Univ. of Alabama Press, 1983.

James, Alice. *The Death and Letters of Alice James.* ed. Ruth Bernard Yeazell. Berkeley & Los Angeles: Univ. California Press, 1981.

James, Henry.

The Art of the Novel: Critical Prefaces by Henry James. ed. R.P. Blackmur. NY: Scribner's Sons, 1934.

Complete Notebooks of Henry James. ed. Leon Edel & Lyall H. Powers. NY: Oxford UP, 1987.

Complete Plays of Henry James. ed. Leon Edel. NY: Oxford UP, 1990.

Complete Stories. (5 vols.) Library of America, 1996–1999.

Henry James Autobiography. ed. Frederick W. Dupee. NY: Criterion Books, 1956.

Henry James Letters. Vols. III, IV. ed. Leon Edel. Cambridge: Belknap Press, 1980, 1984.

Literary Criticism: Essays on Literature, American Writers, English Writers. ed. Leon Edel. Library of America, 1984.

Literary Criticsim: French Writers, Other European Writers, The Prefaces to the New York Edition. ed. Leon Edel. Library of America, 1984.

Portraits of Places. London: Duckworth, 2001.

The Scenic Art: Notes on Acting and the Drama: 1872–1901. ed. Allan Wade. New Brunswick: Rutgers UP, 1948.

NOVELS:

The Ambassadors. 1903. NY: Harpers, 1948.

The Golden Bowl. 1904. NY: Grove Press, n.d.

The Outcry. 1911. NY: Howard Fertig, 1982.

The Sense of the Past. 1917. NY: Scribner's Sons, (New York Ed, XXVI).

Novels 1871–1880. Library of America, 1983. (*Watch and Ward,* 1873, 1878; *Roderick Hudson,* 1876; *The American,* 1877.)

Novels 1881–1886. Library of America, 1985. (*Washington Square,* 1881; *The Portrait of a Lady,* 1881; *The Bostonians,* 1886.)

Novels 1886–1890. Library of America, 1989. (*The Princess Casamassima,* 1886; *The Reverberator,* 1888; *The Tragic Muse,* 1890.)

Novels 1896–1899. Library of America, 2003. (*The Other House*, 1896; *The Spoils of Poynton*, 1897; *What Maisie Knew*, 1897; *The Awkward Age*, 1899.)

Novels 1901–1902. Library of America, 2006. (*The Sacred Fount*, 1901; *The Wings of the Dove*, 1902.)

Kakutani, Michiko. "Casting Henry James as an Artistic Cad." *NYTimes* (Apr. 23, 1999) E 42.

Kaplan, Fred. *Henry James: The Imagination of Genius*. NY: William Morrow, 1992.

Kenton, Edna. "Henry James to the Ruminant Reader: The Turn of the Screw." 1924. *A Casebook on Henry James' "The Turn of the Screw"*. ed. Gerald Willen. NY: Thomas Crowell, 1960. 102–14.

Kincaid, James R. *Child-Loving: The Erotic Child and Victorian Culture*. NY: Routledge, 1992.

Klein, Marcus. "A Portrait of Two Women." *The New Leader* (Jun. 14–28, 1999) 32–33.

Krook, Dorothea. *The Ordeal of Consciousness in Henry James*. Cambridge: Cambridge UP, 1962.

Landau, John. *"A Thing Divided": Representation in the Late Novels of Henry James*. Madison: Fairleigh Dickinson UP, 1996.

Levy, Leo B. *Versions of Melodrama: A Study of the Fiction and Drama of Henry James, 1865–1897*. Berkeley: Univ. of California Press, 1957.

Lewis, R.W.B. *The Jameses: A Family Narrative*. NY: Farrar, Straus & Giroux, 1991.

Lodge, David. *Author, Author*. NY: Viking, 2004.

McCall, Dan. "What Maisie Saw." *Henry James Review* 16.1(1995) 48–52.

Marcus, Steven. *The Other Victorians: A Study of Sexuality and Pornography in Mid-Nineteenth-Century England*. NY: Basic Books, 1966.

Matthiessen, F.O. "The Ambassadors." 1944. *The Question of Henry James*. ed. F.W. Dupee. London: Allan Wingate, n.d. 227–43.

_______. *Henry James: The Major Phase*. NY: Oxford UP, 1944.

Michaels, Walter Benn. "Jim Crow Henry James?" *Henry James Review* 16.3(1995) 286–91.

Mitchell, Juliet. "*What Maisie Knew*: Portrait of the Artist as a Young Girl." *The Air of Reality: New Essays on Henry James*. ed. John Goode.

London: Methuen, 1972. 184–87.

Moody, Andrew J. "'The Harmless Pleasure of Knowing': Privacy in the Telegraph Office and Henry James' 'In the Cage.'" *Henry James Review* 16.1(1995) 53–65.

Monteiro, George. *Henry James and John Hay: The Record of a Friendship.* Providence: Brown UP, 1965.

Morrison, Toni. *Playing in the Dark: Whiteness and the Literary Imagination.* NY: Random House, 1992.

Nixon, Nicola. "Texts and the Single Girl: James' Novels of the Late 1890s." diss., Univ. of Toronto, 1993.

Novick, Sheldon M. *Henry James: The Mature Master.* NY: Random House, 2007.

_______. "Henry James on Stage." *Henry James on Stage and Screen.* ed. John Bradley. NY: Palgrave, 2000. 1–22.

Nowell-Smith, Simon. *The Legend of the Master.* NY: Scribner's, 1948.

Oates, Joyce Carol. *Haunted: Tales of the Grotesque.* NY: Dutton, 1994.

Ozick, Cynthia. *Fame and Folly.* NY: Knopf, 1996.

Palmer, Geoffrey, and Noel Lloyd. *E.F. Benson. As He Was.* Luton Beds: Lennard Publishing, 1988.

Pound, Ezra. *Literary Essays of Ezra Pound.* ed. T.S. Eliot. NY: New Directions, 1968.

Przybylowicz, Donna. *Desire and Repression: The Dialectic of Self and Other in the Late Works of Henry James.* Univ. of Alabama Press, 1996.

Robins, Elizabeth. *Theatre and Friendship: Some Henry James Letters, with a Commentary by Elizabeth Robins.* NY: Putnam's Sons, 1932.

Richards, Bernard. "*The Ambassadors* and *The Sacred Fount*: the artist *manqué*." *The Air of Reality: New Essays on Henry James.* ed. John Goode. London: Methuen, 1972. 219–43.

Rowe, John Carlos. *The Other Henry James.* Durham: Duke UP, 1998.

_______. "Working at Gender: *In the Cage*." *Questioning the Master: Gender and Sexuality in Henry James' Writings.* ed. Peggy McCormack. Newark: Univ. of Delaware Press, 2000. 86–103.

Savoy, Eric. "In the Cage and the Queer Effects of Gay History." *Novel* 28.3 (1995) 284–307.

Sears, Sally. *The Negative Imagination: Form and Perspective in the Novels of*

Henry James. Ithaca: Cornell UP, 1968.

See, Fred G. "Henry James and the Art of Possession." *American Realism: New Essays*. ed. Eric J. Sundquist. Baltimore: Johns Hopkins UP, 1982. 119–37.

Shaw, George Bernard. "Two New Plays." *Dramatic Opinions and Essays with an Apology by Bernard Shaw*, vol. I. London: Archibald Constable, 1907. 7–14.

Sherman, Stuart. "The Aesthetic Idealism of Henry James." 1917. *The Question of Henry James*. ed. F.W. Dupee. London: Allan Wingate, n.d. 86–106.

Shine, Muriel. G. *The Fictional Children of Henry James*. Chapel Hill: Univ. of North Carolina Press, 1968.

Silverman, Willa Z. *The Notorious Life of Gyp: Right-Wing Anarchist in Fin-de-Siècle France*. NY: Oxford UP, 1995.

Thurber, James. "A Final Note on Chanda Bell." James Thurber. *Alarms & Diversions*. NY: Harper, 1957. 143–49.

Thwaite, Ann. *Waiting for the Party: The Life of Frances Hodgson Burnett, 1849–1924*. NY: Scribner's, 1974.

Tintner, Adeline R. *The Museum World of Henry James*. Ann Arbor: UMI Research Press, 1986.

Todorov, Tzvetan. "The Verbal Age." *Critical Inquiry* (Winter 1977) 351–71.

Tóibín, Colm. *The Master*. Scribner, 2004.

Van Leer, David. "Frank and Jim Go Boating: Henry James and the French New Wave." *Henry James on Stage and Screen*. ed. John R. Bradley. NY: Palgrave, 2000. 84–102.

Wade, Allan, ed. *Henry James: The Scenic Art: Notes on Acting & Drama*. New Brunswick: Rutgers UP, 1948.

Wagenknecht, Edward. *Eve and Henry James: Portraits of Women and Girls in His Fiction*. Norman: Univ. of Oklahoma Press, 1978.

Wang, Chun-san. "Desire in the Later Novels of Henry James." diss., SUNY/Buffalo, 1996.

Willen, Gerald. ed. *A Casebook on Henry James' "The Turn of the Screw"*. NY: Thomas Crowell, 1960.

Wilson, Edmund. "The Ambiguity of Henry James." 1934–1938. Edmund

Wilson. *The Triple Thinkers.* NY: Oxford UP, 1948. 88–132.

Wilson, Harris W. "What Did Maisie Know?" *College English* 17(1955–1956) 279–82.

Wolk, Merla. "Narration and Nurture in *What Maisie Knew.*" *Henry James Review* 4(1982–1983) 196–206.

Woolf, Virginia. "Henry James' Ghost Stories." *Collected Essays by Virginia Woolf.* vol. I. London: Hogarth, 1966. 286–292.

Yeazell, Ruth Bernard. *Language and Knowledge in the Late Novels of Henry James.* Chicago: Univ. of Chicago Press, 1976.